CAPITAL of the AMERICAN CENTURY

CAPITAL of the AMERICAN CENTURY
The National and International Influence of New York City

EDITED BY
Martin Shefter

RUSSELL SAGE FOUNDATION NEW YORK

The Russell Sage Foundation

The Russell Sage Foundation, one of the oldest of America's general purpose foundations, was established in 1907 by Mrs. Margaret Olivia Sage for "the improvement of social and living conditions in the United States." The Foundation seeks to fulfill this mandate by fostering the development and dissemination of knowledge about the country's political, social, and economic problems. While the Foundation endeavors to assure the accuracy and objectivity of each book it publishes, the conclusions and interpretations in Russell Sage Foundation publications are those of the authors and not of the Foundation, its Trustees, or its staff. Publication by Russell Sage, therefore, does not imply Foundation endorsement.

Library of Congress Cataloging-in-Publication Data

Capital of the American century : the national and international influence of New York City / Martin Shefter, editor.
p. cm.
Includes index.
ISBN 0-87154-768-6
1. New York (N.Y.) I. Shefter, Martin, 1943–
F128.52.C35 1993
974.7'1—dc20 92-43045
CIP

The paper used in this publication meets the minimum requirements of American National Standard for Information Sciences—Permanence of Paper for Printed Library Materials, ANSI Z39.48-1984.

RUSSELL SAGE FOUNDATION
112 East 64th Street, New York, New York 10021

10 9 8 7 6 5 4 3 2 1

The preparation of this volume was sponsored by the Committee on New York City of the Social Science Research Council.

Contributors

James L. Baughman, University of Wisconsin
Paul DiMaggio, Princeton University
Nathan Glazer, Harvard University
Miles Kahler, University of California, San Diego
James R. Kurth, Swarthmore College
Martin Shefter, Cornell University
David Vogel, University of California, Berkeley
Vera L. Zolberg, New School for Social Research

To Dean Burnham, Martha Derthick, Ted Lowi,
Jim Wilson,
teachers and friends.

Contents

Acknowledgments xi

1. New York's National and International Influence 1
Martin Shefter

2. New York City and the International System: International Strategy and Urban Fortunes 27
Miles Kahler

3. New York City as a National and Global Financial Center 49
David Vogel

4. Between Europe and America: The New York Foreign Policy Elite 71
James R. Kurth

5. New York City and American National Politics 95
Martin Shefter

6. Take Me Away From Manhattan: New York City and American Mass Culture, 1930–1990 117
James L. Baughman

7. New York Culture: Ascendant or Subsident? 145
Vera L. Zolberg

8. The National Influence of Jewish New York 167
Nathan Glazer

9. On Metropolitan Dominance: New York in the Urban Network 193
Paul DiMaggio

Name Index 219

Subject Index 227

Acknowledgments

Capital of the American Century is the final volume in a series sponsored by the Committee on New York City of the Social Science Research Council (SSRC) and published by the Russell Sage Foundation. John Mollenkopf edited *Power, Culture, and Place* (1988) and co-edited, with Manuel Castells, *Dual City* (1991). The third volume in the series, *The Landscape of Modernity* (1992), was edited by David Ward and Olivier Zunz. For making this and the other books possible, grateful acknowledgment is made to the SSRC, the Russell Sage Foundation, which financed the SSRC Committee on New York City, Ira Katznelson and John Mollenkopf, who chaired the Committee, and David Szanton, who handled administrative arrangements.

As the editor of this volume and a contributor to it, I benefitted from the help of a number of colleagues. An unusual event interrupted my work on this project: I was seriously injured in an accident. Ira Katznelson graciously helped me complete the footnotes for the introductory chapter to this volume; Glenn Altschuler and Tim Borstelmann suggested historical references. I am also deeply grateful to my wife, Sudy Shefter, and a number of other friends for generously commenting on drafts and in other ways helping me regain my confidence as a scholar: Amy Bridges, Ben Ginsberg, Peter Gourevitch, Hugh Heclo, Ira Katznelson, Steve Krasner, Jeremy Rabkin, Ron Rogowski, Theda

Skocpol, and Richard Valelly. And finally I would like to thank the scholars to whom this volume is dedicated. I never formally studied under Professors Burnham and Derthick, but along with Professors Lowi and Wilson, with whom I did study, they served as my scholarly models. Over the past few years, these distinguished teachers and scholars have been true friends.

1

New York's National and International Influence

Martin Shefter

If, as Walter Benjamin said, the capital of the nineteenth century was Paris, then the capital of the American Century surely was New York.[1] During the decades following World War II, when American power was at its peak, elites and institutions based in New York exercised enormous political, economic, and cultural influence both at home and abroad. Wall Street lawyers and bankers played a central role in fashioning the policies of containment, collective security, and liberal internationalism that the United States pursued in the international arena. Corporations headquartered in the metropolis brought American products, and extended American business methods, throughout the world. Finally, New Yorkers exercised predominant influence in many areas of American cultural life: the New York School of Abstract Expressionists in the visual arts; the "New York intellectuals" in literary and social criticism; the New York-based companies of George Balanchine and Merce Cunningham in modern dance.

The 1970s witnessed serious challenges to both the dominant position of the United States within the international arena and of New York within the United States. The abandonment of the Bretton Woods sys-

Martha Derthick, Benjamin Ginsberg, Hugh Heclo, Ira Katznelson, Ronald Rogowski, and James Q. Wilson provided valuable comments on drafts of this chapter.

tem of fixed currency-exchange rates, the overthrow of a number of U.S.-backed regimes in Third-World nations, and the resurgence of Marxist literary and social theory signified the decline of American economic strength, political power, and cultural authority. Also, New York's economy contracted sharply and in 1975 its municipal government was placed in receivership; the city's foreign-policy elite fragmented; and Congress imposed restrictions on the activities of New York's charitable foundations.

If the decade of Watergate and the New York fiscal crisis was clearly a traumatic one for the United States and its largest city, the years since 1980 are more difficult to characterize. In some respects the trends of the 1970s have continued. The increasing flow of goods, capital, and immigrants from Asia to the United States has helped Los Angeles and San Francisco to grow, relative to New York, as centers of commerce, communications, and manufacturing. Californians and Texans have moved into positions in the national security establishment that New Yorkers virtually monopolized forty years ago. And the conservative evangelical movement of the 1980s, including its efforts to impose restrictions on art exhibits in the name of "local community standards," can be seen as a provincial revolt against cosmopolitan values commonly identified with New York.

On the other hand, many changes in American national life over the past decade reflect the influence of New York. Wall Street investment banks played a larger role in the reorganization of American industry in the 1980s than at any time since the merger movement of 1898–1904. New York may have lost its privileged access to the State Department, but it retains close ties to the Federal Reserve—and the central bank became a key institution of macroeconomic management under Paul Volcker and Alan Greenspan in the 1980s and early 1990s. Finally, in spite of cultural diffusion there have been centralizing tendencies in the cultural realm in recent years and the focal point of many of these is New York—for example, the emergence of the *New York Times* and *Wall Street Journal* as national newspapers, or the conglomeratization movement in the publishing and entertainment industries.

The chapters in this book seek to make sense of these developments by analyzing the changes that have occurred in New York's influence in economics, politics, and culture over the past half-century. This introductory chapter offers an overview of these changes in New York's influence. Before proceeding to that task, however, it addresses two prior questions. What conditions shape the influence that cities exercise in national affairs? How is it that New York emerged as the most influential city in the United States?

Metropolitan Influence

Scholars have devoted surprisingly little attention to analyzing the influence that cities exercise on American national life. Generally speaking, students of national affairs—national politics, macroeconomics, and national cultural trends—pay little heed to local influences on the developments they examine. And though social scientists in the field of urban studies have analyzed the impact of space and location on social life, two images of the city have tended to dominate their work. The first depicts the city as a microcosm. Urban sociologists and anthropologists commonly regard cities (or their neighborhoods and even street corners) as self-contained worlds whose social relations can be studied in isolation from the surrounding environment.[2] The second major image in urban studies is that of the dependent city. Urban economists and, increasingly, political scientists postulate that businesses and residents would just as soon leave their cities as remain, that municipal governments are constrained from doing anything which might drive employers and taxpayers away, and that consequently cities are buffeted by forces beyond their control.[3] This image implies that the city is more an object than a source of influence.

There are, however, some exceptions to this pattern. A century ago, James Bryce devoted a chapter of *The American Commonwealth* to analyzing the impact on American political and intellectual life of the absence of a capital city in the United States—a city that would serve as the nation's political, economic, and cultural center. Bryce argued:

> In the case both of politics and literature, the existence of a capital tends to strengthen the influence of what is called Society, that is to say, of the men of wealth and leisure . . . whose company and approval are apt to be sought by the men of talent. Thus where the rich and great are gathered in one spot to which the nation looks, they effect more in the way of guiding its political thought and training its literary taste than is possible where they are dispersed over the face of a large country.[4]

In nineteenth-century America, however, Washington was the political capital, New York the business and financial center, and Boston, New York, and Philadelphia shared cultural influence. In this situation, Bryce asserted, "doctrines may be less systematic, programmes less fully reasoned out than when the brisk intelligence of groups gathered in a capital labours to produce them," but they tend to be "more truly representative of all the classes, interests, and tendencies that exist within the nation."[5]

If Bryce discussed how a nation's political and literary culture may be shaped by the interaction of writers, public officials, and men of wealth *within* cities, economic geographers such as Allan Pred have analyzed the relationships *among* different cities.[6] Pred observes that the activities conducted in any given city are a function of those conducted in the other cities with which its firms and organizations interact. Thus the cities in a region, a nation, and indeed, the world may be regarded as elements of a larger system. City-systems generally have a hierarchical structure. Organizations in large cities characteristically supply information and issue commands to those in smaller cities. Thus institutions located in cities at the apex of this hierarchy can exercise influence, through urban networks, that is national—or international—in scope. In the concluding chapter of this book, Paul DiMaggio discusses the implications of the essays in this volume for theories of inter-city relations.

The historical sociologist Charles Tilly has recently analyzed the relationship between urban networks and the development of state structures.[7] Tilly notes that from the fifteenth through the seventeenth centuries, land warfare in Europe was dominated by the mercenary troops of private military contractors, and naval warfare was conducted by warships that were readily converted from merchant vessels. In the most heavily urbanized region of Europe, cities commanded sufficient resources to deploy substantial military and naval forces on their own, or to extract concessions from monarchs in exchange for supplying the loans that would enable the national state to acquire such forces. Hence in Europe's urban heartland, cities were able either to maintain their independence (e.g., Florence, Milan) or to gain direct representation in the ruling structures of national states (e.g., the Netherlands, England). By contrast, in the more peripheral regions of Europe, where cities were weak, absolutist monarchies and empires prevailed.

The work of these scholars suggests that urban systems can function as networks of influence in national and international affairs. It also indicates some directions in which to look when seeking to understand changes in the influence New York has exercised in American national life. Pred's discussion of international communications flows and systems of cities suggests that in seeking to account for shifts in New York's national influence it may be useful to look outward to the changing position of the United States in the world. Tilly's analysis indicates that one should examine the interplay between the American city–system centered in New York and other national institutions. And Bryce's observations suggest that shifting patterns of interaction among elites within the metropolis may alter the character of the nation's economic, political, and cultural life.

The national or international influence that particular New York–based institutions exercise is a function not only of the standing of New York's institutions relative to institutions in other major cities within that domain (e.g., corporate finance), it is also a function of the structure of the domain in question. For example, New Yorkers may not exercise as much intellectual influence in the 1990s as the "New York intellectuals" exercised in the 1940s; less because Philadelphia, Detroit, or Houston have grown in importance relative to New York as sites of intellectual exchange than because universities have come to play an increasingly important role in American intellectual life. Seminar rooms and academic journals in such unlikely places as New Haven, Ithaca, and Palo Alto have become significant centers of intellectual exchange akin to New York City's coffee houses and little magazines of a half-century ago. The following chapters point to this sort of pluralization of the various environments within which New York institutions now operate.

New York's national and international influence in various domains is affected not only by changes in the environments within which New York institutions operate, but also by explicit decisions of the municipal government and social processes within the city. For example, the rise of New York banks and corporations to a dominant position nationally and internationally during the postwar decades was assisted by the municipal government's construction of an elaborate network of highways which facilitated commuting between the city and its bedroom suburbs. In this and other ways, the municipal government fostered the development of dense office districts in Manhattan in which national and international corporations found it convenient to engage in transactions with one another and to acquire legal, financial, and other professional services.

In a recent article, Jason Epstein asserts that these highway projects and office towers destroyed many small manufacturing plants.[8] He argues that the municipal government should have devoted less attention to highway projects and more to policies that would have encouraged the city's manufacturers to develop new markets. In the absence of such policies, the city's manufacturing sector was left to wither. This reduced employment opportunities for recent migrants to the city, opportunities that had encouraged previous immigrants to lead stable lives. Not having much opportunity to find a job, the many recent migrants to the city have had less stable lives than their predecessors and large sections of the city have become ridden with crime.

The problems associated with a population undisciplined by labor markets may undermine the position of New York institutions. The sentiment, "New York is a nice place to visit, but I wouldn't want to live there," used to be attributed by New Yorkers to people they dismissed as hicks. Now an increasing number of executives and professionals, New Yorkers as well as outlanders, are expressing reluctance to move to, or remain in, the city because of blight, crime, and disorder. This may impair New York City's ability to exercise as much influence as formerly in a number of national and international domains.[9]

New York's Rise to Dominance

New York has long been America's "hinge" to the Atlantic world.[10] The key role New York played in managing the flow of commodities and capital between the United States and Europe enabled it to become the nation's largest city by 1805 and was a continuing source of influence thereafter. As New York's transportation, communications, and institutional linkages with the rest of the country multiplied over the next 125 years, its influence expanded accordingly.

New York emerged as the chief commercial city in the United States by virtue of the ties it established with London as Britain was becoming the world's leading economic and political power. In 1755, on the eve of the Seven Years' War, New York was designated as "the general Magazine of Arms and Military Stores" in British North America. As Eric Lampard notes, the "award of government contracts to politically-favored merchant houses for . . . military supplies enabled such firms to accumulate substantial credit balances in London. . . ."[11] That same year, the Board of Trade in London made New York the western terminus of a monthly postal vessel. Lampard observes,

> From the middle of the eighteenth century, therefore, New York City was tied into the burgeoning information network linking Britain and continental Europe, with all its potential for the promotion of communication and commerce. New York was brought from one to two days closer to London, Liverpool, Glasgow, or Amsterdam than Philadelphia or even Boston. . . .[12]

These links survived the American Revolution. The Anglo-French conflict of the 1790s enabled New York merchantmen to take business from European vessels diverted to war. By 1797 New York's export trade exceeded Philadelphia's, and by 1805 it became the nation's most populous city.

Commercial links between New York and Britain multiplied to the city's advantage in the nineteenth century. In the early years of the century, New York merchants made their city the chief port through which America's leading export—raw cotton—was shipped to England by dispatching agents to the South and advancing money to planters on the security of their crops. Jefferson's embargo and the War of 1812 set back the city's foreign trade, but when hostilities ended, the British selected New York as the site for auctioning their surplus textiles. And in 1818 the Black Ball line introduced regularly scheduled sailings between New York and Liverpool.

The transportation revolution of the second quarter of the nineteenth century added to New York's commercial primacy. As canals and railroads reduced the costs of land transportation, inland merchants, farmers, and manufacturers had a declining incentive to ship goods through the closest seaport and greater reason to do business in the city with the best commercial facilities, New York. As Raymond Vernon explains,

> For a time, New York's unique scheduled sailings, its "ship brokers," and its wholesalers could be matched nowhere else. Those who used the New York Port could hold down their costs of doing business by relying on these facilities, these "external economies" which establishments obtain through sharing the services of specialists external to themselves.[13]

New York's dominance of foreign trade gave it advantages in competing for domestic business. Firms that were initially involved in overseas commerce came to deal in domestic products. In addition, as the nation's leading entrepôt for people as well as goods, the city provided employers with an enormous pool of labor possessing a wide range of skills. New York's population was ethnically more heterogeneous than that of any other American city, and its upper classes were less coherent than Boston's or Philadelphia's.[14] The relative fluidity of the city's social structure may have contributed to the entrepreneurialism of its business community.

There was an especially close relationship between New York's commercial primacy and its emergence as the nation's financial capital. Financing foreign trade served as a major source of business for the banks of the metropolis. Moreover, retail merchants throughout the country had to remit funds to New York for the goods they purchased from the city's wholesalers, and consequently the local banks with which they did business found it useful to maintain balances in New York. By the 1850s, 600 of the 700 commercial banks in the United States had correspondent accounts with banks in the metropolis.[15] New York supplanted Boston as the nation's chief market for railroad securities in the late 1850s, because Boston's economy contracted sharply during the depression that followed the Panic of 1857, whereas New York's commerce continued to expand and hence its merchants were in a position to seek new investment opportunities.[16] And access to foreign, especially British, capital contributed to New York's emergence as the major market for industrial securities at the end of the nineteenth century. J.P. Morgan & Co., the nation's most influential investment banking house, had affiliates in London and Paris.[17] Kuhn, Loeb & Co., the city's leading Jewish investment banking firm, had ties to financiers in London and Frankfurt.[18]

Wall Street bankers were largely responsible for organizing the giant national corporations—in railroads, manufacturing, petroleum, and mining—that were created in the United States at the end of the nineteenth century. A substantial proportion of these corporations established their headquarters in New York: In 1895 the metropolis had 298 firms worth more than $1 million, while second-ranking Chicago had eighty-two. As David Hammack explains, "Corporate leaders . . . found that New York offered by far the best combination of marketing facilities, commercial information and financial, professional and technical services . . . all available for face-to-face discussions. . . ."[19] Similar considerations encouraged the wealthy to congregate in the metropolis. At the end of the nineteenth century, close to half of America's millionaires lived in the New York metropolitan area.

New York's commercial primacy contributed to its cultural influence. Because New York's commercial links with Britain and the Continent were the best in the United States, the city's newspapers were the first to gain access to political, economic, and cultural news from abroad, and during the 1820s and 1830s daily newspapers in Philadelphia, Boston, and Baltimore would simply reprint foreign dispatches from the New York press. The frequency of sailings from New York to other American cities gave its newspapers advantage in the publication of domestic news as well. For example, in 1817, news from New Orleans, that on average took thirty-four days to reach Philadelphia, was available a full week earlier in New York. As late as 1841, newspapers in New Haven received their Boston news from New York.[20]

By the 1830s, New York had clearly become America's newspaper capital. In competing with one another, the city's eleven dailies introduced major innovations into American journalism, some of which were borrowed from Britain. In particular, the New York *Sun* and the New York *Herald* were the first successful penny dailies in the United States. They relied on the "London plan" of circulation management to create a mass market for newspapers: single-copy sales (previously, newspapers had been sold by annual subscription), a low price, and hawking by newsboys. The New Journalism of the 1880s—which relied on crusades and sensationalism to further extend the market for newspapers—also emerged out of New York's hypercompetitive environment. These journalistic innovations diffused down the hierarchy of cities, and ambitious journalists (not least, newspaper publishers Joseph Pulitzer, William Randolph Hearst, and Adolph Ochs) advanced their careers by moving up the urban hierarchy to New York.

During the nineteenth century, New York also exercised leadership by example in the realm of elite culture. The concentration of millionaires in New York after the Civil War made it possible to establish museums, orchestras, and opera companies that catered to an upper-class clientele and that institutionalized a distinction between highbrow and lowbrow culture.[21] The New York Philharmonic's conductor, Theodore Thomas, played a particularly important role in this regard. He insisted that audiences acknowledge the distinction between the fine arts and mere entertainment by approaching symphonic music with reverence and restraint.[22]

The names adopted by a number of elite cultural institutions in New York—the American Museum of Natural History, the Metropolitan Museum of Art, and the Metropolitan Opera—indicate that they had pretensions to cultural leadership on a national, not merely local, scale. As Vera Zolberg notes in her chapter in this volume, the nonprofit mode of organization pioneered by the Metropolitan Museum was picked up by elite institutions in other cities. Nonetheless, New York at most occupied a position of *primus inter pares* during the nineteenth century: elite cultural institutions in Boston, Philadelphia, and Chicago could also purchase Old Masters and hire prominent European conductors. Museums and symphony orchestras in other major American cities thus rivaled New York's elite cultural institutions in prestige.

The development of new media of communications and forms of popular culture at the turn of the twentieth century added to New York's influence. Weekly magazines, the popular music industry, and vaudeville booking agencies were all concentrated in New York. Success in these fields required knowing which topics were timely and which styles and performers currently were popular—and anticipating the ones likely to become hot in the near future. Nowhere in the United States could such information be obtained more quickly than in New York, the nation's communications capital. New York also had the largest and most demanding audiences, and the greatest number of theaters in the United States. "Broadway musicals," culminating in the productions of Richard Rodgers and Oscar Hammerstein, became enormously influential forms of American popular culture.

By the turn of the century, as James Baughman argues in his chapter in this volume, New York had clearly become the most influential cultural center in the United States. An increasing proportion of the nation's leading writers and artists worked in New York during the early decades of the twentieth century. With the decline of the genteel tradition, many writers and painters came to regard social life in Boston and Philadelphia as artistically stultifying.[23] In New York they could join one of a number of different social worlds—among them, O. Henry's world of commercial culture; the radical bohemianism of Max Eastman's Greenwich Village; or the sophisticated urbanity of Dorothy Parker's Algonquin Roundtable.[24]

New York depended more on its ties to Britain than links with the national government in Washington to gain economic and cultural influence during the nineteenth century. For this reason, major political forces in the city did not support efforts to strengthen the American national state. During the Jacksonian era, the city's representatives sought to keep the national government from constructing canals and turnpikes that would compete with New York's Erie Canal, and Wall Street bankers undertook to make New York the nation's financial capital by destroying the Bank of the United States, whose headquarters were in Philadelphia. New York was a leading center of free-trade sentiment, and congressmen from the city fought to restrict the tariff rates and revenues of the federal government.

Political parties were the chief vehicles through which New Yorkers exercised influence in American national politics during the nineteenth century. In the 1820s, New York's Martin Van Buren forged an alliance with southern political leaders who shared his goal of limiting the power of the national government—an alliance institutionalized in the Democratic party. To compete effectively, the Whigs and Republicans found it necessary to copy Van Buren's techniques.

New York's dominance of American national life has been subject to greater challenge by significant "second cities" or city-pairs than have the premier cities of other major nations. Initially, Philadelphia and Boston, then Chicago, and now Los Angeles and San Francisco have posed challenges to New York's national influence more significant than Birmingham, Manchester, and Liverpool have presented to London, or Marseille, Lyon, and Bordeaux have presented to Paris.

The Civil War enhanced New York's position. War coverage contributed to Horace Greeley's emergence as the nation's most influential journalist and, as Richard Bensel observes, the war "reinforced the city's importance within the financial system."[25] By roughly 1870, New York City came to exercise enormous influence over the American economy, American national politics, and American cultural life. In 1870, 57 percent of the nation's foreign trade flowed through the port of New York and New York City played almost as significant a role in domestic commerce. The city's port and its control over commerce provided New Yorkers with access to the information that enabled them to play a leading role in American culture. New York's cultural primacy was buttressed by the flood of single business travelers to the city, who swelled the audience for its theaters and music halls. By the mid-nineteenth century, patronage-fueled party organizations modeled on Martin Van Buren's Albany Regency and New York City's Tammany Hall thoroughly dominated American national politics, helping to keep the American national state weak.[26] The weakness of the national state, in turn, left New York–based markets and institutions free to shape American economic, political, and cultural life.

The New York–Washington Axis

The international economic and political order in which New York emerged as the premier American city was characterized by British leadership and a commitment to unfettered markets and limited government.[27] This order was subject to a number of shocks during the early decades of the twentieth century, as the United States moved past Great Britain to become the world's leading economic power. A series of financial panics—in 1907, 1914, and 1929—culminated in the Great Depression of the 1930s, a calamity caused, in part, by the uncertainties attending the transfer of international economic leadership from Britain to America. And Germany's drive to establish itself as the world's leading military power precipitated two European wars into which the United States eventually was drawn.

New York elites responded to the threats and opportunities associated with the new position of the United States in the world by working to strengthen the American national state. These efforts achieved some success during the early decades of the twentieth century but did not fully triumph until the Great Depression and World War II brought about the final collapse of the international economic and political order that Britain had dominated.

At the turn of the century, a group of New York patricians led by Theodore Roosevelt, Elihu Root, and Henry Stimson undertook to strengthen American military institutions and to involve the United States more actively in international affairs. As president, ex-president, and publicist, Roosevelt promoted a strong army and navy, American imperialism, and U.S. intervention in World War I. Root and Stimson each served as secretary of war and as secretary of state and they helped implement Roosevelt's vision.

Roosevelt, Root, and Stimson were the founding fathers of the American foreign-policy establishment, which was dominated by leading New York lawyers and bankers, and committed to America's assumption of world leadership as British power waned. It suffered a serious setback when isolationists blocked American ratification of the Treaty of Versailles. Yet even during the 1920s, presidents drew upon members of that establishment to conduct American foreign policy, giving it, as historians now increasingly recognize, an internationalist cast.[28] Charles Evans Hughes was Warren Harding's secretary of state and Henry Stimson served as Herbert Hoover's. Moreover, the very incapacities of the institutions of American diplomacy encouraged the White House and State Department to rely, in remarkable measure, upon J.P. Morgan & Co. to administer U.S. foreign economic policy in Europe, China, and Latin America.[29]

The changing position of America in the world during the early decades of the twentieth century led New York elites to support strengthening the national government of the United States in a second domain —monetary policy—by pressing for the creation of a U.S. central bank. At the turn of the century, the Bank of England and New York's leading financiers together performed central banking functions for the U.S. economy by providing liquidity and serving as lenders of last resort in financial panics.[30] During such crises, major New York bankers joined together under the leadership of J.P. Morgan to bail out institutions at risk of failing. They obtained the necessary funds by drawing upon, in sequence, the resources of the strongest New York banks, U.S. Treasury deposits, the London money market, and, ultimately, the Bank of England. These procedures successfully managed American financial panics through 1907, but as the U.S. economy grew, the British found it increasingly difficult to meet the demands that the Americans were placing upon them.

Leading New York financiers proposed creating a U.S. central bank to deal with this problem. Agrarian interests in the South and West had their own complaints about the American banking and monetary system, and the 1913 statute creating the Federal Reserve provided greater influence both to Washington and to regional reserve banks than the New Yorkers had advocated. In practice, however, the New York

Federal Reserve Bank, which had close ties to the city's financial community, came to dominate domestic monetary policymaking through the purchase and sale of government securities in the metropolis's money market. And New York Federal Reserve Bank president Benjamin Strong, together with Bank of England governor Montagu Norman, largely ran the international monetary system from shortly after World War I until Strong's death in 1928.[31] In the monetary realm, then, the creation of new institutions by the federal government actually increased the capacity of New York interests to influence events both domestically and internationally.

The relationship between the Federal Reserve and the Bank of England was not institutionalized, however, and did not survive Benjamin Strong's death. In the absence of a central institution willing and able to assume responsibility for managing the world's financial system, the panic precipitated by the 1929 stock market crash was left to spiral out of control, becoming the century's most severe depression.[32] In turn, the Great Depression both enhanced the influence that important New York political forces were able to exercise in Washington and encouraged them to endow the national government with additional power.

The economic crisis of the 1930s catapulted New York governor Franklin Roosevelt into the presidency and led to the election of large Democratic congressional majorities prepared to follow his leadership. Roosevelt brought with him to Washington more than a dozen members of New York City's welfare establishment, and they served as key architects of the New Deal welfare state.[33] Harry Hopkins, for one, designed and administered the New Deal's major work relief programs as head of the Works Progress Administration, and FDR placed Frances Perkins in charge of drafting the Social Security Act. To avoid alienating southerners on Capitol Hill, they found it necessary to grant states and localities a major say in the administration of national welfare programs. Nonetheless, in conjunction with their allies in the New Deal coalition, liberal political forces from New York were able to increase significantly the role that the national government played in American economic and social life.

The economic crisis of the 1930s also brought Hitler to power, precipitating World War II. This military crisis enabled New York's foreign-policy elite to take the lead in constructing America's wartime and postwar national-security state. Seeking to expand the political base of his administration after war broke out in Europe, FDR appointed members of that elite to top defense and foreign policy positions. Harry Truman pursued a similar strategy in mobilizing domestic support for the Cold War. In this way, Henry Stimson, John McCloy, Robert Lovett, Averell

Harriman, and their associates came to be in a position to fashion the institutions and policies through which the United States defeated Germany, contained the Soviet Union, and became the world's leading military power.

New York elites also came to play a significant role in the institutions through which the United States succeeded Britain as the world's dominant power and exercised international economic hegemony following World War II. The U.N. was not a major force, but the placement of its headquarters in New York symbolized the locus of power in the postwar order. The World Bank was situated in Manhattan to facilitate its winning the confidence of the New York financial markets—its chief source of capital. The architects of the postwar monetary system, however, put the International Monetary Fund (IMF) in Washington. As designed, the IMF embodied a rejection of the "key currency" plan favored by the New York financial community. The actual operation of the monetary system, however, pretty much accorded with the key currency plan—an arrangement that gave the U.S. dollar, and hence the major New York banks, primacy in international trade and investment.[34]

Major interests in New York continued to enjoy access to institutions of domestic and foreign policymaking throughout the postwar period, and a broad coalition of social forces in the city supported the national government's assumption of responsibility for promoting prosperity at home and advancing American interests abroad. Thus the New York union leaders who helped make the national labor movement a major pillar of domestic liberalism by organizing CIO unions also were instrumental in bringing organized labor into the Cold War coalition. And the Wall Street lawyers and bankers who shaped American national security policy led the wing of the national Republican party (the Dewey-Rockefeller wing) that was prepared to live with the domestic reforms of the New Deal.

Of course, New Yorkers did not completely dominate American politics during the 1930s, 1940s, and 1950s. A broad array of social forces—southern cotton growers, midwestern industrial workers, California defense manufacturers, among others—were incorporated into the New Deal and postwar coalitions, and New York interests found it necessary to make concessions to these alliance partners. Moreover, after 1938 conservative southern Democrats regularly joined with old-guard Republicans on Capitol Hill to fight efforts, led by New York Senator Robert Wagner and other urban liberals, to extend the New Deal. World War II and the Cold War worked to the advantage of this conservative coalition by focusing the president's attention on foreign affairs more than domestic reform and by enabling its members to discredit the American left with McCarthyite attacks. Consequently, proposals to enact new federal social programs and to expand the planning capacities of the national government fared poorly during the two decades following Pearl Harbor.

A number of conditions enabled liberals to overcome these impediments in the 1960s: the Supreme Court's desegregation decisions and the emergence of the Southern civil rights movement; the Democratic landslide in the 1964 congressional elections following Lyndon Johnson's accession to the presidency; and, not least, the warming of Soviet-American relations after the Cuban missile crisis and the waning of McCarthyism.[35] Institutions based in New York played an important role in the efforts by liberals to strengthen the national government in the 1960s. Liberal foundations and fund-raisers in New York supplied the civil rights movement with much of its financing, and television network coverage of violence directed against demonstrators in Birmingham and Selma was instrumental in securing enactment of the 1964 Civil Rights Act and the 1965 Voting Rights Act. In addition, projects financed by New York's Ford Foundation served as models for the Johnson administration's antipoverty program and its program of providing federal support to the arts.[36]

In sum, New York and Washington were complementary, not competing, centers of power during the New Deal and postwar decades. New York elites worked to strengthen executive institutions in Washington and subsequently exercised a considerable measure of influence over national and international affairs through the institutions they had helped to create.

The institutions of the postwar political order that New York helped establish contributed, in turn, to the city's emergence as the premier center of command and control in the American and global economies. In the late 1950s, 156 of the nation's 500 largest industrial corporations had headquarters in the metropolis, and New York's share of the largest multinational enterprises was even higher. Writing at the time, Raymond Vernon explained why national and multinational corporations located their central offices in the city:

> The needs of the elite group in the central office of a large company are . . . variable and unpredictable. . . . From week to week their interests vary from some esoteric provision of the Internal Revenue Code to the political situation in Cuba; from the effectiveness of spot television commercials to the efficacy of operations research. . . . [I]t is uneconomical for such offices to staff themselves internally to deal with every such problem; the only feasible pattern is to draw upon specialists as the need arises. And the

most efficient locational arrangement is one which permits the specialists and those they serve to be congregated at a common point.[37]

The security umbrella that the United States extended over Western Europe and East Asia following World War II, and the international regime of free trade that America promoted, enabled major American corporations to expand their operations abroad. Moreover, the status of the dollar as the key international currency provided advantages overseas to American banks relative to their foreign competitors. Finally, by limiting the markets in which financial institutions could operate at home, the regulatory restrictions imposed upon Wall Street during the New Deal and postwar decades encouraged major New York banks to cultivate opportunities for profit abroad.

In the postwar era, New York also became a world cultural capital. A number of trends contributed to the growth of New York's cultural influence, but among them were the strengthening of the American national state and the changing international position of the United States. The rise of the New York School of Abstract Expressionist painting provides a notable example.

The New Deal reinforced New York's dominance of the visual arts in America. More than 78 percent of the painters and sculptors supported by the WPA artists project lived in the metropolis. The vitality of its WPA program attracted artists to New York City. More significantly still, it was through the WPA that almost all the members of what was to become the New York school got to know one another and, as Dore Ashton notes, "established the camaraderie that was essential for . . . their prodigious undertakings of the 1940s."[38]

America's emergence as the leader of the Western Alliance in the 1940s added to New York's international standing in the visual arts. The fall of France to the Germans in World War II led many of the world's most prominent painters to flee from Paris to New York, among them Piet Mondrian, Jean Miró, Marcel Duchamp, Fernand Léger, André Breton, and Max Ernst. And the outbreak of the Cold War encouraged the U.S. State Department to sponsor international exhibitions that promoted Abstract Expressionism as exemplifying cultural freedom in the United States.

The Abstract Expressionists also drew on local networks uniquely available in the metropolis and on New York's position as a communications capital to gain a sense of themselves and recognition by progressively broader publics. The painters of the New York school interacted with each other at New York's Artists Club and Cedar Tavern. Their work was exhibited at galleries and museums associated with some of the nation's wealthiest families: the Art of This Century Gallery and the Museum of Non-Objective Art with the Guggenheims, the Museum of American Art with the Whitneys, and the Museum of Modern Art with the Rockefellers. Their presence was announced to the art world by *Art News;* their importance was proclaimed to a general intellectual audience by Clement Greenberg in *The Nation* and Harold Rosenberg in *The New Yorker;* and they were hyped to the mass public by Henry Luce's *Life* magazine.

That Nelson Rockefeller and Peggy Guggenheim, or Henry Luce and Clement Greenberg, joined in promoting the art of Jackson Pollock and Adolph Gottlieb illustrates one final point about the postwar order that New Yorkers helped shape. In general, WASP and Jewish New Yorkers acted together—in the political and economic realms as well as in cultural affairs—during the decades following World War II. (For an analysis of the Jewish "spin" on New York's national influence, see Chapter 8 by Nathan Glazer.) The doctrines associated with the postwar national and world orders—internationalism, liberalism, modernism—can be regarded as the ideology of this WASP-Jewish coalition. They were causes around which the Protestant establishment and upwardly mobile Jews could unite. In the name of those doctrines, the members of the WASP-Jewish coalition came to exercise a remarkable measure of influence in American political, economic, and cultural life.

Global City

The liberalism, internationalism, and modernism advocated by New York elites triumphed to a considerable degree both in the United States and elsewhere in the western world during the quarter-century following World War II. Paradoxically, this very success strengthened economic, political, and cultural centers that challenged New York's hegemony in the 1970s and 1980s. Nonetheless, New York plays a major role in the global order that is emerging as the twentieth century draws to a close, though its influence has become more specialized than it had been in the immediate postwar decades.

The policies fashioned by liberals and their allies to promote growth in America's poorest regions contributed to the emergence of economic centers elsewhere in the United States that competed with New York. Federal public works projects fostered the development of the American South and West by financing the construction of crucial infrastructure—water supply systems, highways, airports—and national defense programs funneled capital into these regions' economies.[39] Moreover, New

Deal transportation regulation worked to the relative advantage of the nation's peripheral regions, while the reorganization of the financial system under FDR made it possible for Americans to engage confidently in anonymous economic transactions across great distances.

Similarly, the postwar international order that New Yorkers helped construct stimulated the growth of rival economic centers abroad. The Marshall Plan helped rebuild Western Europe and Northeast Asia; American military spending overseas provided the international economy with liquidity; and the advent of full currency convertibility under the Bretton Woods system, along with the Kennedy round of tariff reductions, led to an explosion of international trade. America's share of world manufacturing production fell from nearly 45 percent in 1950 to under 32 percent in 1980, and the U.S. trade surplus turned into a persistent deficit. As Germany, Japan, and South Korea prospered, so too did Frankfurt, Tokyo, and Seoul.

These developments contributed to a restructuring of New York's economy during the 1970s and 1980s, undermining some sectors while strengthening others. Foreign competition weakened the city's garment industry and, more generally, eroded New York's position as the nation's premier center of light manufacturing. (See chapter 2 by Miles Kahler.) Also, the growth of the South and West made the cities of these regions increasingly attractive as sites for the headquarters of national industrial corporations. For this reason, among others, New York's share of Fortune 500 head offices declined from 26 percent in the mid-1960s to 11 percent in the mid-1980s.

On the other hand, the internationalization of the U.S. and world economies has enhanced the influence New York exercises as America's hinge to the world. New York remains America's leading center of foreign trade, accounting for 20 percent of the nation's ocean cargo and 40 percent of its international air cargo. Moreover, though in recent decades there has been a decline in New York's share of the largest U.S. *national* corporations, its share of the largest U.S. *multinational* corporations remains undiminished. Currently, forty of the 100 largest American multinationals have their headquarters in the New York metropolitan region, with three-fifths of these located in the city itself. As international trade has risen from 12 to 20 percent of the U.S. GNP over the past twenty years, the economic influence New York firms exercise by virtue of their control over much of that trade has increased accordingly.[40]

Over the past two decades, New York's share of the nation's major investment banks and diversified financial corporations has increased. Closely linked to New York's financial dominance is the influence it continues to exercise in such information-intensive sectors as corporate law, accounting, management consulting, and advertising.[41]

Internationalization has multiplied New York's influence as America's financial capital. The explosive growth of international trade in recent years has compelled the managers of U.S. manufacturing corporations to slash costs and reorganize their operations, or face the prospect of being deposed by outsiders prepared to make such changes. The wave of corporate reorganizations that ensued in the 1980s bespoke a dramatic rise in the influence of Wall Street financiers relative to corporate managements. (The financial community may be less oriented to New York City now than formerly, however. There is a sharp contrast between Wall Street's intense efforts to help New York overcome its municipal fiscal crisis of 1975 and the financial community's largely indifferent reaction to New York City's municipal financial problems in 1991–1992.)[42]

Finally, the deregulation and internationalization of financial markets in recent years has strengthened New York as a global financial center. These trends have increased competition within the financial sector, placing a premium on innovation. As David Vogel notes in chapter 3, the lead that Wall Street investment banks have taken in developing new financial instruments and markets provides New York with its comparative advantage in contending with London and Tokyo to be the financial capital of the world.

New York's experience in the political arena has been broadly similar to its trajectory in the economic realm. By contributing to the growth of the South and West, federal domestic and defense programs enhanced the political as well as economic influence of the nation's peripheral regions relative to New York. Moreover, by the 1970s the city of Washington itself had become a center of political opinion and power independent of New York—a development signified by the use of the phrase "inside the Beltway" to refer to views characteristic of the Washington community. Despite these developments, however, New York's position as a national and global financial capital has served as an important source of political influence for the metropolis in the 1980s and 1990s.

During the late 1960s and the 1970s, as James Kurth notes in chapter 4, political forces in other regions of the country increasingly rejected New York's leadership in foreign policy. Protectionist sentiment grew in the midwestern industrial heartland as American manufacturers faced difficulties coping with competition from abroad. At the same time, the growth of the American balance-of-payments deficit and the concomitant decline of the U.S. dollar reduced the enthusiasm of New York foreign-policy elites for prosecuting the Vietnam War, opening a breach between those elites and political forces in the West and South committed to a more assertive American military posture. As the Cold War consensus shattered, these political forces found it useful to finance centers of foreign policy expertise in Washington staffed by analysts sympathetic to their perspective. The emergence of these disparate regional interests and perspectives regarding American foreign policy has led New York to become, in Kurth's words, "merely first among equals in the constellation of power."

In the arena of domestic policy, the influence of liberal political forces from New York declined during the Reagan-Bush years. As mentioned above, New York–based charitable foundations, communications media, and political activists had played influential roles in the enactment of the social programs and civil rights policies of the Kennedy and Johnson administrations. The growth of federal domestic expenditures in the 1960s and 1970s, in turn, encouraged groups seeking funds for themselves and influence over social policy to cluster in the nation's capital. Previously, trade associations, charitable foundations, think tanks, and other idea-making institutions had been concentrated in New York City.[43] But in recent decades Washington, D.C. has emerged as the focal point of networks of nonprofit organizations and public bureaucracies that dominate the making of many national domestic policies.[44]

The role New York City plays in liberal political activism has declined in one other respect in recent decades. Until recently New York City, especially Jewish New Yorkers, were the major source of contributions in the United States to liberal political causes and liberal candidates for public office. But in recent years the Hollywood entertainment industry has emerged as a major source of liberal political money. The publishing and idea-producing industry has remained in the East, however, so the rise of Hollywood as a source of political contributions has been associated with the fraying of the formerly close relationship between liberal activism and the world of ideas.[45]

One New York–based interest—the Wall Street financial community—came to exercise far greater influence during the Reagan-Bush years than it had previously. In the 1970s, the growth of public spending and the declining strength of the American economy internationally combined to generate an inflationary spiral and a succession of dollar crises. Moreover, as financial markets became increasingly internationalized and billions of dollars flowed across national boundaries in response to changes in currency-exchange rates and national interest rates, it became increasingly difficult for the government to manage the economy. To cope with this crisis, President Carter appointed Paul Volcker, the president of the New York Federal Reserve Bank, as chairman of the U.S. Federal Reserve in 1979.

The power of the Federal Reserve rose to new heights during the 1980s and 1990s, and inasmuch as New York–based financial markets and institutions comprise a major constituency of the Federal Reserve, the greater power of the central bank has meant that Wall Street's concerns have gained greater influence in Washington. Deadlock over fiscal policy between the Reagan-Bush White House and the Democratic-controlled Congress increased the importance of monetary policy as a tool of macroeconomic management. The Federal Reserve's relatively restrictive monetary policies over the past dozen years directly benefited the owners of financial assets by halting an inflationary process that had been gathering momentum for more than a decade. In addition, the policies of the central bank—in conjunction with the Reagan administration's actions regarding taxation, trade, and regulation—weakened the political forces associated with the New Deal coalition, while strengthening the private sector relative to the public sector, management relative to labor, and financial institutions relative to manufacturing corporations. The booming financial markets of the 1980s and early 1990s indicate that Wall Street was pleased with these developments.

Finally, there have been some parallel developments in the cultural realm. New York's standing as America's overwhelmingly dominant cultural center has faced challenges from two quarters in recent years: other cities and the nation's universities. Federal policies that New Yorkers had largely supported contributed to the emergence of each of these challenges.

A number of federal policies of the postwar period strengthened cultural institutions outside New York. Beginning in the 1950s, the federal urban renewal program encouraged cities throughout the nation to turn themselves into office centers, thereby contributing to the creation of a national market for executive personnel. To compete in this market and make themselves more attractive to corporate executives, cities throughout the country had an incentive to bolster their cultural institutions. This endeavor was facilitated by the National Endowment for the Arts, which in the 1960s began to provide grants to artists and subsidies to arts organizations.

Moreover, federal civil rights and immigration policies, and the civil liberties jurisprudence of the federal courts, contributed to the nationwide diffusion of cosmopolitan values that formerly had characterized chiefly New York, increasing the attractiveness of other cities as places for writers and artists to live and work. By the 1960s, as James Baughman suggests in chapter 6, the Hollywood "movie colony" no longer was such an alien presence in Southern California, and more television entertainment programming was produced in Los Angeles than in New York. In ensuing years, the diffusion of cosmopolitan values and the nationalization of American culture transformed cities that were considerably smaller and more provincial than Los Angeles. Thus Jackson, Mississippi, which had been home to the White Citizens Council in the 1950s, came to sponsor an annual international modern dance festival in the 1980s!

The federal government also contributed to the expansion of America's system of higher education during the postwar decades. Federal support for research and financial assistance to students enabled universities to expand, and they hired large numbers of intellectuals and artists both in traditional academic departments and in creative-writing and artist-in-residence programs. Consequently, the locus of much intellectual and artistic activity in the United States has shifted from urban bohemias to universities.[46] New York still sits on top of America's system of cities, but, as noted above, in recent decades academic networks have grown in importance relative to the urban hierarchy in the realm of cultural production.

At the same time, however, New York has maintained its influence over those aspects of the production of culture that are linked to its role as a global financial and communications capital. For example, as Vera Zolberg notes in Chapter 7, New York remains at the center of the American art world and the international art market. Approximately one and a half times as many artists live and work in New York as in second-ranking Los Angeles. Artists are drawn to New York by its galleries, whose sales exceed those of Los Angeles by a factor of almost five. They are also attracted to New York by its critics and curators, who serve as key arbiters of international artistic success. The leading international art galleries and auction houses, in turn, are drawn to New York by *their* customers—international corporations and wealthy collectors, American and foreign.

The internationalization of financial markets under Wall Street's leadership has enabled New York largely to displace London as the capital of the international art market. The wealth concentrated in New York in the 1980s also led it to supplant Paris as the world's leading center of fashion and luxury consumption.[47] The close association between the New York art and financial markets is indicated by the index, regularly calculated by one of the city's major financial houses and published in its financial press, which compares the performance of Old Masters,

French impressionists, and twentieth-century paintings with stocks, bonds, and precious metals as investment vehicles.[48] In the art world, as in many other fields, the central role New York plays in the allocation of financial assets contributes to its influence as a global capital.

Notes

1. "Paris—the Capital of the Nineteenth Century," in Walter Benjamin, ed., *Charles Baudelaire: A Lyric Poet in the Era of High Capitalism*, trans. Quintin Hoare (London: Verso Press, 1983), pp. 155–176.
2. For examples and for discussion, see Suttles, Gerald D., *The Social Order of the Slum: Ethnicity and Territory in the Inner City* (Chicago: University of Chicago Press, 1968); Whyte, William F., *Street Corner Society* (Chicago: University of Chicago Press, 1951); Vidich, Arthur J., Joseph Bensman, and Maurice R. Stein, eds., *Reflections on Community Studies* (New York: Harper and Row, 1964); Keller, Suzanne, *The Urban Neighborhood: A Sociological Perspective* (New York: Vintage Books, 1968).
3. Peterson, Paul, *City Limits* (Chicago: University of Chicago Press, 1981); Tiebout, Charles M., "A Pure Theory of Local Expenditures," *Journal of Political Economy* 64 (1956): 416–424.
4. Bryce, James, *The American Commonwealth*, vol. 2 (New York: Macmillan and Company, 1889), p. 793.
5. *Ibid.*, p. 797.
6. Pred, Allan, *City Systems in Advanced Economies* (London: Hutchinson and Company, 1977).
7. Tilly, Charles, *Coercion, Capital and European States, A.D. 990–1990* (Oxford: Basil Blackwell, 1990).
8. Epstein, Jason, "The Tragical History of New York," *New York Review of Books*, April 9, 1992, pp. 45–52.
9. I owe some of the phrasing in this paragraph to a personal communication from James Q. Wilson.
10. Cf., McNeill, William, *Venice: The Hinge of Europe* (Chicago: University of Chicago Press, 1974).
11. Lampard, Eric E., "The New York Metropolis in Transformation: History and Prospect: A Study in Historical Particularity," in Ewers, Hans-Jurgen, John B. Goddard, and Horst Matzerath, eds., *The Future of the Metropolis: Berlin, London, Paris, New York* (New York: Walter de Gruyter, 1986), p. 36.
12. *Ibid.*, p. 38.
13. Vernon, Raymond, *Metropolis 1985* (Cambridge, MA: Harvard University Press, 1965), p. 9.
14. Jaher, Frederick Cople, *The Urban Establishment: Upper Strata in Boston, New*

York, Charleston, Chicago, and Los Angeles (Urbana, IL: University of Illinois Press, 1982).

15. Conzen, Michael, "The Maturing Urban System in the United States, 1840–1910," *Annals of the Association of American Geographers* 67 (#1, 1977): 92.
16. Chandler, Alfred D., *The Visible Hand* (Cambridge, MA: Harvard University Press, 1977), pp. 91–92.
17. Chernow, Ron, *The House of Morgan* (New York: Atlantic Monthly Press, 1990).
18. Supple, Barry E., "A Business Elite: German-Jewish Financiers in Nineteenth Century New York," *Business History Review* 31 (Summer 1957): 156–157; Carosso, Vincent, *Investment Banking in America: A History* (Cambridge, MA: Harvard University Press, 1970), pp. 81–82, 157.
19. Hammack, David C., *Power and Society: Greater New York at the Turn of the Century* (New York: Russell Sage, 1982), pp. 45–46.
20. Pred, *City Systems in Advanced Economies*, Chap. 2.
21. Levine, Faye, *The Culture Barons* (New York: Crowell, 1976).
22. Kasson, John F., *Rudeness and Civility: Manners in Nineteenth Century Urban America* (New York: Hill and Wang, 1990).
23. Green, Martin, *New York 1913: The Armory Show and the Paterson Strike Pageant* (New York: Scribners, 1988).
24. Taylor, William R., "The Launching of a Commercial Culture: New York City, 1860–1939," in Mollenkopf, John, ed., *Power, Culture, and Place: Essays on New York City* (New York: Russell Sage Foundation, 1988); Jacoby, Russell, *The Last Intellectuals* (New York: Basic Books, 1987).
25. Bensel, Richard, *Yankee Leviathan* (New York: Cambridge University Press, 1990), p. 253.
26. Shefter, Martin, "Party, Bureaucracy, and Political Change in the United States," in Maisel, Louis, and Joseph Cooper, eds., *Political Parties: Development and Decay, Sage Electoral Studies Yearbook* 4 (1978): 211–266.
27. Polanyi, Karl, *The Great Transformation: The Political and Economic Origins of Our Time* (New York: Rinehart & Co., 1944).
28. Costigliola, Frank, *Awkward Dominion: American Political, Economic, and Cultural Relations with Europe* (Ithaca, NY: Cornell University Press, 1984).
29. Chernow, *The House of Morgan*.
30. Broz, J. Lawrence, "The Rise of the United States, International Monetary Instability, and the Origins of the Federal Reserve Act of 1913." Paper delivered at the 1989 annual meeting of the American Political Science Association, Atlanta, GA.
31. Chandler, Lester, *Benjamin Strong, Central Banker* (Washington, DC: The Brookings Institution, 1958).
32. For a discussion, see Kindleberger, Charles P., *Manias, Panics, and Crashes* (New York: Basic Books, 1978).

33. Bremer, William, *Depression Winters: New York Social Workers and the New Deal* (Philadelphia: Temple University Press, 1984).
34. Gardner, Richard, *Sterling-Dollar Diplomacy* (Oxford: Clarendon Press, 1956).
35. Shefter, Martin, "Political Incorporation and the Extrusion of the Left: Party Politics and Social Forces in New York City," *Studies in American Political Development* 1 (1986): 52ff.
36. See, e.g., Moynihan, Daniel Patrick, *Maximum Feasible Misunderstanding* (New York: The Free Press, 1969).
37. Vernon, *Metropolis 1985*, p. 81.
38. Ashton, Dore, *The New York School: A Cultural Reckoning* (New York: Viking Press, 1973).
39. Mollenkopf, John, *The Contested City* (Princeton: Princeton University Press, 1983).
40. Mollenkopf, John, *A Phoenix in the Ashes* (Princeton: Princeton University Press, 1992).
41. Noyelle, Thierry and Thomas M. Stanback, Jr., *The Economic Transformation of American Cities* (Totowa, NJ: Rowman and Allanheld, 1984), p. 144.
42. Shefter, Martin, *Political Crisis/Fiscal Crisis: The Collapse and Revival of New York City* (New York: Columbia University Press, 1992), pp. xi–xvi.
43. Wilson, see note 9.
44. Heclo, Hugh, "Issue Networks and the Executive Establishment," in King, Anthony, ed., *The New American Political System* (Washington, D.C.: American Enterprise Institute, 1978).
45. Wilson, see note 9.
46. Jacoby, *The Last Intellectuals;* Bender, Thomas, *New York Intellect: A History of Intellectual Life in New York City from 1759 to the Beginnings of Our Times* (New York: Knopf, 1987).
47. Winnick, Louis, *New People in Old Neighborhoods: The Role of New Immigrants in Rejuvenating New York's Communities* (New York: Russell Sage Foundation, 1990).
48. For this index see any recent issue of *Barron's*.

2

New York City and the International System: International Strategy and Urban Fortunes

Miles Kahler

In 1945, New York was the largest city in the most powerful country in the world and its predominant standing nationally seemed to be reinforced by the international position of the United States. Forty-five years later, New York remains the largest American city, but central cities are less significant within their metropolitan regions and national politics, and one rapidly growing Sunbelt rival, Los Angeles, seems poised to challenge New York's economic and cultural preeminence. The American economy remains by far the largest in the world, but its edge over other industrialized states has declined, and perhaps more important, it has become far more open internationally.

These national and international developments raise two questions. What role did changes in the international system play in New York City's economic decline prior to its 1975 fiscal crisis and in the city's economic resurgence since? Has New York City had a coherent strategy for coping with the changes it has experienced in its international economic position? Before addressing these questions, however, it is useful to analyze the relationship between cities and the international system in more general terms.

The author wishes to thank Michael Conzen and Amy Bridges for their comments on an earlier version of this chapter.

National and International Urban Development

With the exception of Hong Kong and Singapore, the world's major cities today are embedded in nations. Because relations between the urban and the international are mediated by national political structures, the links between cities and the international system have not been subject to the same scrutiny as relations between national and international, or urban and national, affairs. In the case of American cities, this tendency has been reinforced by the closed character of the U.S. economy for much of the nation's history and the relative insulation of the American polity from international conflict. Neither imperial centers nor targets of conquest, American cities have developed in a relatively benign international setting in contrast to their counterparts in Asia or Europe.

Even when cities and city-states dominated the commanding heights of the world economy, urban fortunes were largely determined by the policies of national or dynastic states. In his history of early capitalism, Fernand Braudel makes it clear that the Portuguese and Spanish monarchies were largely responsible for the movement of world economic mastery from Venice to Antwerp to Genoa. The opening of the New World by Portugal and Spain shifted the locus of world trade northward, eroding the position of Venice and the Mediterranean economy, which it dominated. Antwerp and Genoa, which succeeded Venice as hubs of the world economy, were entirely at the mercy of absolutist monarchs who were technically in their debt but in fact were in charge of their fate.[1]

These examples demonstrate not only the importance of national policies for the fortunes of cities—even in an era when city-states confronted national states on a more equal basis than currently—but also the possibility of conflict between city and nation in setting the terms of integration within the international economy. With the rise of Amsterdam and London as the core cities of the international economy, these conflicts between cities and states were transformed into conflicts *within* national states. Increasingly, the policies of national states have influenced the fate of cities by shaping their interaction with the international system.

Perhaps the oldest national strategy for dealing with the world economy has been the formation of empires. These imperial structures created important economic nodes at both their center and periphery. Seville flourished with the Spanish empire, but now sits high and dry (literally) in the poorest region of a Spain without imperial pretensions. Former colonial capitals, such as Dakar in Senegal, built their livelihood on connections to the metropole, but with decolonization have lost much of their economic hinterland. Other cities have benefited from military threats in the international system. Garrison towns and naval bases—such as Portsmouth, England, and Norfolk, Virginia—receive a steady stream of government resources.

Finally, some cities are built on the peculiarities of breaks in the structure of market regulation erected by nation-states. The border cities of the United States and Mexico profit from the fact that there is not free exchange of goods, capital, or individuals between the two countries: the growth of *maquiladora* industry (duty-free assembly plants), founded on a handful of clauses in the United States tariff code, is a prime example. The fortunes of most international financial centers and many leading mercantile cities have been built on a special status of reduced state regulation, either recognized (the birth of the London Euromarkets is one example) or illicit (smuggling). All of these examples suggest that the incorporation of cities within national states may produce opportunities as well as impose costs.

Whatever the opportunities created by national mediation, cities embedded in nation-states do not have their own commercial policies or their own monetary policies. As Jane Jacobs notes, they cannot set their own exchange rates vis-à-vis the world or other regions. They must instead attempt to influence the national economic and diplomatic policies that do set the terms of their transactions with the international system.

In examining the international relations of New York, three propositions will guide our discussion:

1. Although international economic and political change influences the fate of cities, that change is mediated by national policy regimes.
2. Because the international is mediated by national politics, national policies matter in shaping urban outcomes. By influencing the behavior of economic decision-makers, national policy regimes shape the fortunes of cities.[2]
3. The political and economic choices of urban elites may also affect urban fortunes. In reading the international system and attempting to make gains from it, urban decision-makers can pursue two broad strategies to maximize gains.

First is a strategy of *adaptation*—taking the national policy regime as given, and attempting to capture for the city's residents the benefits of international change. Second is a strategy of *influence* at the national level, which may in turn take two forms: efforts to arrest the effects of international changes damaging to urban interests, or efforts to change national policies which prevent the city from benefiting from international developments. Seeking tariff protection for economic sectors threatened by international competition is a classic example of the former influence strategy; proposals to deregulate the financial sector are an example of the latter. Of course, cities may pursue strategies of both adaptation and influence simultaneously.

In principle, a third strategy might be pursued by cities: a strategy of influence at the international level. Although some subnational political units have attempted their own "diplomacy" abroad, such efforts usually take the overarching national policy regime as given and seek to gain competitive advantages vis-à-vis other subnational entities in attracting tourists, investors, or other economic players to a particular city. Thus these activities can be regarded as a subcategory within strategies of adaptation. They are attempts to capture additional gains from the international economy by advertising a congenial policy regime.[3]

The prerequisites of strategies of adaptation and influence diverge. Adaptation has more demanding requirements within local urban politics: shaping the city to make gains from international change may be difficult if losses are implied for particular groups within the city, or if the gains from international dependence are not widely perceived. Successful influence strategies at the national level, on the other hand, depend on the political weight of urban elites within national institutions and the support that their international policy preferences are likely to garner from potential coalition partners in national politics.

New York and the International System, 1945–1975

The international relations of New York following World War II had economic, local political, and national political roots. Each pointed toward emphatic support for the basic tenets of Cold War liberalism: anti-Communism and a liberalized international economic regime. The city's economic elite, as James Kurth makes clear in his chapter in this volume, had long been internationalist. New York's financial establishment was the vanguard of America's substantial economic involvement in Europe and Latin America. Although New York's financial elites did not endorse all components of the postwar economic order—they initially opposed the Bretton Woods agreement in favor of either gold or a key-currency plan based on sterling and the dollar—the liberal orientation of the postwar policies of the United States matched their preferences.

Not only did they endorse the postwar initiatives, they also staffed the expanded foreign policy apparatus that managed America's new international role.

The second base for New York's support of anti-Communist internationalism was local ethnic politics. Many northeastern and midwestern cities displayed volatile ethnic politics, but New York City's was unusual in its expression of clear-cut foreign policy preferences, grounded in the ties that ethnicity forged to other parts of the world. While German and Irish New Yorkers tilted toward isolationism in the 1930s and 1940s, Jewish New Yorkers were strongly internationalist. Their support for an interventionist American role before World War II was reinforced after World War II by the birth of Israel and later by the plight of Soviet Jews. Their internationalism was expressed through the city's Liberal party (anti-Communist successor to the American Labor party) and labor unions, particularly the ILGWU.

Finally, and perhaps most important, New York's support for liberal internationalism was rooted in the new relationship between Washington and the nation's cities that emerged during the postwar era. As John Mollenkopf notes, the New Deal both rested on political support in northeastern cities and transformed the relationship between the national government and the cities. Under the aegis of the New Deal, a pro-growth coalition was constructed in major cities, incorporating labor unions, middle-class reformers, and traditional Democratic machines.[4] With membership in a national political coalition came support for the policies of that coalition, foreign as well as domestic.

It could be argued that in providing support for the postwar stance of American foreign policy, New York elites read their interests and the interests of their city correctly. A port city backed an international stance committed to expanding international trade; a financial center could aspire to become the capital of international capital; a city of immigrants could welcome an international order committed to the free movement of individuals. Looking back on the effects that international change had on the city during the three decades after World War II, however, one is impressed by the mixed consequences for New York of America's postwar national policy regime. On the one hand, the liberal international order that the United States established enabled New York–based banks and corporations to expand their operations throughout the world. On the other hand, in a number of domains New York was less successful than some other cities in capturing gains from the postwar international order.

World War II and Cold War competition with the Soviet Union raised national military spending and transformed cities in the West: from a status described as "colonial" by one historian, the West and its urban centers developed a strong manufacturing base, encouraged by wartime policies of decentralization. After the impetus given their growth by defense spending during World War II, Sunbelt cities in California and Texas increased their edge in such sectors as aerospace and electronics.[5] Although New York benefited from the wartime and postwar economic expansion, its economic structure was not transformed by an infusion of defense spending. The effects of military expenditures during the postwar decades cannot be attributed only to a politically determined regional bias: The fact that greater Boston and Connecticut managed to capitalize on military spending suggests that the spending followed economic sectors of interest to the military. (During the 1980s, a decade of increased military expenditures, the regional bias, if anything, worked against the Midwest, not the Northeast: in fiscal year 1981, New York State ranked third in prime contract awards from the Department of Defense; Massachusetts and Connecticut were fourth and fifth.[6])

Whatever the causes for the regional distribution of military spending—whether sectoral location or the influence of Sunbelt congressmen—it is clear that New York City benefited relatively little. The lack of development of a defense manufacturing base may simply have reflected deeper competitive disadvantages faced by the city in an era when new manufacturing sectors had different physical requirements. On the other hand, New York's apparent weakness in developing the university-high technology-defense nexus is striking, and cannot be wholly explained as another facet of the erosion of the city's manufacturing base.

The failure of New York to capture its share of a defense budget that was admittedly tilted toward the Sunbelt is less puzzling than the failure of New York's existing manufacturing firms to capitalize on the liberalized trading system, an Atlantic-centered system that boomed during the 1950s and 1960s. Trade among the industrialized countries grew at rates unprecedented in the twentieth century. Yet two key activities that should have benefited from this international change—the production and transport of manufactured goods—began their relative decline within New York's economy in these decades, mirroring the slippage of New York's relative position in these sectors within the national economy.

As Roger Starr notes, "One of New York's best-kept secrets in 1946 was its status as the nation's largest manufacturing town."[7] New York's manufacturing pre-eminence was of long standing: after the Civil War, manufacturing outstripped the port and its ancillary activities as the core of the city's economy, and Manhattan became "the fast-industrializing nation's premier factory town."[8] Many of the features of that key sector set during the late nineteenth and early twentieth centuries persist today. The early dominance of the apparel industry, and an early tendency toward decentralization out of the Manhattan core were two. More important for the future decline of the city's industrial base were the divorce between the business elite of New York and its manufacturers and the dependence of manufacturing on low-wage immigrant labor.

As Emanuel Tobier suggests, what might be called the headquarters business elite of New York—the managers of national and international corporations—and the entrepreneurs who manned its small-scale manufacturing sectors have long been drawn from different social and ethnic strata. Their interests frequently clashed, particularly on questions of land use. The business elite that developed New York's first zoning code in 1916—in part to arrest the march of manufacturing up the island—and masterminded the Regional Plan of 1929, with its "national center" strategy, had little sympathy with the core city's manufacturers. Indeed, they aimed at the displacement of manufacturing from the central business district in favor of office development.[9] The national linkages fostered by the headquarters business elite presaged the international strategy that business leaders would urge for the city in the 1980s. Both of these visions endorsed a future for the city center that had little place for one of the principal economic activities of the city at the end of World War II.

As the nation's industry embarked on two decades of expansion after 1945, New York's diverse manufacturing base began a slow decline that accelerated in the late 1960s and early 1970s. By the late 1950s, real estate, corporate headquarters, and business services had surpassed manufacturing in importance in Manhattan.[10] Many economists argue the inevitability of manufacturing's decline in the postwar era: the cost advantages of suburban or out-of-region locations seem to have been more significant than international competition.[11] Although New York's manufacturing sector was unable to capitalize on a postwar order congenial to manufactured exports, the open trading system sponsored by the United States appears to have had only a minor role in deciding the sector's fate in the central city.

The apparel industry is often cited (particularly by the labor unions) as a prominent exception, but even in the case of this, the largest of New York's manufacturing industries, evidence that liberalized trade and import competition was a principal cause of decline is far from clear. As Roger Waldinger describes, the first steps in exiting New York City were moves to non-union regional locations, such as Pennsylvania and New Jersey, and then moves south and west to states where right-to-work legislation made unionization even more difficult. Labor cost differentials later pushed larger apparel firms to seek overseas production sites or outward processing, but the surge in imports in recent decades was the result of direct retailer-producer contracts that were based on overseas firms rather than American multinationals. Since 1975, while imports to the United States have grown steadily, New York's relative position within the American apparel industry has stabilized.[12]

In two other respects, however, New York's international linkages after World War II may have hastened manufacturing's decline. First, as the city's business elite became increasingly internationalized, the divorce between the elite's urban strategy and manufacturing became final. Whether the national center of the 1930s or the world city of the 1980s, the New York of the business elite had little place for small-scale manufacturing. As Starr points out, the political elite echoed this set of assumptions: Before the war, politicians had nurtured the manufacturing sector through such measures as housing subsidies and cheap mass transit; after 1945, other issues dominated the public agenda.[13] Second, labor costs in New York were driven up by a central feature of the postwar policy regime in Washington: the McCarran-Walter Act of 1952 retained national-origins quotas and tight restrictions on immigration. Waves of immigration from overseas, which had sustained New York manufacturing with low-cost labor and entrepreneurial talent, would not resume until thorough reform of the immigration laws in 1965.[14]

In the liberalized trading system after 1945, New York's role as a center for the movement of goods was also undermined. The port of New York has long demonstrated the effects of public policy on the ability of a city to capture gains from international trade and trade-related services. In the early nineteenth century the Erie Canal connected the burgeoning economy of the upper Midwest to the world economy through New York City, confirming New York's position as the dominant metropolis on the eastern seaboard. Railway terminuses and business services followed the growth of port activity. Like the manufacturing sector, the port emerged from the war displaying a deceptive prosperity. Its disadvantages in cost and congestion increased, however, as trucks supplanted railroads. In addition, public-policy decisions undermined the port's position, particularly the decision to build the St. Lawrence Seaway, severing New York's connection to part of its hinterland.[15] Modernization by the Port Authority, which would have hastened the transition to containerized cargo, was thwarted by the power of labor unions, a key part of the postwar political coalition.[16] As for airports and marine terminals, dominant business interests were reluctant to support city control of these vital infrastructural links to the international economy: When New York City attempted to develop its own airport authority, the Port Authority—an agency dependent on two state governments for its charter—mobilized both the airlines and the investment banks to thwart the city's plan.[17]

In a final sector, the conflict between urban influence and the postwar national policy regime produced an even more startling outcome. Finance has been one of the pillars of New York's support for internationalism since the 1920s. Yet in the 1950s and early 1960s, the federal government enacted a series of measures to restrict capital outflows from the United States in an effort to prop up the dollar. This imposed considerable costs on New York as an international financial center. Many activities that might have located in New York during the 1960s instead located in London, where American banks and multinationals were critical in establishing a flourishing international capital market. New York banks followed financial activity and their clients to London in the 1960s; the benefits to the city itself were slender during the early years of the Euromarkets. Washington's peculiar interpretation of the necessities of international leadership impeded New York's claim to international financial primacy.

When the erosion of New York's economic base became clear in the late 1960s and early 1970s, the city's highly organized public sector precluded the Lindsay and Beame administrations' pursuing a policy of adaptation. Rather, the city relied on external financing, first from the national government and finally from commercial bankers. The banks grew increasingly skeptical, however, and finally, in 1975, closed the financing window on the city.[18] The renewed influence that forced austerity awarded to international business interests served to crystallize a new outward orientation in New York.

International Strategy and the "New" New York Economy

The shock of the fiscal crisis and the political accommodations required to overcome it temporarily disguised structural changes that accompanied the recovery of the New York economy after 1977. The outlines of those changes are relatively clear. In terms of employment, the city's economy demonstrated a clear shift to business services, finance, insurance, and real estate. Coincident with the growth of these sectors, manufacturing continued its relative decline: By 1982, only two of the top ten industries in the city were in manufacturing—apparel and publishing—and the latter no longer sustained substantial blue-collar employment. The growing sectors were highly concentrated in Manhattan and in larger firms; Manhattan also lost proportionately less of its manufacturing base than other boroughs, particularly Brooklyn.[19] At the same time, the number of Fortune 500 firms' headquarters in the city continued to decline, from a level of between 130 and 140 during the 1950s and 1960s, to sixty-six in 1982. Optimists noted that many corporations departing the city remained in the region, sustaining the market for business services in New York, and that business service firms and foreign corporations located in the city, compensating for the loss of Fortune 500 headquarters.[20]

The transformation of New York (or at least Manhattan) into a "super service center" resembled changes in other American cities, the "postindustrial transformation" described by Mollenkopf in which central cities are increasingly characterized by headquarters, business services, the professions, and public and "third sector" entities. In the case of New York, this transformation is connected to the internationalization of the American economy.

Matthew Drennan has stated the paradox of New York's economic performance since the mid-1970s most succinctly: ". . . New York City has become smaller, poorer, and less important in some economic activities in the region and the nation. At the same time, it has become more important or at least maintained a position of dominance in some booming economic activities often linked to the international economy."[21] Drennan notes that while New York has lost relative share in the headquarters of firms that engage in national goods production, it has retained its share of headquarters for the most internationalized multinational corporations and the most internationally dependent corporate service firms.[22] Mollenkopf echoes this view, arguing that New York displayed "powerful competitive advantages" in "providing a key link between the United States and the rest of the world."[23]

In two areas in particular, changes in international linkages after the 1960s seem to have played a significant role in these developments. One—widely noted—is the internationalization of financial markets, a trend that has benefited both London and New York, and is now influencing Tokyo's rapid emergence as a financial center. As David Vogel indicates in his chapter of this book, regulatory changes at the national level helped New York benefit from international trends—the introduction of offshore banking in 1979, and the elimination of withholding tax on interest paid to foreigners to encourage foreign financing of the federal deficit. Whether international developments will remain as favorable for growth in this sector as they had been during the past decade is considered in greater detail below.

A second international trend, less noted by the heralds of New York's new international position, has had a very different impact on the city's economy, though perhaps an equally positive one: the renewal of large-scale immigration into the city after the enactment of new immigration legislation in 1965. The new immigration has had marked effects on other American cities, such as Miami or Los Angeles, but, as in finance, New York has captured a high proportion of this new international flow. Despite the relative decline of the port and the economic distress of the 1970s, New York remained a favored destination for the new immigrants from Asia, Latin America, and the Caribbean: the city retained a competitive advantage in accommodating newcomers. When compared to earlier waves of immigrants, the newcomers were better educated and about 20 percent held white-collar or professional jobs (the balance were employed in service or blue-collar occupations).[24]

As might be expected, the new immigrants found employment in expanding sectors of the city economy: health services, eating and drinking establishments, banking, and real estate. Their role in one key sector, however, suggests that their contribution to the city's economic prospects was more significant than simple aggregate statistics suggest. One-third of the workers in the garment industry in 1980 were post-1965 immigrants; that industry's relative stabilization after 1975 (measured as a share of national employment) depended in important respects on these newest New Yorkers.[25]

After 1975 the New York apparel industry—which remains the largest manufacturing sector in the city—found a market niche resistant to the national and international trends that had reduced the industry's size for decades. As Waldinger describes, while the city had lost mass production segments of apparel manufacture in preceding decades, more "style-sensitive" items closely connected to the city's fashion industry came to dominate production in the 1970s and 1980s. These portions of the garment industry were more resistant to competition from low-cost producers in the United States and other countries.

The new immigration increased the competitiveness of the apparel sector in New York by providing, as it had in the past, low-cost (some would say sweated) labor to the industry.[26] It also provided an infusion of entrepreneurs, a contribution that was arguably even more significant. One explanation for the decline of the city's manufacturing base in the late 1960s and 1970s was the passing of the cohort of entrepreneurs drawn from the great waves of immigration in the early twentieth century. Waldinger's evidence suggests that few of those entrepreneurs, at least in the apparel industry, passed on their businesses to their children, who generally moved into white-collar jobs or the professions. Only with the new immigration after 1965 did a new generation of entrepreneurs, predominantly Chinese and Dominican, appear. The possibility for success was increased by a renewed labor force as well, but low-wage labor alone does not explain the recent resilience of the garment industry.[27]

New York's International Strategy and Its Prospects

Although domestic economic developments contributed to the prosperity of the city's service sector, New York's improved economic prospects in the 1980s resulted in significant measure from its pursuit of an international strategy of adaptation. The Koch administration adopted urban policies that were more favorable to business than previous administrations, and these policies were in effect guaranteed by the oversight of New York's finance by outside agencies. Like a developing country experiencing a fiscal crisis, New York undertook a rigorous adjustment program that involved reducing its budget deficit and restraining public-sector wages in exchange for external financing to avoid bankruptcy. Fiscal autonomy was diminished in favor of creditors and external fiscal monitors—in New York's case, the Municipal Assistance Corporation and Emergency Financial Control Board. Poorer and less organized sectors of the population bore most of the costs of adjustment in New York, as in many debtor countries. In New York, however, these policies were successful in stimulating private investment and economic growth.

Business firms linked to the international economy also made their mark in the city's planning, particularly in Manhattan. International banks had undertaken to revive the financial district in the late 1950s through the Downtown–Lower Manhattan Association, an initiative of David Rockefeller that produced a "private master plan for lower Manhattan."[28] The city's economic resurgence in the late 1970s permitted the completion of a number of immense projects directed toward fostering tourism and the international financial sector: South Street Seaport, the Convention Center, and Battery Park City.[29]

Regarding immigration, the city has been more passive. The politicians who reformed immigration law in 1965 did not expect an influx of new immigrants from Asia and Latin America. New York did have established advantages in assimilating immigrants, but its stance to the new immigration has largely been one of laissez-faire.

The growing importance of New York's links to the international economy has led local officials to pursue policies designed to strengthen the city as a global financial, communications, and cultural center. As Irving Leveson has observed:

> There has been an unstated but quite impressive attempt to use service industries as a basis for economic development. This is seen in the attempt to encourage tourism, through the 'I Love New York' campaign, the growth of show tours, the World's Fair, Op Sail, and other activities. It is seen in the development of a banking free-trade zone, a reinsurance pool, and a convention center.[30]

Despite widespread acceptance of a "world city" strategy, however, its implications and the probability of its success have not been carefully evaluated.

First, the economic prospects of the increasingly internationalized financial and business service sectors must be assessed. These sectors of the city's economy burgeoned during the sustained expansion of the national economy after the 1981–1982 recession (although their growing contribution to the city's economy predates the most recent recovery). An international bull market in financial assets accompanied the expansion. Although many talk of "recession-proof" services, the cyclical history of New York's financial sector does not warrant such optimism. Global growth in the financial sector has also depended on the deregulation and internationalization of financial markets over the past decade. How much growth will subsequently flow from what may have been a one-time set of events is unclear.

Whatever the outlook internationally for those sectors central to the New York economy, an equally significant issue—and one subject to influence by public policy—is what *share* of these activities will be captured by New York rather than other locations. One possibility, of course, is that all core cities may lose their hold over service-sector jobs, just as they did over the location of manufacturing: the advantages of agglomeration in services may prove to be temporary. Certainly there are indications that the "global office" may succeed the global factory for some operations, an extension of the movement of "back office" operations out of central cities and away from headquarters.[31] The cost advantages of overseas locations for certain activities, such as data entry, are already considerable. More significant for the future of New York's international service strategy, however, is the shift or loss of share in high-skill or professional jobs to other urban areas.

In the case of alternative financial centers, at least one threat to New York's relative position is closely connected to the eroding economic dominance of the United States. The rapid rise of Tokyo as a financial center, unforeseen a decade ago, is related to a regional shift in the world economy—rapid economic growth in the Asia-Pacific region—and to changes in the Japanese economy, particularly financial deregulation and the persistence of large current-account surpluses (in turn the result of a high national savings rate) that have underpinned growing Japanese overseas investments in the 1980s.

The rise of Tokyo as a world financial center could erode New York's position by attracting a larger share of the international financial and business service activities. The principal attraction of Tokyo as a financial center is Japan's vast pool of savings; firms may find it useful to be close to such important customers as Japanese institutional investors. In other respects, however, its advantages over New York may not be great. Certainly there are no cost advantages to doing business in Tokyo. Despite the rise in prominence of Japanese financial institutions (seven of the world's ten biggest banks are now Japanese), the competitive advantage of Japanese banks, at least in their overseas operations, is as "low-cost producers in bulk, commodity-type loans to big firms and local authorities. . .[32] Tokyo and Japanese financial institutions, unlike New York and its institutions, have not been centers of financial innovation. That edge in innovations is likely to persist and to favor the New York financial market, though innovations in this sector cannot be copyrighted or patented, and imitation by rivals soon follows. The economic basis of Japanese financial predominance may also be temporary. Japanese trade surpluses and the savings rate are declining; the aging of the Japanese population (increasing the number of dissavers) will also erode the export of capital. And despite their impressive size, Japanese banks may suffer from their deep involvement in the risky Tokyo property market.[33]

In many respects, Los Angeles poses a more plausible threat to New York's international strategy. Eight of the top twelve Japanese financial institutions have based their American operations in California (five in Los Angeles); they are following their clients—Japanese corporations—who use Los Angeles as the anchor for their involvement in the American economy.[34] Los Angeles now ranks second to New York in deposit totals (surpassing Chicago since 1986), and the rate of increase in Los Angeles is far higher than in New York.[35] Los Angeles has also retained a far more significant manufacturing sector than New York or many other American cities; as in New York, the new immigration provides low-wage labor for its apparel and furniture factories. However, Los Angeles does not host the headquarters of many large corporations, whether manufacturing, services, or financial institutions, and this weakens its ability to compete with New York as a center for business services.[36] Nevertheless, its underlying manufacturing base, the largest port in the United States, and the growing importance of the Japanese (and Pacific) beachhead have convinced some that Los Angeles may challenge New York for metropolitan dominance in the next century.

Although the internationalization of financial markets and business services has benefited New York, many would argue that it has produced firms that are more footloose than in the past and that those firms are happy to stimulate competition among possible business locations. As such firms become more sophisticated and cities become more intent on retaining their key service industries, municipal governments have had to offer ever larger subsidies to attract and retain firms. The recent decision by Chase Manhattan to move back-office operations to Brooklyn rather than to Jersey City is only one example: New York City retained Chase's back-office employment only with the help of "far more valuable government incentives than ever offered to a New York City company. . ."[37]

Subsidies are only one measure of the pro-business strategy of adaptation that New York and other cities have undertaken to attract increasingly discriminating firms and their payrolls. As noted above, economic development programs in New York during the 1980s have been directed toward international financial services and tourism. Increasingly, in both its economic structure and public-policy orientation, New York has come to resemble a "monocultural" economy with a narrowing economic base of potentially volatile sectors.

These choices within a strategy of adaptation have imposed costs and may have foreclosed opportunities. Despite the prominence and glamour associated with the world city strategy, the city has neglected that other key element of international influence on its economy during the past decade—the new immigration and the contribution that it has made to the manufacturing base of the city. Manufacturing has been the stepchild of New York's development strategy in the past decade. Some observers have simply written it off, while others have argued that New York needs the diversification and the entry-level jobs that only this sector can provide. Two industries in particular—what might be called the cultural-manufacturing nexus of fashion/apparel and printing/publishing—remain significant employers in the city. In certain respects, the argument over the role of manufacturing in New York echoes a national debate over whether "manufacturing matters," particularly in sustaining service-sector jobs.[38] The city's current strategy has squeezed manufacturing, however: In the competition for urban space, small-scale manufacturing often loses to residential and service uses.[39] Competing (and more politically influential) uses have made it difficult for newcomers in "cultural" sectors, such as publishing, advertising, or fashion, to get a start in Manhattan.

The economic costs and choices implicit in the international orientation of the city are also reflected in politics. Critics of the world city argue that it produces a dual city, one that is more clearly divided between poorly paid service jobs and high-income professional employment than a structure based on manufacturing. That bifurcation is probably exacerbated by an internationally oriented service strategy. The economic consequences of such a development path—high levels of immigration and growing social inequality—may eventually produce new forms of political conflict.[40]

The strategy of adaptation pursued by the Koch administration must be sustained in urban politics, and with the departure of Ed Koch and the election of David Dinkins as mayor, several threats to that strategy can be discerned. Since the fiscal crisis of the 1970s, the city's development strategy has been based on a set of negotiated bargains to ensure competitiveness and a satisfactory business climate. That strategy has incorporated elements of both inclusion and exclusion. To date, the bargains struck with public-sector unions have more or less stuck. Whether they will continue to do so, particularly if higher inflation returns, remains an open question. Those excluded from the post-1975 bargain and many of its benefits—particularly the black and Hispanic poor—can also threaten its continued success: Any renewal of urban violence on the scale of the 1960s would undoubtedly produce capital flight and disinvestment and seriously damage the tourist industry as well. (This is a lesson that many developing countries, such as Jamaica, have learned.) Political mobilization around social welfare demands, a more likely alternative, could meet resistance from revenue-providers, particularly organized business.

Business itself, despite renewed influence following the fiscal crisis, remains fragmented in New York. Fainstein and Fainstein note that "perhaps because of the global scope of their interests, [New York business elites] have shown less concern with developing their urban environment than have their counterparts elsewhere."[41] Business fragmentation makes it difficult for economic elites to develop sustained involvement in the city's political process. Sustained participation in ongoing political coalitions is even less likely as the role of foreign investors in New York grows.

Finally, the world city strategy has produced some backlash in residential neighborhoods (notably Manhattan's Upper West Side) that resist the effects of commercial development. New York has been spared much of the conflict between downtown and the neighborhoods that San Francisco and other American cities have endured, since most of the development required for its international strategy has taken place in established commercial areas. If expansion continues, however, political backlash may grow. Extending arguments made by Peter Katzenstein about small states in the international system, one might argue that a successful urban strategy based on specialized links to the international economy requires a set of underlying political bargains to offset the costs of volatility in the international economy and the adjustments that such dependence imposes.[42] New York's socially fragmented and ethnically divided politics may be unable to produce such a solution.

Since 1975 New York's international strategy has chiefly been one of adaptation. Local officials have not regarded it as necessary to pursue a strategy of influence over national policy because the national policy regime—one of liberalized trade and capital movements and close ties with other industrialized countries—has been favorable to the city's interests. Despite threats of growing protectionism, it is likely that national policies governing American links to the international economy will not change drastically.

In one area, however, New York's weakness within the national political system sets it apart from its urban rivals in Europe and Japan: financial deregulation. The ties between metropolitan financial institutions and the national regulatory authorities are far closer in Tokyo or London than in New York. In Japan the consensus in favor of financial deregulation faced opposition from provincial banks that had strong political connections in the Diet; finally, however, the alliance between the central bureaucracy and major financial institutions pushed forward regulatory changes. In London, links between the City and the Bank of England, principal regulator of the financial sector, are even cozier than in Japan. In the United States, by contrast, political suspicion of metropolitan finance is reflected in a fragmented regulatory structure, in which Congress (representing the interests of many smaller banks) plays a central role. If a regulatory issue pits New York financial institutions against foreign competitors (such as offshore banking), New York views are likely to prevail. If it pits New York finance against its domestic rivals, particularly regional and local banks, New York is more likely to lose.

On the key question of interstate banking, New York has not prevailed. The pattern of gradual reduction of interstate barriers has served the interests of the regional banks.[43] They have been able to grow in expanding regional markets while excluding larger financial institutions. This failure of New York finance to shape domestic banking regulation has had two effects. First, by encouraging money-center banks to seek profits in international banking, it exposed them to the Third World debt crisis. That in turn has provided the possibility for a takeover of some major New York banks by fast-growing "super-regional" banks: One observer predicted that "by 1990 at least two of the eight money-centre banks will have disappeared, taken over by or merged with either a super-regional bank or another money-centre."[44] Thus the advent of national banking will mean that not only will New York banks be able to operate in other regions, but also the headquarters of a larger number of major banks will be located elsewhere.

Conclusion: New York and the Requirements of Internationalization

Following World War II, New York elites assumed that because their city was the leading metropolis of the world's most powerful nation, its fortunes would rise with those of the United States. However, several established sectors in the city's economy—in particular, the port and manufacturing—did not gain from America's international predominance; in addition, the city did not capture a large share of defense spending and London became a leading international capital market. Like the United States, New York assumed that its position nationally and internationally was secure and, especially in the late 1960s and early 1970s, did not take cognizance of challenges to its preeminent position as a link between the national and the international economies.

After the crisis of 1969–1975, New York had an international strategy thrust upon it, and its success in attracting international services, real estate investment, and tourism has reinforced its dependence on the international economy. Despite this success, trends in the international economy are sufficiently uncertain that diversifying the city's economy should be a major concern. The contribution that the new immigrants have made to entrepreneurship and skilled labor (especially in the manufacturing sector) should be encouraged. New York's political and business leadership must also grasp the political requirements of greater openness to the winds of international change.

Internationalization has benefited New York, but has also produced urban rivals. Competition, however, need not mean decline. Modern metropolises might contemplate two cities—one as a caution, the other as a guide. The first is Venice, beautiful Adriatic port, a museum city that was unable to adapt successfully to changing trade routes or industrialization, a city that has failed to reinvigorate itself by influencing national policy. The second is London, the symbol of what a modern metropolis can be, a gateway to the international economy, open to immigrants and their talents, repeatedly successful in reading the international economy and benefiting from changes in it. Urban fortunes do not depend wholly upon a city's international strategy. But growing international dependence makes a clear assessment of such a strategy, one instrument for New York's avoiding the fate of Venice and shaping a future resembling London's.

Notes

1. Braudel admits that Antwerp's central position was "not generated from within" but rather was thrust upon the city from the outside. Genoa remained a significant financial center after the seventeenth century, but its central role in the world economy ended with the Spanish bankruptcy in 1627. Braudel, Fernand, *Civilization and Capitalism, 15th–18th Century*, vol. 3, *The Perspective of the World* (New York: Harper & Row, 1984), pp. 144, 173.2.
2. For a discussion of economic shifts from northeastern cities to sunbelt cities, see Mollenkopf, John, *The Contested City* (Princeton: Princeton University Press, 1983), chap. 6; for a discussion of the influence of government policies within the New York region, see Danielson, Michael, and Jameson Doig, *New York: The Politics of Urban Regional Development* (Berkeley: University of California Press, 1982), pp. 8–31.
3. For a more detailed account of such "global para-diplomacy," see Duchacek, Ivo D., *The Territorial Dimension of Politics* (Boulder, CO: Westview Press, 1986), pp. 246–254 and "Toward a Typology of New Subnational Governmental Actors in International Relations," Institute of Governmental Studies, University of California, Berkeley, May 1987.
4. Mollenkopf, *The Contested City*, pp. 80–81.
5. The effect of World War II on western cities is described in Nash, Gerald D., *The American West Transformed: The Impact of the Second World War* (Bloomington: Indiana University Press, 1985), especially chap. 2. On the advantages of Sunbelt cities in attracting military spending, see *Ibid.*, p. 217.
6. DeGrasse, Robert W., Jr., *Military Expansion, Economic Decline* (Armonk, NY: M. E. Sharpe, 1983), Table 1.2, p. 25.
7. Starr, Roger, *The Rise and Fall of New York City* (New York: Basic Books, 1985), p. 68.
8. Tobier, Emanuel, "Manhattan's Business District in the Industrial Age," in Mollenkopf, John Hull, ed., *Power, Culture, and Place: Essays on New York City* (New York: Russell Sage Foundation, 1988), pp. 78, 82.
9. *Ibid.*, p. 94; see also Fitch, Robert, "Planning New York City," in Alcaly,

Roger E. and David Mermelstein, eds., *The Fiscal Crisis in American Cities* (New York: Vintage, 1977), pp. 247–248, 261.

10. Tobier, "Manhattan's Business District," p. 100.
11. See, for example, *Ibid.*, p. 100, and Drennan, Matthew P., "Deconstruction of the New York Economy," paper prepared for Dual City Working Group, SSRC Committee on New York City, June 1988, p. 13.
12. Waldinger, Roger D., *Through the Eye of the Needle: Immigrants and Enterprise in New York's Garment Trades* (New York: New York University Press, 1986), pp. 54–88.
13. Starr, *Rise and Fall*, p. 68.
14. Tobier, "Manhattan's Business District," p. 99.
15. On the historical role of the port, see Danielson and Doig, *New York*, pp. 41–43; on its postwar decline, see Starr, *Rise and Fall*, pp. 50–52.
16. Starr, *Rise and Fall*, p. 53.
17. Doig, Jameson W., "Airports, Bus Terminals, and Great Bridges: The Port Authority and Its Strategies to Rein in and Reshape Robert Moses," paper prepared for the Conference on Robert Moses and the Planned Environment, June 1988, pp. 31–33.
18. This period is well described in Shefter, Martin, *Political Crisis/Fiscal Crisis* (New York: Basic Books, 1985), chap. 5.
19. Good accounts of the changed structure of the city's economy are given in Ehrenhalt, Samuel M., " New York City's Labor Force: Change and Challenge," *City Almanac* 17 (December 1983): 1–12; and Klebaner, Benjamin J., ed., *New York City's Changing Economic Base* (New York: Pica Press, 1981).
20. Stanback, Thomas M., Jr., "New York City and the Services Transformation," in Klebaner, ed., *New York City's Changing Economic Base*, p. 52.
21. Drennan, "Deconstruction of the New York Economy," p. 4.
22. *Ibid.*, pp. 20–22.
23. Mollenkopf, John, "The Postindustrial Transformation of the Political Order in New York," in Mollenkopf, John, ed., *Power, Culture, and Place*, p. 230.
24. On the new immigration in New York, see Bogen, Elizabeth, *Immigration in New York* (New York: Praeger, 1987), chap. 3.
25. On employment of the new immigrants by sector, see *Ibid.*, pp. 83–85; for data on employment in the garment sector, see Waldinger, *Through the Eye*, pp. 89–90.
26. *Ibid.*, pp. 103–104.
27. *Ibid.*, chap. 5.
28. Fainstein, Norman I. and Susan S. Fainstein, "Governing Regimes and the Political Economy of Development in New York City, 1946–1984," in Mollenkopf, ed., *Power, Culture, and Place*, p. 175. Newfield, Jack and Paul DuBrul, *The Abuse of Power: The Permanent Government and the Fall of New York* (New York: Viking, 1977).

29. Fainstein and Fainstein, "Governing Regimes," p. 185; Fainstein, Norman I. and Susan S. Fainstein, "The Politics of Urban Development: New York City Since 1945," *City Almanac* 17 (6 April 1984): 19–20.
30. Leveson, Irving, "Strategies for New York City Economic Development," in Klebaner, ed., *New York City's Changing Economic Base,* p. 153.
31. A recent evaluation of this trend is given in Lohr, Steve, "The Growth of the 'Global Office,'" *New York Times,* 18 October 1988, sect. C, pp. 1, 15.
32. Emmott, Bill, "International Banking: Survival of the Fittest," *The Economist,* 26 March 1988, p. 34.
33. *Ibid.*, pp. 58–59.
34. Kotkin, Joel and Yoriko Kishimoto, "The Japanese Are Banking on Los Angeles," *Los Angeles Times Magazine,* 26 July 1987, p. 19; "The Moneymen's Pursuit of Money," *The Economist,* 5 March 1988, pp. 83–84.
35. Lockwood, Charles and Christopher B. Leinberger, "Los Angeles Comes of Age," *The Atlantic Monthly,* January 1988, p. 35.
36. *Ibid.*, p. 36.
37. Lueck, Thomas J., "Chase Bank, with $235 Million Incentive Deal, Picks Brooklyn," *New York Times,* 10 November 1988, sect. A, p. 25.
38. Cohen, Stephen S. and John Zysman, *Manufacturing Matters* (New York: Basic Books, 1987).
39. On this point, see Waldinger, *Through the Eye,* p. 193.
40. Mollenkopf, "The Postindustrial Transformation of the Political Order in New York City," p. 231.41.
41. Fainstein and Fainstein, "Governing Regimes," p. 192.42.
42. Katzenstein, Peter J., *Small States in World Markets: Industrial Policy in Europe* (Ithaca, NY: Cornell University Press, 1985).
43. Emmott, "International Banking," p. 21.
44. *Ibid.*, p. 38; see also "The rebuilding of New York's rickety banks," *The Economist* 23 (April 1988): 77–78.

3

New York City as a National and Global Financial Center

David Vogel

This chapter explores the impact of changes in the domestic and international economy on New York City's standing as a global financial center. It specifically focuses on three interrelated developments.

First, we are currently in the midst of a historic shift in the global center of economic gravity from the Atlantic to the Pacific basins. In the early 1980s, for the first time in American history, the trade of the United States with Asia surpassed its trade with Western Europe. If the current differential between the growth rates of the economies bordering each of these oceans persists, within a generation the Pacific GNP will be equal to that of the Atlantic. In light of the fact that New York City has historically played a critical role in financing trade and investment between the United States and Europe, how will it fare as Asia, rather than Europe, becomes America's most important economic partner?

Second, the relative position of America in the world economy has eroded in recent years. After running a merchandise balance-of-trade surplus for nearly a century, America has run negative trade balances every year but two since 1971. This trend accelerated after 1980, with the trade deficit doubling between 1981 and 1983 and doubling again between 1983 and 1985. Despite the subsequent decline in the value of the dollar, it set still another record in both 1986 and 1987. Since 1988, the size of America's trade deficit has steadily declined; the merchandise trade deficit totaled only $60 billion in 1991. Nonetheless, America's cumulative trade deficits have resulted in a significant shift in the direction of global capital flows: After exporting capital during the three decades following World War II, the United States has now become a net capital importer. In 1986, for the first time since World War I, America's foreign debt exceeded its assets overseas. In 1981 the United States was the world's largest new creditor; it has since become the world's biggest debtor. What effect will these developments have on New York City's importance as a financial center?

New York City's prominent position in international finance dates from the 1940s and was intimately linked to the replacement of Great Britain by the United States as the world's hegemonic power. The United States, however, was able to occupy this role for only a relatively brief period of time, namely between 1945 and 1973. Over the past decade, the relative decline of the American economy has been mirrored by the growing economic strength of Japan. Japan is now the world's largest creditor. It has run a positive trade balance for more than two decades, with its trade surplus totaling a record $99 billion in 1991. It is unlikely that Japan will ever come to occupy a position in the world economy comparable to that previously enjoyed by Great Britain and the United States; however, the steady improvement in Japan's relative position in the world economy vis-à-vis the United States does make Tokyo's financial markets an increasingly important competitor to those of New York City.

There is also a third development whose significance for New York City needs to be explored. This has to do with changes taking place in the United States. Thanks in part to the relaxing of restrictions against interstate banking and an increase in banking mergers and acquisitions, a number of regional financial centers are emerging throughout the United States, most notably in the Southeast and Los Angeles. Not coincidentally, both of these areas are in the Sunbelt, where a disproportionate share of the growth of the American economy has taken place since the early 1970s. To the extent that New York City's historical role as the financial center of the United States has been due to the traditional economic dominance of the Northeast, its dominance may well be threatened as the nation's center of economic gravity shifts south and westward.

In this context, Los Angeles, with its geographic proximity to the Pacific Basin, may find itself in a particularly advantageous position to challenge New York as a major domestic and international banking center. At the same time, Chicago, historically the center of the nation's trading in commodities, has recently pioneered the development of trading in stock index and foreign exchange futures. Do these developments prefigure the emergence of more domestic competitors for New York City?

This chapter consists of two parts. The first section deals with New York City's international role. It begins by tracing the emergence of London as a global financial center and then examines how its role was affected by the replacement of Britain by the United States as the world's dominant power. It then turns to an assessment of New York City's strengths and weaknesses as a global financial center and seeks to measure the significance of Tokyo's challenge to New York City's postwar role as the "capital of capital." The second section explores the domestic challenges to New York City's stature as the financial center of the American economy. The chapter concludes by suggesting that, while New York City's importance as a domestic financial center is likely to decline, no one city will replace it. Rather, the distribution of financial power will likely become increasingly decentralized.

London

One way of approaching the relationship between New York City's future as a financial center and the international competitiveness of the American economy is to trace the impact of the decline of British industry on the City of London. London's emergence as a major financial center in the eighteenth and nineteenth centuries was closely linked to Britain's role as the world's first industrial nation. The two developments reinforced one another. The earnings from British exports of manufactured goods provided much of the capital for the development of British financial institutions, while the quality of Britain's financial infrastructure in the eighteenth and nineteenth centuries facilitated the development of British industry. As Walter Bagehot wrote of the City of London in 1873:

> This efficient and instantly ready organization gives us an enormous advantage in competition with less advanced countries—less advanced, that is, in this particular respect of credit. In a new trade English capital is instantly at the disposal of persons capable of understanding the new opportunities and making good use of them. . . . All *sudden* trade comes to England (his emphasis).[1]

Through the first two-thirds of the nineteenth century, a larger share of the world's manufacturing production was located in Britain than in any other country; as late as 1880, Britain accounted for 40 percent of the world's trade in manufactured goods.

While neither the London Stock Exchange nor British banks were important sources of capital for British industry, London's financial institutions did play an important role in financing Britain's overseas trade and investments. Britain's emergence as a major center of the insurance industry was due to the enormous volume of foreign trade that passed through London. Likewise Britain's merchant banks originally developed to finance Britain's overseas trade by providing credits for countries wishing to import Britain's industrial output. As Britain began to export increasing amounts of capital in the latter quarter of the nineteenth century—between 1880 and 1913 nearly half of Britain's savings were invested outside Britain—London became the center of the international long-term capital market. It supplied the funds that financed much of the world's industrial development, including that of the United States. During this period,

> the City had become the focus of the world's international financial system. Sterling, as the currency in both short- and long-term lending was denominated, was deemed as good as gold. And the Bank of England found itself the guardian of a truly international money system, the gold standard.[2]

Significantly, in 1907, it was to London that New York banks turned to borrow the funds to cope with a panic in American financial markets. London's importance as an international financial center suffered as a result of the relative decline of the British economy that began during the later third of the nineteenth century. This first became apparent during World War I. After 1914, London had difficulty in maintaining its role as a center for foreign reserves and a source of short- and long-term credit. Consequently, New York City began to "carry some of the load for financing the world's commerce."[3] Kindleberger has argued that much of the instability of the world economy in the interwar period can be traced to "Britain's inability to serve as a lender of last resort for Europe and the U.S. unwillingness . . . to take over this task." He concludes: "The 1929 depression was the consequence of an ineffective transition of the financial center from London to New York."[4]

The Bretton Woods system established after World War II marked the replacement of sterling by the dollar as the world's reserve currency and New York City's emergence as a major international financial center. Due to Britain's relatively slow rate of growth in the postwar period, the relative size of the London equity market has progressively shrunk: it now ranks in third place behind New York and Tokyo. The relative size of British-owned financial institutions has also declined. By the late 1980s only four of the world's fifty largest banks were British, and currently none of the world's twenty largest security firms are headquartered in London. Consequently, top London officials have recently shown a growing concern about the City's future as a financial capital. With the mobilization of capital through computers and satellites, they are concerned that business could just as easily be done in New York, Tokyo, or elsewhere.

Yet at the same time, it is also apparent that the decline in Britain's share of world GNP—Britain's current GNP is less than that of half of the other member states of the European Community—has not been accompanied by a similar decline in London's importance as a financial center. On the contrary, the City has held its own in recent decades as a leading financial center. London may be located geographically in the United Kingdom, but "economically [it] may just as well be in international waters or in orbit."[5] Britain is no longer one of the world's three industrial nations, but London is unequivocally one of the three major centers of global finance. In spite of the decline of the role of the pound in international transactions, London remains the center of international currency trading: Its daily volume accounts for one-third of the world's turnover—greater than that of both New York and Tokyo. It also dominates trading in a number of metals, including gold, tin, copper, zinc, and lead, as well as in tropical agricultural products such as cocoa and peanuts. Notwithstanding the relatively small size of British banks, London also remains a key center of international banking. Foreign asset deposits in London banks are as large as those in New York and Tokyo. "The massive size of the United Kingdom as a banking center can be gathered from the U.S. $1 trillion in borrowing reached in 1989, up from U.S. $489.2 billion in 1982; lending to foreigners increased from U.S. $462.8 billion in 1982 to U.S. $894 billion in 1989."[6] And though the British stock exchange now ranks third in the world, it nonetheless witnessed a tenfold increase in annual volume traded during the 1980s.

London also continues to dominate the Eurocurrency market, a position it has held since it pioneered the creation of that market in the early 1960s: In 1985, $163 billion in new capital was raised on the Eurobond market and trading volume in all Eurocurrency instruments amounted to $2.35 trillion. In 1987, three-quarters of the secondary-market turnover in Eurobonds took place in London—even though none of the five leading trading firms were British. The stocks of about 500 firms are now traded actively on more than one equity market, and London has become a major center for international equity trading. For example, in 1985, the gross transaction volume of American equity trading in London amounted to $38 billion—the equivalent of half the comparable volume of domestic equity trading on the London stock exchange.

How has this been possible? First, due to the equity-based nature of Britain's financial system, the relative size of its equity market has remained disproportionately larger than the relative size of its GNP. It is, in fact, more than twice as large as any other industrial nation in Europe, despite Britain's relatively small GNP. From September 1988 to December 1989 alone, the market value of equities of domestic firms in Britain increased from $676 billion to $823 billion. Over the past decade, more than 100 non-British companies have requested listings on the London stock exchange. By 1986, 10 percent of the trading in French stocks and 15 percent of the trading of German shares took place in London, leading one banker to describe London as "the financial capital of the world."[7]

Moreover, Britain continues to be an important center of international business. For example, forty-five of the world's 500 largest corporations are headquartered in London—even if much of their profit is made overseas. In particular, during the 1980s, Britain resumed its role as an important source of international capital: From 1979 to 1988 Britain more than doubled both its imports and exports of direct investment. Britain also remains the largest foreign investor in the United States, with assets totaling more than $100 billion in 1991.

Second, the time zone in which London is located fits well with Tokyo and New York in a 24-hour trading clock. London is located precisely in the middle of the world's time zones. Within the space of a working day, foreign-exchange dealers based in London can communicate with their counterparts in every other currency market, from Paris to New York to Hong Kong to Tokyo. This has given London a major competitive advantage. In addition, thanks to London's 400-year history of involvement in international trade and finance, its commercial and merchant banks have considerably more international experience than their counterparts in either Japan or the United States. As the *Economist* put it, "America's huge domestic economy guarantees its financial firms a flow of capital market business; so, increasingly, do West Germany's and Japan's huge capital exports. With no natural hinterland, the City of London must live on its excellence."[8]

Another reason has to do with public policy. The British government in the postwar era has been highly supportive of the city, first by its efforts to maintain the high value of sterling, later by its policies toward

Eurodollar trading, and on October 27, 1986, by the deregulation of its financial markets. The Eurocurrency market

> emerged not as a product of irresistible economic forces but as part of England's policy to maintain England as an international financial center despite the decline of Sterling as an international reserve currency. Such a policy required that London-based banks be free to conduct their operations in the new international money, dollars.[9]

Compared to both the United States and Tokyo, Britain's financial markets have been comparatively unregulated; with the exception of a brief period in the mid-1970s, the British government has not restricted foreign borrowing or lending since the end of World War II. This is in sharp contrast to America and Japan—both of which have often made it relatively difficult for foreigners to borrow funds in their currencies at the same rates available to domestic borrowers. (This is what allowed London to become a major center of trading in dollar-dominated commercial paper in the 1960s.) In contrast to the United States, the British government has never restricted interest rates on savings deposits. In addition, unlike both Japan and the United States, British law does not divide investment banking from commercial banking. Furthermore, in sharp contrast to the Japanese, the British have historically welcomed the participation of non-British institutions in London's financial markets. As a result, London continues to host far more foreign banks than Japan, and is second only to New York City. It is also just behind Tokyo in total international banking business.

The importance of government regulation in affecting the competitiveness of the city can be clearly seen in the response of the international financial community to "Big Bang" day, October 27, 1986. On that day, Britain opened its gilt (government securities) markets to foreign firms, abolished fixed brokerage commissions, and allowed the same firm—whether foreign or British—to both trade stocks and represent customers. It also allowed foreign companies to join the London stock exchange. As a result of this deregulation, both American and Japanese investment and commercial banks, as well as securities firms, have dramatically increased their presence in London. For example, American firms have acquired a major interest in thirteen of the top twenty British brokerage firms. As a member of the executive committee of Salomon Brothers put it: "Aiming to be a global player and avoiding London is like deciding you want to be in the U.S. investment business and not in California. We would absolutely lose worldwide if we were not in London."[10] There are currently more than 500 branches of foreign banks in London.

In sum, London continues to be a major financial center and its contribution to the British economy has never been greater—even if much of its trading and lending are now dominated by Japanese and American firms. In 1989, the financial sector contributed £15.2 billion to Britain's balance of payments and accounted for 10.5 percent of the British GNP (up from 6 percent in 1975). In 1990, it employed over 3 million people, an increase of more than 350,000 since 1988. In the words of a former British chief economic advisor, "The City should be a stagnant backwater. But . . . since the 1960s the City has more than held its own as the most important international finance center."[11]

New York City

The relative erosion of the American economy vis-à-vis that of Japan over the last fifteen years has certainly been far less dramatic than that of the British economy vis-à-vis that of the United States over the last half-century. The United States remains the world's largest economy and its share of world GNP has been relatively stable over the last two decades. At least in the short run, the importance of New York City's financial markets and institutions appears to have been only marginally affected by the instability of the dollar and the emergence of Japan as the world's leading creditor nation. In 1987 the finance and business services complex employed nearly 1 million workers, or about one out of every four workers in New York. The securities industry has been an especially high growth sector in the financial complex: employment more than doubled between 1980 and 1987. In general, "the complex of finance and business services is a key growth sector, accounting for about 44 percent of Manhattan's payroll."[12]

New York City has been America's financial center since the first quarter of the nineteenth century. The completion of the Erie Canal in upstate New York in 1825 enabled the city to become a major exporter of agricultural commodities, while in the antebellum period financial intermediates located in New York City brokered both the export of southern cotton and the import of manufactured goods from Europe. However, unlike the case of London, New York City's growth as a major financial center was due to its central role in financing domestic industrial growth. From the end of the Civil War through the 1930s, Wall Street and the American industrial economy grew together. Even as American banks followed American corporations overseas in the postwar period, financing the domestic economy has remained the primary activity for New York–based commercial and investment banks.

Thanks both to the substantial growth of the American economy and the dependence of American corporations on private capital markets, Wall Street became preeminent in the world of corporate finance. New York City dominates trading in both corporate bonds and commercial paper. The New York Stock Exchange represented 34 percent of total world capitalization at the end of the 1980s, despite the substantial aggregate expansion of all equity markets around the world during that decade. Due in part to the recent decline of the Tokyo Stock Market, it is currently the world's largest capital market, with a total value of nearly $3 trillion. As one observer notes:

> A roll call of the new instruments of today's world capital markets—variable rate and convertible bonds, bonds with warrants and deep-discount bonds, financial options and futures, securitized mortgage and automobile-leasing pools—is a catalogue of innovations by American banks in American markets. Any major international company considering launching itself on the global stock market thinks of issuing simultaneous share offerings in New York as well as its home market. . . . In being able to handle huge issues without a hiccup, the New York Stock exchange has shown what "liquidity" means.[13]

New York City's capital markets have become more international over the past decade. The large amount of capital available in the United States—United States pension fund assets now stand at more than $1.5 trillion—has led increasing numbers of foreign companies to turn to Wall Street as a source of funds. Foreign investment in U.S. pension funds increased dramatically over the last decade from $3 billion in 1980 to over $100 billion in 1990. Foreign purchases of U.S. treasuries doubled between 1985 and 1986 from $24.2 billion to $50 billion, though they have since declined substantially. For a large number of non-American-based companies, more of their shares are traded each day in New York City than on their domestic exchanges. The number of foreign investment companies with offices in New York City has also expanded enormously in recent years—in large measure motivated by a desire to tap American private savings.

The deregulation of America's financial markets has also made New York City a much more important center for international bank lending—although it still trails behind London. Since the lifting of both interest rate restrictions and reserve requirements on foreign lending, New York City has captured a growing share of the banking that formerly took place in offshore centers such as the Bahamas and the Cayman Islands: American bank lending increased from $400 billion in 1982 to $600 billion in 1989. While the amount of foreign currency traded in New York City is only half that of London, the continued importance of the dollar-based world trade and financing has encouraged a growing number of banks to open branches in New York: Between 1973 and 1990 the value of foreign bank assets in New York increased by nearly twenty-fold. In 1990, New York was host to 342 foreign bank offices with assets worth $536.5 billion.

Ironically, America's increased dependence on foreign investors to finance its budget and trade deficits has proved to be a boon to New York City's financial institutions and markets. In order to encourage overseas investors and financial institutions to purchase more government bonds, the United States government has repealed the 30 percent withholding tax on interest paid to foreigners—a levy which had been partially responsible for the growth of the $250 billion Eurobond market. According to the chairman of Dillon, Read Ltd. of London, "The disappearance of the withholding tax will strengthen New York as a financial center."[14] Both European and Japanese banks have shown increased interest in directly financing America's government debt as primary dealers in U.S. Treasury Bonds—particularly since the Treasury announced that it is considering issuing bearer bonds. (These will allow holders to remain anonymous, thus increasing the appeal of Treasury bonds to European investors.)

For a variety of reasons—in part historical, in part geographical, and in part due to public policy—the importance of London as a major financial center has survived the decline of British industry. Does this suggest that New York City's importance as an international financial center will be unaffected by the decline in the international competitiveness of American industry? The answer is not obvious. For while America's relative economic wealth has declined, in absolute terms it still remains the world's largest and wealthiest economy—hence, the comparatively large size of America's capital markets and the continued attractiveness of Wall Street to corporations and investors throughout the world. But what if the relative size of sums available for investment generated by the American economy were to shrink steadily over the next half-century? Would the financial institutions based in New York City be able to fashion an alternate role like their counterparts in London? Would Wall Street be as successful as the city in maintaining an important role in international bank lending and international currency transactions even if the dollar were to become a much less important global currency and if the relative size of American-owned financial institutions were to continue to shrink? One way of beginning to answer these questions is to examine the emergence of the world's third major financial center, namely, Tokyo. For if New York City's financial institutions and markets are successfully challenged over the next few decades, that is from where the competitive threat will come.

Tokyo

Tokyo's emergence as an important international financial center is relatively recent. Japan has been an important capital exporter since 1982. Through the early 1980s, there was comparatively little Japanese investment outside of Japan. Consequently, Tokyo's capital markets were of little interest to the rest of the world. Moreover, the Japanese government, throughout the postwar period, imposed very tight restrictions on Japanese capital markets. They sought to keep them as insulated as possible in order to lower the costs of capital for Japanese firms. By favoring domestic over foreign companies and corporate borrowers over individual savers, the Japanese government helped promote the competitiveness of its manufacturing firms—but at the price of retarding the internationalization of both its financial markets and financial institutions.

However, due to the rapid expansion of Japan's domestic economy and the growing international presence of Japanese firms, by the late 1980s, Tokyo had become a major financial center and a potential threat to New York's hegemony. For nearly two decades, the growth of the Tokyo stock exchange seemed irrepressible; in 1987 it became the world's largest. In 1988, Tokyo's stock market was capitalized at $3.3 trillion, seventeen times higher than in 1970 and $1 trillion more than the New York Stock Exchange. In 1989, at its peak, Tokyo accounted for 45 percent of the total capitalization of all the world's stock markets, and the market capitalization of Japan's top sixteen commercial banks was six times greater than the fifty largest U.S. commercial banks.[15]

The dominance of the Tokyo Stock Exchange proved short-lived: In 1990 it slipped back into second place behind New York and its relative size vis-à-vis that of New York has since steadily declined. In April 1992 the Nikkei stock index fell below 18,000, a decline of 55 percent from its all-time high in December 1989. Depending in part on the confidence of foreign investors, the Nikkei could fall as low as 10,000 or less before it stabilizes.[16] Even at its current level, Japanese banks are turning away borrowers out of fear that they lack adequate funds. As Shigeru Masuda, president of Zeron Capital Management Inc., warned: "Below 20,000, Japanese banks have a big problem. Industry has a big problem. The nation has a big problem."[17]

In other measures the importance of Tokyo as an international finance center remains more constant. Since the late 1980s, Tokyo banks have dominated the global market. In 1990 *Fortune* reported that eight of the top ten banks in the world were Japanese, including the seven largest banks.[18] The top thirty Japanese banks control assets worth $5.6 trillion, more than the banks of the United States, France, West Germany, Britain, and Italy combined. Japanese banks account for 55 percent of foreign-controlled banking assets in the United States. And Japanese bank assets in the United States total $433 billion, or 11.7 percent of all bank assets in the United States. However, Japanese banks are considerably less profitable than American and British ones, and the rising costs of capital in Japan are likely to reduce their future overseas expansion.

International use of the yen has increased significantly since the 1970s. From 1975 to 1988, the percentage of Japanese exports denominated in yen increased from 17.5 to 34.7, while the increase for Japanese imports was from 0.9 percent to 14 percent. Likewise, the proportion of international bonds denominated in yen increased more than fivefold during the 1980s, bringing the yen's world share up to nearly half that of the dollar by 1992. Between 1980 and 1987, the proportion of the official reserves of the world's central banks held in yen nearly doubled. The value of yen-denominated bonds issued in the Euromarket increased by twenty-fold between 1983 and 1985. In 1987, the volume of fixed-rate Euroyen bonds exceeded Eurodollars issues for the first time. There is now more trading in yen on the Eurocurrency market in London than in any currency other than the dollar—with much of it being done by Japanese firms.

Following the lead of the Americans and the British, the Japanese have finally begun to liberalize their markets. In 1980 Japan abolished foreign-exchange controls, thus enabling foreign firms to borrow yen. Twenty-two foreign companies are now members of the Tokyo stock exchange, constituting one-fifth of the total. In addition, by 1988, 119 foreign banks and fifty security firms had branches in Japan. Japan has allowed three new yen instruments to be traded—bankers' acceptances, bond futures, and Euroyen bonds—and has permitted a market for American treasury bonds in Tokyo. In 1985, nine foreign banks were allowed into the Japanese trust and bank markets, and foreign firms are now allowed to advise Japanese pension funds and corporations on their investments as well as to distribute Japanese government bonds. Due to a modification of listing requirements, over 100 foreign stocks are now traded in Tokyo, and foreign investors now account for a larger share of the market and trading value of the Tokyo stock market than of the New York Stock Exchange.

Tokyo's comparative advantage as a financial market lies in one extremely important development: the substantial sums of money available in Japan for international lending and investment. Just as London became an international financial center in the latter third of the nineteenth century by exporting British capital, and New York emerged as an important center of international banking in the postwar period by its role in exporting American capital, so Tokyo's growing financial importance is due to Japan's sudden prominence as an international lender. Japan, thanks to its massive trading surpluses over the past decade, has become the world's largest creditor nation. In 1986 it exported $131.5 billion in long-term capital, nearly eight times its level only three years earlier (though this figure had declined slightly by 1988). In 1988 Japanese loans abroad totaled $15 billion, and securities and external bonds stood at $67 billion. In the United States, Japanese transnational banks increased their lending by nearly $13 billion during 1990, while lending by domestic banks in the United States declined during the same time. Significantly, between 1983 and 1989, the dollar's share of international lending by global banks fell from 72 to 53 percent. However, Japan's net-capital flows have steadily declined since 1987, and in 1991 it actually imported more capital than it exported.

Since Tokyo's emergence as an important financial center is so recent, it is difficult to assess the extent of its challenge to New York City. Yet in one important respect it may prove a more important rival to New York City than New York City has been to London. A major reason why the City has been more affected by the decline of the British economy is that it was not heavily engaged in supplying the British economy with funds to begin with—a strategy which some observers have cited as an important reason for Britain's industrial decline in the first place. But ironically, precisely because Wall Street has historically been so supportive of the American economy, it may suffer more seriously from the latter's decline. In a sense, New York City may be seen as a "victim" of its own success: America's postwar policy of promoting the economic growth of its political allies—a policy that was inspired by New York's foreign policy establishment and in part financed by New York's banks—proved to be successful beyond anyone's wildest expectations. In particular, New York facilitated Japan's emergence as an economic rival to the United States.

Despite the recent collapse of the Tokyo Stock Market, and with it a significant decline in the funds available for overseas expansion by Japanese manufacturing firms and financial institutions, there are strong grounds for optimism about Japan's long-term economic prospects. Most important, Japan's share of world GNP has grown steadily since the early 1950s, while America's share has remained stable. Notwithstanding Japan's recent economic difficulties, its growth rates continue to exceed those of the United States. Should this trend continue, Japan's GNP will exceed that of the United States by the end of the first decade of the twenty-first century.

At the same time, it is important to distinguish between the role of Japanese financial institutions and the role of Tokyo as a financial center. There is no question that Japanese financial institutions will play an increasingly important role in both New York and London. Three of the seven major underwriters of Eurobonds are now Japanese firms while two of the thirty-five authorized primary dealers of U.S. government securities are now owned by Japanese companies. In 1986, Sumitomo Bank purchased a 12.5 percent interest in Goldman, Sachs, and in 1987, Nippon Life Insurance Company purchased a 13 percent interest in Shearson Lehman Brothers. Known as the Big Four, Japan's four largest security houses—Nomura, Daiwa, Kikko, and Yamaichi—account for 20 percent of all long-term U.S. government bond trading in New York, and during the 1980s, they purchased 30–40 percent of all new Treasury issues at auction. Japanese banks now account for 25 percent of all British banking assets and handle more than one-third of Britain's international banking transactions. However, Tokyo is still unlikely to replace New York as the world's dominant financial center. There are four reasons for this.

First, although Japanese financial markets have become significantly more open in recent years, they still remain far more restricted than those of both London and New York. The interest rates on 80 percent of the deposits in Japanese banks continue to be set by the government, and Japan is the only major capitalist that imposes fixed commissions on equity transactions, though they have been recently reduced. The Big Four have a tight hold over the Tokyo Stock Exchange, controlling almost 40 percent of all shares traded, their profits protected by fixed commissions. Japanese rules, regulations, and customs continue to limit foreign participation in Tokyo's financial markets. For example, foreign banks in Japan hold only about 5 percent of the total domestic banking accounts.

While these restrictions are gradually being lifted, the pace of liberalization continues to lag behind both New York and London. To the extent that this situation persists, non-Japanese financial institutions are unlikely to play as important a role in Tokyo as Japanese firms play in either New York or London. As a result, much of the internationalization of Japanese financial markets will continue to take place outside of Japan, thus, ironically, reinforcing both London's and New York City's importance as global financial centers.

Second, the yen appears unlikely to replace—or even rival—the dollar as a major international currency. The use of the yen remains limited to Japanese foreign trade: it does not serve as a transaction currency for trade between third countries. All the world's major commodities, including oil, continue to be denominated in dollars. The yen's role in Japan's international trade, after rapidly escalating, appears to have stabilized somewhat: Roughly 35 percent of Japanese exports and 10–15 percent of imports were denominated in yen from 1986 to 1989. (By contrast, 96 percent of America's exports and 85 percent of its imports are denominated in dollars while 80 percent of West Germany's exports and half of its imports are denominated in D-marks.) Analogously, the role of the yen as an investment currency, while it has significantly increased in recent years, is still small: In 1990 13.5 percent of external bonds were denominated in yen, while 33.3 percent were denominated in dollars. Likewise, in 1990 only 1.7 percent of foreign and international bank loans were denominated in yen; by contrast, 17.9 percent were made in pounds and 57.9 percent were in dollars.

For all its economic strengths, Japan still lacks one important attribute of a world financial leader: it is unwilling to allow its currency to function as a global currency. "Ceding a certain amount of control over the domestic economy is part of the price for being a global central bank and meeting the obligation of financial leadership."[19] This is a price, however, that Japanese financial authorities remain reluctant to pay. They fear—correctly—that allowing huge outflows of yen or permitting the development of a large Euroyen market comparable to that of the Eurodollar market would reduce their ability to control domestic interest rates. It is important to recall that the transfer of the world's financial center from London to New York paralleled the replacement of the pound by the dollar as the world's major reserve currency. Thus, as long as the Japanese government discourages the use of the yen outside Japan, Tokyo is unlikely to replace New York as the world's financial center.

The third set of reasons are cultural and social. For all the internationalization of Japanese business, Japanese society and culture remain relatively insular and provincial. Compared to either London or New York, Tokyo is a much less cosmopolitan city, with relatively little to offer foreigners in the way of shopping, culture, and the other amenities of upper-class life. For this reason, as well as its unusually high prices and population density, it is a much less pleasant and appealing place for foreigners to live and work. As a result, Tokyo will find it relatively difficult to attract an expatriate community of the size and scope that is necessary for a city that aspires to become the "capital of capital."

Finally, the future role of Japan in the world capitalist system needs to be kept in perspective. For all its well-publicized problems, America's long-term economic prospects remain far better than Britain's were a century ago. At the same time, for a variety of reasons Japan appears both unable and unwilling to assume the geopolitical responsibilities commensurate with its growing economic importance. To the extent that this reluctance continues, Japan is unlikely to replace—or even rival—the United States as the world's most politically and militarily powerful capitalist nation.

Nonetheless, there can be no question that, in the long run, due to Japan's substantial overseas investments, the growing size and importance of its global corporations and its high domestic growth rates, Tokyo will become an increasingly important competitor to New York City. It will not overshadow New York City in the way that New York supplanted London. But on the other hand, rather than remaining at the apex of the global economy, New York City may increasingly come to occupy the status of one of its three major financial centers.

The Domestic Challenge

To date, New York City appears to have been relatively unaffected by the problems of the American economy—though this is unlikely to continue indefinitely. But what of New York City's position as a financial center within the United States? Has it been similarly unaffected by the relative decline of the industrial Northeast and the growing importance of Pacific Basin–related trade?

New York City continues to remain the nation's banking center, being headquarters for four of the five and six of the ten largest American banks. From 1976 to 1986, New York banks increased their share of deposits among the top 200 U.S. banks from 57.1 percent to 68.8 percent. In contrast, in 1986 Los Angeles hosted only two of the ten largest banks in the United States, whereas there were none in Chicago. The deposit share for Los Angeles and Chicago banks in the nation's top 200 was only 2.9 percent and 8.5 percent respectively. New York City's share of national employment in banking and finance has remained constant at about 12 percent, more than double that of any other U.S. city. Equally important, New York remains the nation's leading foreign banking center, holding 47 percent of all foreign bank shares and 68.4 percent of all foreign assets in 1990. The equivalent figures for the entire state of California are 21.9 percent and 17.2 percent.

Why has no other city emerged to challenge New York's dominant position in banking? One explanation is that the source of strength for banks headquartered in other cities—namely, the relative prosperity of their region—has also been a source of vulnerability. For example, Dallas, in the heart of the Sunbelt, appeared to represent a major competitive challenge to New York City during the 1960s and 1970s. But the recent decline in the price of oil has severely hurt the economy of the Southwest, and the banks headquartered in Dallas have suffered accordingly. The story of the Bank of America—formerly the nation's largest bank—is a similar one: its dominant position in commercial lending in California enabled it to grow along with that state's economy, but also made it extremely vulnerable to the decline of both oil and agricultural prices. In a sense, New York City's major banks occupy a position vis-à-vis the Northeast similar to that occupied by London's banks vis-à-vis the entire British economy: neither's fate is tied to the prosperity of the region in which they happen to be physically located. New York City's banks have not been hurt by the decline of the industrial Northeast because neither their loans nor their assets have been concentrated there. Significantly, although America's high-technology revolution was centered in northern California, 40 percent of all venture capital funds raised in the United States come from New York City.

There is another factor at work: the revolution in telecommunications. In the long run, it is possible that the development of telecommunications might pose a threat to New York City, since it means that a particular financial transaction can take place anywhere. But to date, it appears to have strengthened New York's importance since it means that its location on the East Coast is no longer a handicap in enabling it to compete for either global or domestic business. As a result, New York City is no less well positioned to play a critical role in financing trade and investment in the Pacific Basin than is Los Angeles. A generation ago, this would not have been the case. But the sophistication of a region's telecommunications network now matters more than where its customers are located.

Since the deregulation of the nation's telecommunications systems, New York City has developed a telecommunications infrastructure that is far more sophisticated than that of any other American city.

> New York Telephone has built a 48,000 circuit Ring Around Manhattan fiber optic network that links twelve major switching centers and telecommunications systems in Manhattan and has recently launched an Interborough Fiber Network that will link the counties adjacent to Manhattan. More than one-third of all the Bell System's optical fiber has been installed in New York Telephone's service area, a consequence of the demand of advanced communications systems within the largest American city and its surrounding metropolitan area.[20]

Kenneth Phillips, vice president of Telecommunications Policy for Citibank, observes:

> A literal revolution has taken place rendering the bits and bytes entering New York via large satellite dish, or flowing under the streets of Manhattan at the speed of light, in a fiber optic cable, which are part of a multimillion dollar electronics funds transfer, indistinguishable from those transmitting the notes of the Bach B-Minor Mass. The turf on which this revolution is taking place is largely from 59th Street, on the North, to Battery Park on the South, and of course stretches clear across the island from the Hudson to the East River. This comparatively small area of land has over twice the telecommunications switching capacity of the average foreign country, more computers than a country the size of Brazil, and more word processors than all the countries of Europe combined. Capital investment by business users in private telecommunications systems, communicating word processing systems, computer mainframes, minis, and micros is currently in the billions of dollars and is growing annually.

He adds:

> New York has become the major synapse in the nervous system of the world's major information flows. During an average business day the VISA Card user in Paris, the job applicant in San Francisco, the emergency-room physician in Stockholm, the stock market investor in Zurich, indeed the telephone user anywhere in the country will be switched in and out of dozens of databases at the speed of light, right here in Manhattan.[21]

As a result, the contemporary telecommunication revolution, like the invention of the telephone and the telegraph, appears to have strengthened New York's dominance.

At the same time, New York City, like London, enjoys an important comparative advantage for those financial transactions—domestic as well as global—that continue to require face-to-face interaction. By any conceivable index, New York remains America's most cosmopolitan and sophisticated city. No other American city compares to it in its appeal to foreign executives. At the same time, no other American city compares to it in either its concentration of influential decision-makers from industry, finance, and law, or in the extent and depth of its support services for domestic and international financial transactions. Explaining why his company employs 750 people in New York, Yoshi Terasawa, executive director of Nomura Securities Company of Tokyo, stated, "The human touch is important. It's better to meet people, to have personal relations, and to be able to have lunch together."[22] A

British executive notes that New York remains "a key outpost for any company with international ambitions," while an Italian executive adds, "There is no place equal to New York in terms of financial transactions. Things happen there before anywhere else."[23] These developments give New York an important comparative advantage. In fact, an increasingly important source of revenue for New York City's financial institutions now lies in the marketing of information about assets, rather than in the distribution of financial assets themselves.

Moreover, Wall Street has become much more important to the future of the American economy for another reason: the recent merger wave. After having been relatively stable since the Great Depression, the balance of power within the American corporate community has recently been in a state of flux and uncertainty. Regardless of the geographic base of the current generation of corporate raiders and speculators—which in fact appears to be rather diverse—or of the consequences of their efforts on the physical location of corporate headquarters within the United States—which is so far unclear—there can be no question that the recent wave of corporate restructuring has been an enormous boon to New York City's financial sector. Not only are mergers and acquisitions extremely profitable, but physical proximity does seem to matter in these negotiations. Anyone interested in either defending or instigating a corporate takeover has no choice but to enlist the services of investment bankers and corporate lawyers in New York City—even if the "king" of junk-bond financing was based in Beverly Hills. Thus, due to New York City's overwhelming domination of the nation's private equity markets, its position in the structure and organization of the American economy remains an extremely strategic one. Moreover, an important effect of leveraged buyouts has been to strengthen the role of investment banks in business management. And virtually all investment banking firms involved in LBO's are based in New York City.

Nevertheless, domestically, as well as internationally, New York's role as dominant financial center is being challenged. Chicago has been able to parlay its experience in commodities futures markets into financial futures, most notably in foreign exchange, equity indexes, and interests. As of 1986, 85 percent of America's trading in futures was taking place on the floor of either the Chicago Board of Trade or the Chicago Mercantile Exchange. It has forged a direct trading link with the Singapore Monetary Exchange, thus allowing trading to take place 24 hours a day—while the New York Stock Exchange is not scheduled to have around-the-clock operations until the year 2000. Furthermore, the Chicago Mercantile Exchange has garnered the exclusive right to the Nikkei averages (the Japanese equivalent of S&P) in North America and Asia, and is in the process of introducing futures based on an over-the-counter stock index, the European currency unit, and zero coupon bonds.

The New York Stock Exchange's importance as a center of American equity trading has significantly eroded. In 1981 the NYSE handled more than 75 percent of the trading in all U.S. stocks (measured by dollar volume); by 1991 this figure had declined to 50 percent. Even the NYSE's share of trading in its own listed shares has declined: between 1981 and 1991 it fell from 82 percent to 67 percent. The NYSE has primarily lost business to newer, frequently electronic, competitors, many of whom offer cheaper, more automated, or in some cases, less regulated transactions. The Exchange's competitors include regional and overseas exchanges, electronic markets such as the over-the-counter Nasdaq market, commercially run trading systems, and the in-house matching services of a few large American brokerage firms. Its ability to arrest this decline will depend on how quickly the Exchange can modernize its operations; by 2000, the NYSE hopes to offer around-the-clock trading. Ironically, the banking deregulation strongly promoted by New York City–based financial institutions such as Citibank and Merrill Lynch did help create one important regional rival to New York, namely, Los Angeles. Between 1980 and 1985, deposits in banks in Los Angeles increased from $60 billion to $136 billion, making it the country's second largest money center with only $45 billion less in deposits than New York City. In addition, 126 foreign banks now have offices in Los Angeles and five of the twelve major Japanese banks in the United States are based there. The growing importance of Asian-American trade has enabled Los Angeles to replace New York as the nation's leading center of import-export ocean-borne cargo. The value of international trade passing through the Los Angeles customs district increased three-fold (in constant dollars) between 1975 and 1985, although it still ranks behind that of the New York region. Significantly, 60 percent of America's trade with the Pacific Rim enters the United States through Los Angeles's two ports and its international airport. And like New York City two generations ago, Los Angeles has become a major center of immigration. According to an article in the *Atlantic,*

> some Angelenos boast that greater Los Angeles is the largest Mexican metropolitan area outside Mexico, the second largest Chinese metropolitan area outside of China, the second largest Japanese metropolitan area outside of Japan, the largest Korean metropolitan area outside of Korea, the largest Philippine metropolitan area outside the Philippines, and the largest Vietnamese metropolitan area outside of Vietnam.[24]

It is also becoming an increasingly important cultural center.

Conclusion

In sum, New York City's future as a financial center cannot but be affected by the growing economic importance of the Pacific Basin. It is certainly not coincidental that both its most important international and domestic rivals, namely, Tokyo and Los Angeles, are integral parts of the economy of this region. Nonetheless, at this point neither of these cities appears likely to ever enjoy the kind of dominance over either the global or national economy that New York City exercised in the past. Rather, it is far more likely that the distribution of financial power—international as well as domestic—will become increasingly decentralized. New York City's relative importance will decline like London's earlier in this century, but like contemporary London, it will remain a major financial center. Indeed, for the foreseeable future, it is likely to remain both America's and the world's *most* important financial center.

Notes

1. As quoted in Sassen, Saskia, *The Global City: New York, London, Tokyo* (Princeton: Princeton University Press, 1991), p. 98.
2. McRae, Hamish and Frances Caincorn, *Capital City* (London: Methuen, 1973), p. 6.
3. Kindleberger, Charles, *Economic Response* (Cambridge, MA: Harvard University Press, 1978), p. 124.
4. *Ibid.*
5. Coakley, Jerry and Laurence Harris, *The City of Capital* (Oxford: Basil Blackwell, 1983), p. 47.
6. Sassen, *The Global City,* pp. 178–179.
7. "Hail Britannia, Britannia Waives the Rules," *Washington Post National Weekly Edition,* November 10, 1986, p. 19.
8. "Capital of Capital," *Economist,* October 11, 1980, p. 13.
9. Zysman, John, *Political Strategies for Industrial Order* (Berkeley: University of California Press, 1977), p. 212.
10. Bleakley, Fred, "The Yanks Muscle In On the City," *New York Times,* September 28, 1986, section 3, p. 8.
11. Walters, Alan, "Bully for the City," *The International Economy* (November/December 1991): 75.
12. Sassen, Saskia, "Finance and Business Services in New York City: International Linkages and Domestic Effects," *International Social Science Journal* 125 (August 1990): 295.
13. Hamilton, Adrian, *The Financial Revolution* (New York: Free Press, 1986), p. 117.

14. "Why the Big Apple Shines in the World's Markets," *Business Week,* July 23, 1984, p. 104.
15. Zielinski, Robert and Nigel Holloway, *Unequal Equities: Power and Risk in Japan's Stock Market* (New York: Kodansha, 1991), pp. 3–4.
16. *The Economist,* April 4, 1992, p. 91.
17. Holden, Ted and William Glasgall, "Fear Stalks the Nikkei," *Business Week* February 3, 1992, p. 70.
18. Field, Nora E., "Japan Is Still No. 1," *Fortune,* June 30, 1990, pp. 324–325.
19. "Japan's New Era, Same Old Bulls," *Economist,* January 14, 1989, p. 71.
20. Moss, Mitchell, "Telecommunications and the Future of Cities." Prepared for presentation for the conference on Landtronics, June 19–21, 1981, London, England, p. 3, mimeographed paper.
21. Phillips, Kenneth, "Testimony Before New York City Commission in the Year 2000," May 9, 1987, pp. 2, 3.
22. Lueck, Thomas, "New York City Is Challenged as Giant of Global Economy," *New York Times,* June 27, 1988, p. 1.
23. *Ibid.*
24. Lockwood, Charles and Christopher Leinberger, "Los Angeles Comes of Age," *Atlantic,* June 1988, p. 41.

4

Between Europe and America: The New York Foreign Policy Elite

James R. Kurth

In recent years, there has been much discussion about two great trajectories arcing across the twentieth century: the rise and decline of the dominance of America in the world,[1] and of New York in America. New York's foreign-policy elite provides the link between these two trajectories. It is this elite which almost fifty years ago brought forth men such as Averell Harriman, Robert Lovett, Dean Acheson, John McCloy, and George Kennan, who were "present at the creation" of the liberal international order under American leadership and were the founding fathers of "the American Century." And it is this New York foreign-policy elite which today, like New York in America and like America in the world, is merely first among equals in the constellation of power.

Some have ascribed the diminished role of the New York foreign-policy elite to a particular tragedy—Vietnam.[2] Before Vietnam there was a foreign policy consensus; since Vietnam, there has been none. As we shall see, Vietnam is part of the explanation, but it is not the whole story. Others have ascribed the decline of the New York foreign-policy elite to the diffusion of foreign-policy expertise and influence from one center, the Council on Foreign Relations in New York, to a plurality of centers, many of them in Washington.[3] This, too, is part of the explanation, but not the whole story.

The best perspective with which to view the shifting fortunes of the New York foreign-policy elite is to view the shifting relations between New York's and America's interests in the rest of the world. In geographic terms, these interests can be conceived of as the four major regions of the United States, i.e., New York and its hinterland in the Northeast, the Midwest, the South, and the West. In economic terms, these interests can be conceived of as four major sectors of the American economy, i.e., finance, industry, agriculture, and (since World War II large enough to warrant separate consideration) defense, or what President Eisenhower termed the "military-industrial complex."[4] Each of these geographic sections and economic sectors has had its own interests in regard to the rest of the world, its own foreign policy. When the interests of New York (and in particular of finance) were compatible with those of the other sections and sectors, the New York foreign-policy elite ascended and assumed leadership of the foreign policy of the nation. When the interests of New York (and of finance) diverged from those of the other sections and sectors, the New York foreign-policy elite lost that leadership.

The Origins of the New York Foreign-Policy Elite

For more than two centuries, New York has been a place lying somewhere between Europe and America. The New York foreign-policy elite originated in the role that New York played as the broker between the two worlds.

New York versus America

For the first century of the United States, New York was viewed by most of the rest of the country as, well, un-American. During the American Revolution, New York was the most pro-British city in the colonies. During the Civil War, New York was the most antiwar city in the Union. (At the very moment, July 1863, of the great Union victories of Gettysburg in the East and Vicksburg in the West, the largest antidraft riots in American history erupted in New York.) During the Populist era, New York was seen as the ally of British finance. And at the end of the nineteenth century, New York had the largest concentration of foreign-born (and foreign-language) inhabitants in the nation. For many Americans, New York was part of the foreign problem, not part of the American solution.

New York vis-à-vis Europe

Indeed, by the turn of the century, the most distinguished New Yorkers (i.e., the new financial elite, exemplified by J.P. Morgan) thought of New York as almost part of Europe. They formed an urban, and urbane, patriciate, whose standards of excellence and elegance were set in Europe and especially in England. The material foundation of this patriciate was the close ties between the new financial elite of New York and the older one of the City of London, the former being a sort of junior partner of the latter. But around this financial connection there developed British-like social and cultural institutions and a transatlantic world-view. This world-view was memorialized in the architecture of the day, and it can still be seen in the New York town houses, the Hudson River country estates (such as Franklin Roosevelt's Hyde Park), and the neo-Gothic Episcopal churches of the region, which are all variations on a British theme. But the most consequential embodiment of the transatlantic world-view was probably the preparatory schools (whose exemplar was Groton), where the New York patriciate educated its young, and which were modeled on the British public schools. It was here, from about 1890 to 1914, that the future foreign-policy elite of the 1940s was formed.[5] Thus, the architects of the American Century were molded within the most British of American institutions.

Free Trade versus Protectionism

Although many Americans considered New York to be part of the foreign problem rather than part of the American solution, there had always been exceptions. In particular, the commercial and financial elites of New York provided crucial services to the agricultural elites of the South, in support of southern trade with England, both before and after the Civil War. This economic coalition between New York finance and southern agriculture provided a continuing base for the Democratic party and its policy of free trade. It was opposed, of course, by another great economic combine, the industry of New England, Pennsylvania, and the Midwest, which provided the base for the Republican party and its policy of protectionism.

From World War I to the Depression: New York, Internationalism, and Isolationism

This contest between the free trade and the protectionist coalitions was accentuated by World War I. The United States became a creditor nation in 1914, and New York banks loaned vast sums to the allies, especially Britain, during the war. When the war was over, the only way the allies could pay their debts to the New York banks was to export their industrial goods to American markets. This put European industry and American banks in direct conflict with American industry. The New York free traders and internationalists lost the first round of this conflict, the fight over ratification by the U.S. Senate of the Versailles Treaty and the League of Nations. The Senate rejected the Treaty and the League in March 1920.

New York and the Council on Foreign Relations

In response to this defeat and in order to organize better for future battles against isolationism and protectionism, New York internationalists founded the Council on Foreign Relations in 1921. The origins of the Council lay in the many meetings which had been held between the staffs of the American and the British delegations at the Paris peace conference in 1919. Having discovered that they shared many conceptions and goals about the postwar world, these American and British foreign-affairs experts decided to establish permanent organizations within their respective countries, which would be composed of men who were leaders either in international finance and commerce or in the professional study of international affairs. These organizations would continue the mutual communication and cooperation which had developed between the Americans and the British in regard to international issues. In Britain, this became the Royal Institute of International Affairs. In America, it became the Council on Foreign Relations. The necessity for such an American organization became especially clear to New York international businessmen after the defeat of the Treaty and the League in the U.S. Senate and the defeat of the Democrats and free trade in the U.S. presidential election of 1920.[6]

The new Council on Foreign Relations was composed of bankers (e.g., Russell Leffingwell, Norman Davis, and Paul Warburg) and lawyers (e.g., Paul Cravath) in New York, as well as distinguished academics from universities stretched out along the eastern seaboard, from Harvard (Archibald Cary Coolidge) to Johns Hopkins (Isaiah Bowman). The council's first president was John W. Davis, a Wall Street lawyer and the Democratic candidate for president of the United States in 1924. But the council also sought the support of Elihu Root, another Wall Street lawyer, who had been Theodore Roosevelt's secretary of state and was now a Republican elder statesman. It arranged for the new Woodrow Wilson Foundation to give Root a $25,000 award for his contributions to international cooperation, which he in turn would give to the Council to fund its new journal, *Foreign Affairs*.[7] Thus, from its beginning, the Council sought to construct a bipartisan coalition in support of free trade and internationalism.

New York also provided two of the Republican secretaries of state in the 1920s, Charles Evans Hughes and Henry L. Stimson; both had been Wall Street lawyers. However, they and the other New York internationalists within the Republican party could not overcome the heavy weight of protectionist industry, which continued to dominate the party throughout the decade.

Finance versus Industry

Although the foreign policy disputes of the 1920s have often been characterized as being between internationalists and isolationists, this is not wholly accurate. The "isolationists" were often ready to support U.S. military interventions in Central America and the Caribbean, as well as a more modest gunboat presence in China. They were really only isolationist in regard to Europe.

The pattern of foreign-policy differences conformed to the pattern of economic sectors. New York banks were in the business of lending money. Although they were willing to lend to anyone with a good credit rating, it was natural that the most numerous and the biggest borrowers would be found in the most advanced economies of the day, i.e., in Europe (and prospectively Japan); thus the focus of the New York foreign-policy elite on Europe. But for the borrowers to be able to repay these loans, they would have to export their goods to the United States; thus the focus of the New York foreign-policy elite on free trade.

The perspective of American industrialists was quite different. They were in the business of selling goods. Although they were willing to sell to anyone willing and able to buy, it was natural that the best customers would be found in economies which did not produce these goods themselves. These were the less advanced economies of the day, especially those not bottled up in some European colonial empire, i.e., Latin America and China; thus the willingness of the American industrial elite to support intervention in these countries. As for Europe, however, it represented only hostile competitors in markets which Americans might otherwise have to themselves; thus the focus of the industrial elite on protectionism.

The Privatized Foreign Policy of New York Finance

Although the protectionists within the Republican party made sure that the U.S. government in the 1920s did not engage in an internationalist foreign policy toward Europe, this did not prevent New York banks from carrying out such a policy on their own, a sort of privatized foreign policy, which was composed of large-scale American bank loans to European countries, especially to Germany. The New York banks were the creators of the Dawes Plan (1924) and the Young Plan (1929), the most important elements of American relations with Europe in the 1920s. These plans provided for a grand recycling of funds, composed of American bank loans to the German government; German war-reparation payments to the British and French governments; and British and French repayments of war debts to American banks.[8]

These loans were a fundamental pillar of the political stability of the Weimar Republic and of the economic stability of Europe in the 1920s. As such, they were in some ways a prototype of the Marshall Plan a generation later. But although the New York bank loans were part of the solution for the European economy, they were only part of the problem for American industry.

The Consensus Foreign Policy of Finance and Industry

There was, however, one part of the world where American finance and industry could agree on an internationalist, and interventionist, foreign policy by the U.S. government, and that was Latin America. Although the biggest borrowers were found in Europe, New York banks had been engaged in loans to Latin America since the turn of the century, and they saw every reason to continue. On its part, industry saw Latin America as a natural market and not as a competitor. Thus, finance and industry could form a consensus on the Latin American policy of the U.S. government. As such, this was in some ways a prototype of the consensus and bipartisan foreign policy toward both Europe and Latin America a generation later.

Thus the New York foreign-policy elite experienced successes as well as failures in its efforts in the 1920s. The Council on Foreign Relations soon became a solid and established organization. In 1929, the Council bought a new building at 45 East 65th Street to house its expanding operations. (It happened to be next door to the New York town house of Franklin Roosevelt.)[9]

The World Economy Between Britain and America

The international economic order of the 1920s, however, was an unstable equilibrium. Charles Kindleberger, a leading economic historian, has argued that the decade was a period in which there was no longer an economic hegemon, i.e., one great economic power which brings order to the world economy.[10] In Kindleberger's conception, a stable world economy requires an economic hegemon which performs three functions and therefore assumes three burdens. The hegemon must provide for other countries a large and open market for their exports; long-term loans for their economic development; and short-term loans or support for the currencies of countries that undergo foreign-exchange crises that can detonate a banking crisis.

Before World War I, Britain (in particular, the City of London) performed these functions and assumed these burdens, and the world economy consequently operated smoothly and grew substantially. The war, however, greatly diminished Britain's economic assets and power. After the war, Britain still had the will, but it no longer had the ability, to carry out the functions of an economic hegemon.

Conversely, World War I greatly increased the economic assets and power of the United States. After the war, the U.S. had the ability, but it did not yet have the will, to carry out all of the functions of an economic hegemon. The New York banks, as we have seen, did perform one of these functions to a degree, i.e., long-term lending (such as in the Dawes Plan). But the New York banks had not been able to overcome the opposition of American industry to a second function, opening the American market to foreign industrial goods. And they were not willing to strengthen the Federal Reserve System to the point that it could perform the third function, providing foreign-exchange support in a severe currency and banking crisis.

The world economy of the 1920s thus was suspended between a dying world, that of British hegemony, and a world not yet born, that of American hegemony. The shared conceptions of British and American international elites, of the Royal Institute of International Affairs and the Council on Foreign Relations, could cover over the structural gap between the declining hegemon and the ascending one in a time of economic prosperity. But this cover would be blown away in the gale of a severe economic crisis, and this came with the New York stock market crash of 1929.

New York and the Great Depression

With the stock market crash, a vast amount of American capital suddenly disappeared and was no longer available to provide long-term loans. There was now no one able to perform this hegemonic function. This resulted in the collapse of the great recycling project as American bank loans to Germany dried up; Germany defaulted on its reparation payments to Britain and France; and Britain and France defaulted on their loan payments to American banks. Loans to Latin America also disappeared, and Latin American countries also defaulted on their loan payments.

The disappearance of American capital also led to the decrease in domestic demand for American goods, and the disappearance of American loans led foreign nations to maintain their needed foreign exchange by increasing their exports to the United States. American industry was thus faced both with the rapid shrinking of the U.S. market and with foreign producers dumping their goods on that market. This double whammy drove industry to organize and achieve even greater political power than before and to push Congress into enacting the famous Smoot-Hawley Tariff of 1930, the most protectionist trade law in U.S. history. The United States was now even less willing to perform a second hegemonic function than before, and other countries joined the U.S. in closing their markets to international trade.

The rapid shrinkage of foreign markets generated a series of foreign-exchange and banking crises, which occurred first in smaller, export-oriented countries but which then spread throughout the world in a chain that reached from Austria in 1931 through Germany, France, and Britain to America in early 1933. But the U.S. Federal Reserve System was not able, and the New York banks were not willing, to perform the third hegemonic function, i.e., to provide short-term loans to other banks at the early and still manageable stage of the crisis.

Together, the stock market crash, loan defaults, and banking crises of 1929–1933 greatly diminished the financial assets and economic power of the New York financial elite; this in turn undermined the political power of the financial elite and of the New York foreign-policy elite within it. At the same time their traditional adversary, American industry, in organizing to enact the Smoot-Hawley Tariff, had enhanced its own political power. By 1932, the New York foreign-policy elite was at the nadir of its political fortunes.

New York and the New Deal

With the election of Franklin Roosevelt as president in 1932, however, the old Democratic free trade coalition of New York finance and southern export agriculture returned to power. Roosevelt appointed as his Secretary of State Cordell Hull, a congressman from Memphis, Tennessee, who had long been active in encouraging cotton exports. Hull's major project became the construction of Reciprocal Trade Agreements. More generally, the program of the New York internationalists began to be adopted as U.S. foreign economic policy. But as long as the Great Depression continued, American industry demanded protection, and progress toward free trade and internationalism was slow and fitful.[11]

Still, New York during the New Deal continued to embody the transatlantic world-view, and in an even more cosmopolitan form than before. New Deal New York was personified in Franklin Roosevelt as president, Herbert Lehman as governor, and Fiorello La Guardia as mayor. These three respectively represented, in ethnic terms, the New York WASP elite, the New York Jewish elite, and the New York ethnic populations;[12] and they typified the New York foreign-policy elite, the New York financial elite, and the New York labor unions. Presiding over and integrating them all, of course, was "Dr. New Deal," Franklin Roosevelt himself.

At the very end of the Great Depression (and at the very beginning of World War II), the cosmopolitan world-view of New Deal New York was celebrated in one of the most splendid public spectacles ever seen in the United States—the New York World's Fair of 1939–1940. The fair showed what New York offered to America and what, therefore, the New World could offer to the Old. Here could be seen, in a gleaming alabaster city, the New Deal promise of enlightened political leadership, progressive capitalist corporations, and public-spirited labor unions, all united in looking confidently and acting generously toward the rest of the world. It was at the New York World's Fair that one could first actually gaze upon what the (not yet named) American Century was supposed to look like, and what the United States would offer to Europe in the Marshall Plan and the liberal international order a decade later. But, of course, before that could occur, everyone at the World's Fair had to pass through the next world war.

From World War II to the Cold War: New York, the Grand Coalition, and the American Century

It was World War II that at last brought about a grand coalition of the three great sectors of the American economy—finance, industry, and agriculture—and the respective three great sections of American geography—the Northeast (led by New York), the Midwest, and the South. It was a coalition personified in Henry Stimson (the Republican lawyer and statesman from New York) as secretary of war, Frank Knox (a Republican newspaper publisher from Chicago) as secretary of the navy, and Cordell Hull (the Democratic congressman from Memphis) as secretary of state. Reaching out and integrating them all, of course, was "Dr. Win-the-War," Franklin Roosevelt.

New York and World War II

Even during the war, however, there was an echo of the prewar disputes. This was in the debate over which military theater should receive the focus of the U.S. war effort, i.e., "Europe-first" or "Pacific-first." The former generally was supported by the Democratic party and also by the New York financial and foreign policy elites. The latter generally was supported by the Republican party and also by the midwestern and western regional elites. Not surprisingly, the actual result during the first two years of the war was to split the war effort into two roughly equal parts, half going to Europe and half to the Pacific. With this, the grand coalition at home was maintained.[13]

Franklin Roosevelt was also the perfect person to maintain another grand alliance, the one with Britain. There was no political leader in America whose personal background had more in common with the British upper class and therefore with the British foreign-policy elite than the American president, who was also a New York patrician and "the squire of Hyde Park." And as it happened, Winston Churchill was also the perfect person to maintain the grand alliance with America. There was no political leader in Britain whose personal background had more in common with the American foreign policy elite than the British prime minister, who was not only an architect of an Anglo-American alliance but the child of one (his father was English, and his mother was an American, indeed a New Yorker).

The Council on Foreign Relations immediately recognized that the new world war created both the necessity and the opportunity to correct the errors that the United States had made after the first one. In December 1939, the council set up its War and Peace Studies project, an ensemble of four working groups to discuss and determine the goals that the United States should seek for the postwar world. The council groups met frequently and steadily with the staffs of the U.S. departments of State, War, and the Treasury during the war.

The War and Peace Studies project addressed the problem of postwar international security by recommending the resurrection of Woodrow Wilson's concept of the League of Nations. The project also addressed the problem of the postwar international economy, in particular the interwar experience of the absence or collapse of the three hegemonic functions of international trade, long-term development loans, and short-term currency support. The Council saw the solution to these three crucial economic needs to be the establishment of three respective international economic organizations, that would be under the leadership of the United States and would negotiate agreements, enforce rules, and provide funds to bring about an open, liberal, international economic order.[14]

The extent to which the Council proposals directly influenced U.S. policymakers is a matter of dispute; it is clear, however, that the actual policies which these policymakers pursued and achieved in regard to international security and the international economy were very similar to those proposed by the Council. By 1944, policymakers expected international security to be organized within the United Nations, and the international economy to be organized within the International Trade Organization (ITO), eventually realized as the General Agreement on Tariffs and Trade (GATT), the International Bank for Reconstruction and Development (the World Bank), and the International Monetary Fund (the IMF).

The War and Peace Studies project brought a great expansion in the staff and the activities of the Council on Foreign Relations, and the preeminent role of the United States in the postwar world promised to do the same. Once again, the Council acquired a new building to house its expanding operations, this time at 58 East 68th Street (just off Park Avenue and known as the Harold Pratt House), which it moved into in 1945 and which has remained its New York headquarters until the present day.

New York and the Cold War

It was Europe's physical destruction in World War II (far more extensive than in World War I) which actually provided the base for continuing the grand coalition of finance, industry, and agriculture into the postwar, or Cold War, era. After World War I, European industry had posed an immediate threat to the American markets of American industry. After World War II, however, shattered European industry itself provided an immediate market for American industry. New York finance and southern agriculture continued to benefit from a secure and prosperous Europe, but now were joined in this objective for the first time by their ancient adversary, midwestern industry.

The 1940s were the heroic age of the New York foreign policy elite. It was they who created the great institutions that reorganized the postwar chaos into a new liberal world order.[15] This reorganization extended over three arenas.

First, there was the arena of international security. This was addressed first by the creation in 1945 of the United Nations and then, after the U.N. became stalemated by the Soviet-American conflict, by the creation of the Marshall Plan in 1947 and the North Atlantic Treaty Organization (NATO) in 1949. The principal architects of the Marshall Plan and NATO were Dean Acheson and John J. McCloy (lawyers) and Averell Harriman and Robert Lovett (investment bankers).

Second, there was the arena of the international economy. This was addressed by the creation in 1944–1948 of three institutions, one for each of the three crucial economic, and hegemonic, functions—international trade, development loans, and foreign-exchange support. These became respectively the GATT, the World Bank, and the IMF. Together, these comprised the Bretton Woods system, named after the conference which was held between American and British economic experts at Bretton Woods, New Hampshire, in the autumn of 1944 and which laid the foundation for these institutions. The principal architects were Henry Morgenthau, Jr. (a publisher), and again Dean Acheson and John McCloy.

The new international security and economic order, however, had to be supported by a hegemonic power. This led to the third arena, that of the U.S. national government. The New York foreign-policy elite created the institutions which reorganized the U.S. government in 1947 into a national-security state that could sustain the new liberal world order—the National Security Council, the Department of Defense, and the Central Intelligence Agency. Here the principal architects were James Forrestal, Ferdinand Eberstadt, and Robert Lovett (investment bankers).

Finally, giving policy direction and moral meaning to all of these new institutions were the new policy of containment and the new strategic concepts to back it up—nuclear deterrence, commitment, and credibility. Here the principal authors were Averell Harriman, George Kennan (a foreign service officer), and Paul Nitze (an investment banker). Apart from Kennan, every one of these architects of the postwar world order was a New Yorker.

New York Leadership and Regional Divisions

These creative innovations abroad and at home, in foreign policy and defense policy, were supported by the grand coalition of New York finance, midwestern industry, and southern agriculture. The coalition was personified within the Truman administration by the New Yorkers previously mentioned, by President Harry Truman himself (a former senator from Missouri), and by Assistant Secretary of State Will Clayton (a cotton exporter from Mississippi, who continued the Cordell Hull tradition). They were joined by Arthur Vandenberg, who was a Republican senator from Michigan and who was chairman of the Senate Foreign Relations Committee in the 80th Congress (1947–1948). On all the creative innovations of the time, the midwestern and southern members of the coalition deferred to the leadership of the New York foreign-policy elite. This was the great era of "bipartisanship" and "consensus" in foreign policy. This era was to last through the administration of Dwight Eisenhower, who perfectly combined European orientation, New York experience (as president of Columbia University), and Republican support.

However, just as the "isolationism" of the 1920s–1930s really only applied to Europe, so did the "bipartisanship" and "consensus" of the 1940s–1950s also really only apply to Europe, Latin America, and to that most westernized part of Asia, Japan. It did not apply to the rest of East Asia, particularly China. There, the old division between the New York foreign-policy elite and the midwestern regional elite continued throughout the 1940s and the 1950s. Not surprisingly, the latter bitterly attacked the former for "losing" or even "selling out" China. It was the midwestern elite who revered that most Asian and Republican of American generals, Douglas MacArthur. And it was the same midwestern elite, and not some formless and mindless "populist" and "paranoid" mass, which provided that least civil and least progressive of Wisconsin senators, Joseph McCarthy, with crucial support.[16]

Within the New York foreign-policy elite itself, there were particular differences about how to carry out the policy of containment. The figures that we have mentioned all agreed upon the necessity for the United States to protect Europe and Japan (and their prospective hinterlands of the Middle East and South Korea) from the expansion of the Soviet Union and its allies, and they agreed that this protection should be achieved with a combination of nuclear deterrence and conventional forces. But other members of the foreign-policy elite sometimes departed from this consensus position.

The author of the containment policy itself, George Kennan, thought that containment should largely be carried out with political and economic means, rather than with military ones; he was not in favor, for example, of the creation of NATO. But Kennan was not really a member of the New York elite in the literal sense; he did not have a career in banking or in law but rather was a career foreign-service officer. Dean Acheson dismissed Kennan as being woolly-minded, "vague," and "mystical."[17]

Conversely, John Foster Dulles, who was a leading Republican member of the New York elite and was Eisenhower's secretary of state, thought that containment should be extended beyond Europe and Japan (and the Middle East and South Korea) to protect an arc of countries between them. These included Taiwan, Indochina, and Thailand (e.g., the Republic of China Treaty and the SEATO Treaty). Dulles also thought that containment could be achieved principally with nuclear deterrence (the threat of "massive retaliation") and that conventional forces could be de-emphasized and reduced. But Dulles was really trying to construct a compromise with the midwestern elites of the Republican party. As we have seen, these had always been interested in establishing an American position in Asia. But as fiscally conservative businessmen, they did not want to spend what would be required to maintain large conventional forces abroad year after year. From their perspective, it was much more practical to rely upon nuclear deterrence or "more bang for the buck," as Charles Wilson, Eisenhower's secretary of defense and a former chairman of General Motors, put it.

The Rise of the West and of Washington

Seen from the perspective of economic sectors and geographic sections, it was only a matter of time until the great achievements of the New York foreign policy elite—the liberal world order and the national security state—would bring into being forces that would undermine the leadership of that elite and the political consensus which it had constructed.

The liberal world order established the conditions for the revival of European and Japanese industry, the expansion of international trade, and therefore the emergence of foreign threats to American industry. This potential materialized in 1961, when the dollar shortage which Europe had experienced in the 1940s and 1950s was replaced with a dollar surplus; it has grown steadily ever since.[18] Those American industries which had invested in Europe (e.g., automobiles, computers) would remain in the internationalist coalition, but those industries which kept their production in the United States (e.g., textiles in the South, steel in the Midwest) abandoned internationalism and turned toward protectionism. They provided part of the base for Barry Goldwater and the opposition to Nelson Rockefeller in 1964.

The national-security state brought about the creation of a fourth great economic center, the aerospace industry and the defense industry more generally, which was largely located in the West. The West, too, would defer to the New York foreign-policy elite so long as that elite supported the Cold War. But if détente should become the preferred policy of New York, the West would also look elsewhere for its foreign policy leadership.[19]

The national-security state also established the conditions for a great expansion of the importance of Washington. It was natural that around the Defense Department, the State Department, and the Central Intelligence Agency there would grow up offices of military contractors and centers of foreign policy experts. In the long run, these centers would challenge the leadership of New York's Council on Foreign Relations.

From the Heroic Age to the Academic Age of American Foreign Policy

We have seen that the architects of the American Century were drawn largely from New York itself, particularly from the financial and legal communities of Wall Street or what might be seen as the first and second estates of the New York foreign-policy elite. In the heroic age of American foreign policy, the heroes were the rather unlikely figures of bankers and lawyers.

A Tale of Two Cities: New York and Cambridge

With the transition from the 1950s to the 1960s and from the Eisenhower administration to the Kennedy administration, a new era in the history of the American empire and of the New York elite began. Now, for the first time, major foreign-policy makers were selected from the third estate of the New York foreign-policy elite, the universities (in particular, Harvard, MIT, and Columbia). The elevation of the professors coincided with the elevation of the president's National Security advisor, from being largely a committee rapporteur under Truman and Eisenhower to being a coequal with the secretaries of State and Defense and the director of the CIA under Kennedy and later presidents. The National Security advisor was now one of "the awesome foursome," as these four foreign-policy officials were called in the 1960s. And he was also one of "the best and the brightest," as the academics appointed to foreign policy positions called themselves in the 1960s.[20]

The first of the professional and powerful National Security advisors was McGeorge Bundy (Harvard), followed by Walt Rostow (MIT), Henry Kissinger (Harvard), and Zbigniew Brzezinski (Columbia). Together, they added up to a twenty-year reign (1961–1981) for the professorial regime.

The heroic age of American foreign policy was thus succeeded by its academic age. And given the contrast between the accomplishments of the 1940–1950s and those of the 1960s–1970s (e.g., the Marshall Plan versus the Alliance for Progress, the Atlantic Alliance versus "flexible response," the Bretton Woods system versus the Smithsonian Agreement, and of course the Korean War versus the Vietnam War), it appears that the golden age of American foreign policy was succeeded by its silver or bronze one. "The brightest," it turned out, were not the best.

The Apprenticeship of the Academics: Dr. Faustus as a Student Prince

Although the foreign-policy makers of the 1940s–1950s were authentic, or at least economic, members of the New York foreign-policy elite while the National Security advisors of the 1960s–1970s were only academic members, three of the latter had undergone an apprentice relationship with an authentic member. These professors, each of whom had a reputation for monumental arrogance with their academic colleagues and their own students, had also each been the dutiful and pliant tutee of someone of great distinction or at least great wealth. McGeorge Bundy had served as the memoir writer for Henry Stimson; Henry Kissinger as a speechwriter and report writer for Nelson Rockefeller; and Zbigniew Brzezinski as a research organizer and report writer for David Rockefeller. It was as the protégés of lawyers and bankers that these professors reached high office.[21]

The twenty-year regime of the academics, which more or less corresponded to a twenty-year crisis in American foreign policy stretching from the Vietnam War to the Iranian hostage crisis, was finally brought to an end by Ronald Reagan. He was the first president since Warren Harding who appeared to have little connection to or interest in New York.

From the Vietnam War to the Great Diffusion: New York versus the New Foreign Policy Centers

It has already been noted that the very achievements of the New York foreign policy elite in the 1940s, the liberal world order, and the national security state, had created the conditions for the foreign-policy consensus to be eventually replaced by foreign-policy cleavages.

New York and the Vietnam War

As it happened, the growing U.S. military involvement in the Vietnam War at first arrested the emergence of these cleavages. In the early

1960s, the political and economic elites of each of the four great regions supported the war, each for their own reasons, perhaps, but all believing in the grand concepts formulated by the New York foreign-policy elite—containment, deterrence, commitment, and credibility. In July 1965, the most distinguished members of the New York elite, now known as "the wise men," advised Lyndon Johnson to deploy several hundred thousand U.S. combat troops to Vietnam. The leaders in this advice were Lovett, Acheson, and McCloy. In turn, the regional elites gave this Vietnam policy strong support.[22]

The Vietnam War, of course, set in train forces which would break apart the consensus era in American foreign policy and the grand coalition upon which it had been based. For our purposes, a crucial factor was the economic turmoil that soon developed—inflation and balance of payment deficits, culminating in early 1968 with runs on the dollar. The war had become a crisis for New York financial institutions. The reasons that the New York foreign-policy elite changed its position on the war are many. They include a concern that the war was driving apart the United States and its European allies; that it was producing divisions within the liberal political base of the elite, particularly in the media and in the universities; and that it was diverting the flow of government spending from where it was now needed, i.e., for social programs to put out the fires of urban riots. But the decisive and most urgent reason, the one that "wonderfully concentrated the mind" of the New York elite and the only one that had fully developed by early 1968, was the crisis of the dollar. In March 1968, at a famous meeting with Johnson, the same distinguished "wise men" turned against the war as decisively as they had supported it in July 1965.[23]

It is not surprising that Lyndon Johnson, and the regional elites, felt betrayed. These other elites each still had good reasons to support the war and indeed to prosecute it with even greater use of American air power. It was the "liberal Eastern Establishment," the same people who had led the way into the war, who now stood in the way of winning it. Once again they seemed to have sold out Asian countries in order to advance their European interests. Never again would the New York foreign policy elite receive the deference that it had received (and earned) from 1940 to 1965.

The New Foreign-Policy Centers

As it happened, at this same time (the late 1960s) new centers of foreign policy expertise and influence were being established outside of New York and its Council on Foreign Relations.[24] The first of these, a great expansion of the foreign policy and defense policy staffs of the Brookings Institution in Washington, did not seem very threatening at the time. Nor did a similar expansion of the Carnegie Endowment for International Peace. The ideas and positions of the Brookings Institution and the Carnegie Endowment were virtually identical to those of the Council on Foreign Relations. However, they were in Washington rather than in New York, and they provided the models for other institutions with the same geography as Brookings and Carnegie but with a different ideology.

The transformation of the Brookings Institution and the Carnegie Endowment was followed in the 1970s by a similar expansion and transformation of the American Enterprise Institute (AEI) and the Georgetown University Center for Strategic and International Studies (CSIS), both also in Washington. AEI tended to propound views congenial to American industry generally and CSIS views congenial to the defense industry more particularly. Now, in effect, both the Midwest and the West had their own centers of foreign policy expertise and influence, and they were in Washington, where that influence counted most. Why should the elites of these regions follow the lead of anyone in New York, or indeed pay them any attention at all?

Thus, the Vietnam War dramatized the failure of the New York foreign-policy elite, and the new Washington centers (and others, such as the Hoover Institution at Stanford) institutionalized the diffusion of foreign-policy expertise.

From Detente to the Second Cold War: New York versus America Again

The consequences of the Vietnam War and the diffusion of foreign-policy expertise were confirmed by the continuing differences between New York finance and other American economic interests. In each of the great foreign-policy issues from the early 1970s to the mid-1980s, the New York foreign-policy elite opposed the interests of some regional elite.

The Soviet Union and Arms Control

The New York international banks were the first major American economic interest to support détente in the early 1970s and the first to support a new détente in the mid-1980s. In the early 1970s the New York banks anticipated that they would benefit from lending to the Soviet Union and its East European allies. At the time, it appeared that the Soviet Union and Eastern Europe would be the area of the next great European boom, comparable to that in Western Europe in the 1950s and 1960s, which had been so profitable to New York international banks and to the multinational corporations which they serviced.[25] In addition, arms control agreements with the Soviet Union (such as SALT I in 1972) would permit a reduction in U.S. defense spending and therefore an easing of the problems of the dollar.

In the case of the second détente, that of the mid-1980s, the importance of these factors was reversed. Few now anticipated that the Soviet bloc would be the site of a great economic boom, but the economic reforms of the Gorbachev era did promise new opportunities for profitable loans and investments for New York banks and corporations, especially for those with subsidiaries in Western Europe. By the mid-1980s, however, the more important consideration was the great concern of New York banks over the U.S. budget deficit. This drove them once again to seek cuts in U.S. defense spending and therefore arms control agreements with the Soviet Union.

The Council on Foreign Relations provided support for these two openings to the Soviet Union. In the early 1970s, it set up the "1980s Project," its largest single policy-research undertaking since the War and Peace Studies project of the early 1940s. Again in the mid-1980s, the Council organized membership meetings and research workshops and published books and policy analyses on Soviet-American relations and security issues. In both the early 1970s and the mid-1980s, these Council projects made the case for greater cooperation and less confrontation with the Soviets, for arms control agreements, and for a U.S. focus on North-South rather than East-West issues.[26]

In supporting détente with the Soviet Union, and a corresponding reduction in defense spending, the New York foreign policy elite of course opposed the interests of the defense industry and of a good part of the elites of the West and the South. These regional elites, in turn, provided the economic support for the new Cold War, which lasted roughly from 1979 to 1985, i.e., the last half of the Carter administration and the first Reagan administration. These western and southern elites now took their foreign policy guidance not from the Council on Foreign Relations, but from organizations such as the Georgetown Center for Strategic and International Studies, the Heritage Foundation, and the Hoover Institution.

The Middle East and the Arab-Israeli Conflict

New York international banks, along with the major multinational oil companies, were the first major American economic interest to collaborate with OPEC in the early 1970s and to accept Arab positions in the Arab-Israeli conflict. In regard to OPEC, they opposed the interests of energy-intensive heavy industry and a good part of the elites of the Midwest. On the Arab-Israeli conflict, they opposed the interests of many in the Jewish community who had previously accepted their leadership on a variety of issues.

The conflict between the international banks and the multinational oil companies, on the one hand, and the Jewish community on the other, inflicted a grave wound upon the New York foreign policy elite, for it brought about a schism within that elite itself. The schism was reflected in the enhanced role in foreign policy debates of the journal *Commentary*, which although published in New York took positions directly opposed to those of *Foreign Affairs*. It was also reflected in the enhanced role of the American-Israel Public Affairs Committee (AIPAC), which was located in Washington.

The collapse of oil prices in the 1980s brought about a decline of Arab economic power and a corresponding decline in the interest of New York international banks in supporting Arab political positions. By now, however, the Jewish community could turn to foreign policy centers and journals that supported their interests much better than the Council on Foreign Relations and *Foreign Affairs*.

The World Market and Free Trade

As we have seen, the New York international banks and multinational corporations have consistently supported free trade. By the mid-1970s, however, much of the industry located within the United States could no longer compete in the world market. This was the case with the textile industry (principally located in the South) and with the steel and automobile industries (principally located in the Midwest). These industries thus came into conflict with the New York banks and corporations and with the New York foreign policy elite. Some firms in these industries (particularly General Motors and Ford) were themselves multinational corporations, and the interest of their management in free trade did not diverge much from that of New York. But the New York foreign-policy elite was now in opposition to the interests, expressed in protectionism, of management in the textile and steel industries and of industrial labor in general. Labor had previously accepted the leadership of the New York elite on many foreign policy issues.

Unlike the defense industry and the Jewish community, protectionist industry and labor never developed their own strong centers and journals to represent their foreign-policy positions. This in part explains why they have achieved some protectionist measures from Congress but not a fundamental change in U.S. foreign economic policy, as implemented by any president and his administration.

The Creation of the Trilateral Commission

In the early 1970s, the Chairman of the Council on Foreign Relations, David Rockefeller, initiated a two-part change in that organization. The Council, as organizations are wont to do, had gradually expanded its membership over the years; by the early 1970s, with some 1,500 members, it was hardly limited to an elite. Given the spirit of the time, the Council was under pressure to admit even more members from a variety of diverse groups, including women and minorities.[27]

The solution to this double bind was simple, but also double. On the one hand, Rockefeller created the Trilateral Commission in 1973, composed only of truly elite figures drawn from the United States, Europe, and Japan. As it happened, the new Trilateral Commission had about the same number of American members (fewer than 100) as the Council on Foreign Relations had when it was founded as a truly elite organization sixty years before. On the other hand,Rockefeller opened the membership of the council itself even wider, expanding the number of members to about 2,200. In addition, the Council began to engage in public education programs. As such, it began to look and act rather like its longtime, more public, and less elite ally, the Foreign Policy Association. It is often the case with organizations, however, that the more numerous are their members, the less weighty is their influence. For this reason alone, the Council on Foreign Relations would have lost a good deal of influence on foreign policy in the 1970s. In any event, it was no longer a very good place to look for a New York foreign policy *elite.* One could find the elite there, it is true, but it was rather like finding a diamond in the rough.

Nor, as it turned out, could one find a *New York* foreign-policy elite in the Trilateral Commission. Here, one could certainly find a foreign-policy elite, but even the American members were drawn as much from the rest of the country as they were from New York. Given the diversity, indeed the conflict, of interests between its American, West European, and Japanese members and between its American members themselves, the Trilateral Commission has never been able to compose the coherent and implementable policies that characterized the New York foreign-policy elite from the 1920s to the 1960s.

Finally, in the 1980s, there came changes within the New York financial elite itself, the very core of the New York foreign policy elite. The deregulation policies of the Reagan administration greatly changed the world of New York finance. With all the new innovations and opportunities on Wall Street, the new generation of New York financiers and lawyers was largely uninterested and uninvolved in foreign affairs. As John McCloy remarked in 1982, "they're all too busy making money."[28]

Conclusion: From the New York Foreign Policy Elite to a National Foreign Policy Elite

In brief, the New York foreign-policy elite lost first the allegiance of the regional elites of the South and the West in the 1960s, and then that of the regional elite of the Midwest in the 1970s. As a result, it lost the foreign-policy leadership of the country. Then, also in the 1970s, the New York foreign-policy elite lost the allegiance of the Jewish elite. But the Jewish elite was important within the politics of New York itself. Thus, the New York foreign-policy elite lost the foreign-policy leadership of the city. Finally, the New York foreign-policy elite lost the allegiance of the younger Wall Street bankers and lawyers in the 1980s. Thus, the New York foreign-policy elite lost the leadership of its core constituency.

Yet, by the late 1980s, the foreign policy of the Reagan administration was characterized by cooperation with the Soviet Union, cooperation with Arab governments, and vigorous support of free trade, the same positions which had long been advocated by the New York foreign-policy elite. At the very moment that this elite was disappearing, its policies were embraced by that most Californian of administrations. These policies were continued by the Bush administration, which was something of a blend of regions (rather like George Bush, who is from both Connecticut and Texas, himself).

The explanation for the existence of New York kinds of foreign policies even with the decline of the New York foreign-policy elite lies in the spread of financial interests and institutions during the 1980s from New York to other regions of America, particularly to Chicago, Atlanta, Miami, and the cities of the West Coast. The financial elite of the United States is no longer identifiable with New York alone, but has become national or at least multiregional in its location. This provided a new national foundation for a new consensus foreign policy. But the most natural locus, and focus, for influence and expertise directed at that new national foreign policy is the national capital, Washington.

Thus, when the elites of the different regions now coalesce around the same foreign policies, they do not do so in New York. Rather, they coalesce in Washington. Indeed, they most probably will convene for drinks and dinner at 2400 N Street, NW, near Dupont Circle. For there, at the center of a circle whose one-mile radius encompasses the Brookings Institution, the Carnegie Endowment, the American Enterprise Institute, and the Georgetown Center for Strategic and International Studies, can now be found the Washington office of the Council on Foreign Relations.

Notes

1. Depicting decline are: Kennedy, Paul, *The Rise and Fall of the Great Powers: Economic Change and Military Conflict from 1500 to 2000* (New York: Random House, 1988); Mead, Walter Russell, *Mortal Splendor: The American Empire in Transition* (Boston: Houghton Mifflin, 1987); Calleo, David P., *Beyond American Hegemony: The Future of the Western Alliance* (New York: Basic Books, 1987). Denying it are: Nau, Henry R., *The Myth of America's Decline: Leading the World Economy in the 1990s* (New York: Oxford University Press, 1990); Nye, Joseph S., *Bound to Lead: The Changing Nature of American Power* (New York: Basic Books, 1990).
2. Isaacson, Walter and Evan Thomas, *The Wise Men: Six Friends and the World They Made* (New York: Simon and Schuster, 1986).
3. Destler, I. M., Leslie H. Gelb, and Anthony Lake, *Our Own Worst Enemy: The Unmaking of American Foreign Policy*, revised and updated (New York: Simon and Schuster, 1985).
4. Kurth, James R., "The Military-Industrial Complex Revisited," in Kruzel, Joseph, ed., *American Defense Annual, 1989–1990* (Lexington, MA: Lexington Books, 1989), pp. 195–215.
5. Isaacson and Thomas, *The Wise Men*, chap. 1.
6. Schulzinger, Robert D., *The Wise Men of Foreign Affairs: The History of the Council on Foreign Relations* (New York: Columbia University Press, 1984), chap. 1; Silk, Leonard and Mark Silk, *The American Establishment* (New York: Basic Books, 1980), chap. 6.
7. Schulzinger, *The Wise Men of Foreign Affairs*, p. 10.
8. Aldcroft, Derek H., *From Versailles to Wall Street, 1919–1929* (Berkeley: University of California Press, 1977).
9. Schulzinger, *The Wise Men of Foreign Affairs*, p. 30.
10. Kindleberger, Charles P., *The World in Depression, 1929–1939* (Berkeley: University of California Press, 1973), chap. 14.
11. Dallek, Robert, *Franklin D. Roosevelt and American Foreign Policy, 1932–1945* (New York: Oxford University Press, 1979), parts 1 and 2.
12. Roosevelt, of course, was of Dutch ancestry, and not Anglo-Saxon in the most literal sense; La Guardia had an Italian father and a Jewish mother.

13. Dallek, *Franklin D. Roosevelt and American Foreign Policy*, part 4; Schurmann, Franz, *The Logic of World Power* (New York: Pantheon Books, 1974), part 1.
14. Schulzinger, *The Wise Men of Foreign Affairs*, chaps. 3–4.
15. Isaacson and Thomas, *The Wise Men*, chaps. 11–14.
16. Rogin, Michael Paul, *The Intellectuals and McCarthy: The Radical Specter* (Cambridge, MA: MIT Press, 1967). Interpretations of McCarthyism that stress populism and paranoia are Hofstadter, Richard, *The Paranoid Style in American Politics and Other Essays* (New York: Vintage Books, 1967) and his *The Age of Reform* (New York: Knopf, 1956); Lipset, Seymour Martin, and Earl Raab, *The Politics of Unreason* (New York: Harper and Row, 1970).
17. Isaacson and Thomas, *The Wise Men*, pp. 474, 580.
18. Hodgson, Godfrey, *America in Our Time* (New York: Doubleday, 1976), p. 7.
19. *Ibid.*, pp. 127–133.
20. Halberstam, David, *The Best and the Brightest* (New York: Random House, 1972).
21. Henry Kissinger dedicates his memoirs to "the memory of Nelson Aldrich Rockefeller" and calls him "the single most influential person in my life" who "introduced me to high-level policymaking;" Kissinger adds that he was "intoxicated" by his "proximity to power—and I daresay wealth." Kissinger, Henry, *White House Years* (Boston: Little, Brown, 1979), p. 4. Also see Brzezinski, Zbigniew, *Power and Principle* (New York: Farrar, Straus and Giroux, 1983).
22. Isaacson and Thomas, *The Wise Men*, pp. 649–657.
23. *Ibid.*, pp. 698–706.
24. Destler, Gelb, and Lake, *Our Own Worst Enemy*, chap. 2.
25. Gershman, Carl, "Selling Them the Rope: Business and the Soviets," *Commentary* (April 1979): 35–45; and "The Rise and Fall of the New Foreign-Policy Establishment" *Commentary* (July 1980): 13–24.
26. Schulzinger, *The Wise Men of Foreign Affairs*, chap. 8; Council on Foreign Relations, *Annual report, July 1, 1986–June 30, 1987* (New York, 1987).
27. Schulzinger, *The Wise Men of Foreign Affairs*, pp. 213–214.
28. Quoted in Brinkley, Alan, "Minister Without Portfolio—The Most Influential Private Citizen in America: The Life and Times of John McCloy," *Harper's* (February 1983): 46.

5

New York City and American National Politics

Martin Shefter

New York has been America's financial capital since the 1830s and its premier cultural center since the 1890s. In contrast to London, Paris, and Tokyo, however, it is not a political capital. Consequently, economic and cultural elites in New York do not have the same opportunities for daily interaction with national governmental leaders as do their counterparts in other world cities. Nonetheless, New York–based interests have not been without means of exercising influence in the national political arena.

There have been three major phases in New York's national influence. During the nineteenth and early twentieth centuries political parties were the most important channels of New York's political influence. Then from the 1930s through the 1970s, the presidency was the chief vehicle through which New Yorkers shaped American politics. Since 1980, the Federal Reserve and the Treasury have been the agencies through which New York interests have gained their most significant representation in national affairs.

Conditions of Political Influence

Generally speaking, the influence that any political force is able to exercise in national affairs is a function of three conditions: the resources it commands relative to those controlled by other contenders for national power; the alliances it cultivates; and the institutions available for gaining access to the national government. The resources, alliances, and institutions available to New Yorkers have varied over time, but through much of American history they have enabled metropolitan interests to play a major role in national politics.

Wealth is the most obvious resource upon which New Yorkers have been able to draw in contests for national power. For example, the administration of Abraham Lincoln depended so heavily on New York banks to finance the Civil War that, as historian David Montgomery has noted, "the bond, banking, and currency enactments of 1863 to 1865 were not so much legislated by Congress as negotiated between the government and the bankers."[1] And in the 1940s and 1950s, the Republican party's dependence upon New York money to finance its campaigns enabled internationalists and moderates to prevail over isolationists and conservatives in GOP factional struggles; indeed it was only in the late 1970s, when direct-mail techniques enabled Republicans to raise large sums of money from other sources, that Sunbelt conservatives were able to achieve a dominant position in the GOP.[2]

Similarly, New York's position as America's communications capital has given metropolitan elites substantial influence over national opinion. From Horace Greeley and James Gordon Bennett, through Joseph Pulitzer and William Randolph Hearst, to Henry Luce and William Paley, the nation's most prominent publishers and broadcasters have operated from New York. And from Greeley's 1861 "Forward to Richmond" campaign, through Hearst's "Remember the Maine," to network news interpretations of the 1968 Tet offensive, national opinion regarding major events and issues has been influenced by news organizations based in New York.[3]

Votes are yet another resource upon which metropolitan interests have been able to rely to gain a voice in national politics. New York City casts a larger proportion of its state's vote than any other American city, and from the middle of the nineteenth century through at least the middle of the twentieth, New York State was crucial to the Democratic party's fortunes nationally. Consequently, in fifteen of the twenty presidential elections between 1868 and 1944, the Democrats nominated for the White House public figures from New York who were thought to be attractive to voters in the city and state.

However substantial their political resources, New Yorkers have never been in a position to govern on their own and have found it necessary to forge coalitions with other political forces as a condition of exercising power nationally. During much of the nineteenth century, for example, politicians allied with New York commercial and financial interests were able to play a major role in national affairs by joining forces with southern planters within the Democratic party.[4] And during the thirty-year period following the outbreak of World War II, the Wall Street lawyers and bankers who came to be known as the Wise Men were able to shape American foreign policy by joining with industrialists, defense contractors, organized labor, ethnic minorities, and southerners in an expanded version of Franklin Roosevelt's New Deal coalition.[5]

Finally, over the course of American history, New York interests have gained access to the national government through a variety of institutions. As mentioned above, New Yorkers successively exercised influence through political parties, the presidency, and the Federal Reserve and U.S. Treasury. Coincident with these changes were shifts in the coalitions New Yorkers entered, the resources they deployed, and the policies they sought in the national arena.[6]

Party Representation, 1820s–1920s

In the early years of the republic, political leaders linked to New York's mercantile elite made an unsuccessful bid to use the new national government to serve the exclusive interests of that elite and its counterparts in other seaboard cities.[7] The economic program and alliance with Great Britain fashioned by New Yorkers Alexander Hamilton and John Jay benefited the nation's commercial entrepôts at the expense of its overwhelmingly agrarian population. This effort to advance the exclusive interests of a narrow metropolitan constituency divided the coalition of southern planters and northern merchants that had drafted the Constitution. Opponents of Hamilton's financial program and Jay's Treaty organized the Jeffersonian Republican party, mobilized support among subsistence farmers in the countryside and artisans in the cities, and gained control of the national government in 1800. Subsequently, the Federalist party collapsed and the Republican party withered. The system of nonparty politics that ensued was dominated by Virginians, and New Yorkers did not play a central role in American national politics.[8]

In the 1820s and 1830s, Martin Van Buren undertook to reconstruct the old Republican party. Van Buren led a faction of New York politicians that was known upstate as the Albany Regency and that in New York City was called Tammany Hall. By constructing the nation's strongest party organization, the Regency was able to compete effectively with its major rival for power in New York.[9] Van Buren argued to his associates that by cultivating alliances with their counterparts in other states, they could increase their power nationally and serve the interests of "their friends at home" who "stood in want of their influence abroad."[10] Towards that end, Van Buren and his allies put together the political coalition that secured the election to the presidency of Andrew Jackson in 1828 and 1832, and of Van Buren himself in 1836, and that became institutionalized as the Democratic party. The success of the Democrats led their opponents to organize as well.

For much of the next century, political parties served as the central mechanism through which New York City's political and economic leadership converted the electoral, financial, and organizational resources of the metropolis into political power. In the 1840s and 1850s, the Democrats and Whigs established national committees, headquartered in New York, to raise and disburse campaign contributions. In the 1870s and 1880s, the parties established centralized campaign organizations in the metropolis, modeled on the city's emerging national corporations, to conduct truly national campaigns. (The Democrats, under the leadership of New Yorkers Samuel Tilden, Abram Hewitt, and Daniel Lamont, took the initiative in this regard, and the Republicans followed shortly thereafter.) And in the 1900s and 1910s, the parties began to run national publicity campaigns that communicated to voters by borrowing techniques from, or making use of, the metropolis's tabloid newspapers, mass-circulation magazines, public relations firms, and advertising agencies.[11]

Political parties also linked New Yorkers to allies elsewhere in the nation and provided them with access to national policymaking institutions. The major parties, of course, fashioned different programs to bind together their national coalitions, and these party programs and coalitions changed over time. Generally speaking, however, the Democrats sought to unite New York's commercial interests and immigrant voters with allies in the white South by advocating states' rights and opposing national banks and tariffs, federal spending on internal improvements and military pensions, and national standards for citizenship and suffrage.[12] The Whigs and Republicans won support among midwestern and northeastern (including New York) financial, manufacturing, and agricultural interests with a stake in the home market, and among Union veterans and pietistic voters, by advocating a somewhat more active role for the federal government in these domains. However, the very hegemony of party in the nineteenth-century political system contributed to the weakness of the American national state.[13] This, in turn, left New York–based markets and institutions largely free to shape and reshape American economic and cultural life.

Presidential Representation, 1930s–1970s

Although political parties came under attack and national administrative capacities were enhanced during the Progressive Era, it was in the 1930s and 1940s that truly major changes occurred in the institutions through which New Yorkers exercised their greatest influence in American politics and in the impact metropolitan political forces exerted upon the nation's governance. The presidency became the chief vehicle for New York's national influence, and major interests in the city undertook to strengthen the American national state. Working through the national executive, New Yorkers played major roles in constructing the New Deal welfare state in the 1930s and America's national-security state in the 1940s, and in expanding the role the federal government played in American national life in the 1960s.

The New Deal

The first two of these initiatives were led by Franklin Delano Roosevelt. FDR, like Martin Van Buren, came from the Hudson Valley, had ties to both New York City and upstate, and used New York's state government as a springboard to national power. Roosevelt, however, was allied with a different set of New York interests than had previously played a central role in American national politics.

FDR had close ties with what might be termed New York's social-policy complex. In the 1930s, New York was one of the nation's two major intellectual and organizational centers of social-policy formation (the other was Wisconsin). More than a dozen organizations concerned with social policy had their headquarters in the city—chiefly in the United Charities Building on East 22nd Street or within a few blocks of it—and their members interacted with one another intensively.[14] This complex included social-service agencies that directly provided relief to the poor (e.g., the Association for Improving the Condition of the Poor); organizations that drafted social legislation and lobbied to secure its enactment (e.g., the National Consumers' League); the national professional association of social workers (the American Association of Social Workers); and the national journal of charitable organizations (the *Survey*). When Roosevelt entered the White House, he brought sixteen members of this complex to Washington to help design and administer New Deal relief programs.

Leading members of New York's social-policy establishment were associated, in turn, with a loose network of economists, lawyers, union leaders, and businessmen in consumer industries, who over the course of the 1930s became convinced that prosperity could be achieved only if the federal government actively stimulated consumption.[15] Towards this end, they advocated federal jobs and income-maintenance programs, legislation encouraging unionization, and ultimately, planned federal deficits.

New York was an important node in this network. Many of the labor relations practices later propagated by the Roosevelt administration were first developed in negotiations between the city's garment industry and the Amalgamated Clothing Workers Union.[16] Board meetings and study groups of New York's Russell Sage Foundation and Twentieth Century Fund hammered out ideas on government planning, public finance, and consumer credit that gained general acceptance in New Deal circles.[17] These organizations also served as recruiting grounds in the 1930s and 1940s for the National Resources Planning Board, Reconstruction Finance Corporation, Federal Home Loan Bank Board, and the departments of Labor, Commerce, Justice, and State.

The most influential members of the Roosevelt administration recruited from these interlocking networks were Harry Hopkins and Frances Perkins. Hopkins headed the New Deal's major relief and public employment agencies—the Federal Emergency Relief Administration, and its successor, the Works Progress Administration—and then became Roosevelt's personal diplomatic emissary during World War II.[18] Perkins served as secretary of Labor and chaired the Committee on Economic Security, which drafted the New Deal's most enduring welfare initiative, the Social Security Act. Along with FDR himself, and the committee's executive director, Edwin Witte of Wisconsin, Perkins was the key architect of the social security system.[19]

The Wall Street lawyers and bankers who comprised New York's foreign-policy elite also gained access to the national government through the Roosevelt administration. As Europe and then the United States plunged into World War II, President Roosevelt halted his attacks upon "economic royalists" and undertook to unite the nation behind his foreign and defense policies by bringing Wall Street bankers and lawyers—Republicans as well as Democrats—into his administration. To mobilize support for the Cold War, FDR's successors in the White House did the same. In this way, the New Yorkers who later were known as the Wise Men—most prominently, Henry Stimson, James Forrestal, Robert Lovett, Averell Harriman, and John McCloy—came to shape American foreign policy. They helped fashion the doctrines and institutions of containment, collective security, and liberal internationalism that characterized America's relations with the rest of the world during the postwar decades.[20]

New York's social-policy and foreign-policy elites commanded a number of resources that made it worthwhile for FDR to work along with them in constructing the New Deal state. The institutions they led controlled greater expertise and possessed superior planning capacities than the federal government at the time. It was for these reasons that the Committee on Economic Security turned to New York's Industrial Relations counsellors when it needed experts on unemployment compensation, and the State Department commissioned the Council on Foreign Relations to serve, in effect, as its policy-planning division during World War II.[21] Similarly, the experience these elites had acquired in their previous careers could be invaluable to the president. The skills Harry Hopkins developed coordinating relief efforts for the American Red Cross were just what Roosevelt needed in an official charged with organizing the federal government's relief program and, subsequently, lend-lease aid to Great Britain.[22] Similarly, the contacts and reputation Henry Stimson established as New York's leading corporation lawyer were of enormous value to a president seeking the cooperation of industrialists in mobilizing the nation's economy for war.

The domestic programs and foreign policies fashioned by these metropolitan elites appealed to millions of working- and middle-class New Yorkers, whose votes and labor unions provided FDR and his successors with some of their most reliable sources of support. Elected officials and politicians from New York were central figures not only in the urban-liberal wing of the national Democratic party (Ed Flynn, Robert Wagner), but also in the liberal and internationalist wings of the GOP (Fiorello La Guardia, Thomas Dewey). The city's garment union leaders (especially Sidney Hillman) played a key role in labor's electoral mobilization on behalf of Roosevelt in the 1930s and 1940s (hence FDR's "Clear it with Sidney"), and, along with New Yorker George Meany, they made the AFL-CIO a pillar of the Cold War coalition in the 1950s and 1960s.[23]

Of course, the regime that governed the United States during the New Deal and postwar years had ties not only to New York but also to numerous interests outside the metropolis. Southern cotton growers were bound to the postwar system with agricultural subsidies. Midwestern industrialists and their unionized employees benefited from policies of free trade and "commercial Keynesianism," which boosted demand for their products and kept labor markets tight.[24] Sunbelt defense contractors flourished as military spending increased. And throughout the nation, suburban homeowners were served by federal mortgage insurance and highway construction programs.

A number of these interests exercised considerable influence in Congress, and New Yorkers found it necessary to reach accommodations with them—and not infrequently to accept defeat at their hands.[25] In the mid-1940s, a conservative coalition of Republicans and southern Democrats in Congress terminated all federal job programs, abolished the National Resources Planning Board, and defeated proposals by Senator Wagner and other northern liberals to expand the welfare state and commit the federal government to a policy of full employment. During the two decades following World War II, Congress was willing to enact social programs (e.g., urban renewal, grants for hospital construction) only if they channeled federal funds through state and local governments and did not enable federal administrators to upset the balance of political forces locally.[26]

The 1960s

The political stalemate of the 1940s and 1950s was frustrating to liberal political forces. But the access to New York's institutions of culture and communications enjoyed by liberals helped them place the issues of civil rights and urban poverty on the national political agenda and to overcome this deadlock in the 1960s.

A key element in the civil rights movement's success was Martin Luther King, Jr.'s extraordinary appeal not only to southern blacks but also to northern whites.[27] King was able to mobilize support among sympathetic whites by virtue of his links to New York's world of liberal political activism and his access to the metropolis's communications media. Mass meetings in Madison Square Garden, concerts in Carnegie Hall, open letters to the *New York Times,* and grants from New York's Taconic and Field foundations and the J.M. Kaplan Fund helped finance the major campaigns of the civil rights movement.[28] And the coverage the movement received in the print and electronic media enabled King to address a national audience. *Time* magazine featured King on its cover as early as 1957, the *New York Times Magazine* published his articles, and the three networks televised images of civil rights demonstrators being beaten by southern law-enforcement officers. This coverage transformed national opinion, compelled the Kennedy administration to take up the issue, and ultimately secured enactment of the 1964 and 1965 civil rights laws.

New York opinion leaders and charitable foundations also helped focus national attention on the problems of racial minorities in northern cities.[29] Leonard Bernstein's enormously popular *West Side Story,* Paul Goodman's *Growing Up Absurd* and Michael Harrington's *The Other America* made urban delinquency and poverty objects of national concern. The "gray areas" program of the Ford Foundation and New York's Mobilization for Youth project served as prototypes for the urban programs of the New Frontier and Great Society.

The Ford Foundation developed its gray areas program in the late 1950s and early 1960s in an effort to "circumvent the stultification of national policy."[30] The foundation sponsored the creation of organizations that sought to improve conditions in poor neighborhoods in six cities by directly providing social services to neighborhood residents and by inducing municipal bureaucracies to alter the way they dealt with the poor. These agencies stood apart from the regular hierarchy of city government and were run by boards of directors drawn from nonprofit organizations, municipal bureaucracies, and residents of the neighborhoods being served. "In effect," as Daniel P. Moynihan has observed, "the Public Affairs Program of the Ford Foundation invented a new level of American government, the inner-city community action agency."[31]

In fashioning a federal program to combat juvenile delinquency, the Kennedy administration found this approach attractive—one that "took the conventions of institutional practice as the principal target of reform."[32] An official of the Ford Foundation brought the gray areas program to the attention of the Kennedy administration and also informed it about Mobilization for Youth, a similar project on Manhattan's Lower East Side that was run by Columbia University's School of Social Work and financed by a number of New York foundations, the city government, and the National Institutes of Mental Health. The Kennedy aide commissioned to draft the administration's anti-delinquency proposal recruited people from Ford and MFY to assist him. Their bill, enacted in 1961, established what in essence was a federal version of the gray areas program. It is significant, however, that between 1961 and 1964 the President's Committee on Juvenile Delinquency (PCJD) was able to spend only $10.7 million on local antidelinquency projects, while the Ford Foundation's grants to gray areas projects totaled $20 million.

Such constraints on federal domestic initiatives were lifted by the assassination of John F. Kennedy and, more importantly, the Democratic landslide in the 1964 national elections, which broke the power of the conservative coalition in Congress. The first major piece of social legislation that the new Johnson administration proposed and Congress enacted was the 1964 Economic Opportunity Act, whose central component—the community action program—was largely fashioned and subsequently administered by the staff of the PCJD, and essentially provided for a vast expansion of the federal antidelinquency program. Many of the Great Society's subsequent urban programs also resembled

MFY and the gray areas projects in structure, focus, and content.[33] And in a broadly similar fashion, the program of providing support for performing arts organizations that the Ford Foundation initiated in 1957 served as a model for the National Endowment for the Arts.[34]

Obviously, New York–based charitable foundations, communications media, political activists, and cultural elites were not alone responsible for the enactment of civil rights and antipoverty legislation, nor even for federal aid to the arts. Nonetheless, in the 1960s, the foundation-financed "demonstration project" became a major source of innovation in the realm of federal social policy. And in the 1970s, grants from the Ford, Rockefeller, Carnegie, Stern, and Field foundations, in conjunction with favorable media coverage, helped public-interest groups reshape federal environmental policy.[35] In all of these instances, the ideas, financing, and publicity that liberal political forces gained by virtue of their access to New York institutions and alliance with metropolitan elites contributed to the success of their lobbying efforts and influenced the content of the programs they sought to enact.

There was, it should be noted, a smaller electoral component to the influence that New York–based institutions exercised in national politics during the 1960s than there had been in the 1930s and 1940s. One indication of this is that the only New York City politician to make a mark in national politics during the 1960s was Mayor John V. Lindsay. As a leader of the National Urban Coalition and vice-chairman of the National Commission on Civil Disorders (the Kerner Commission), Lindsay became a national spokesman for the racial liberalism and cultural cosmopolitanism of New York civic elites. Unlike Ed Flynn and Sidney Hillman in the 1930s, however, Lindsay did not lead an organization with an extensive popular base. And unlike Mayor Fiorello La Guardia and Senator Robert F. Wagner, he never received the support of a majority of the city's voters. Lindsay won the mayoral elections of 1965 and 1969 with little more than 40 percent of the vote in sharply divided fields, and throughout his years in office the number of New Yorkers who hated their mayor almost certainly was greater than the number who loved him—a striking contrast with the situation three decades earlier.

Financial Representation: The 1980s and 1990s

In the late 1970s, the social, foreign, and cultural policies that New Yorkers had taken a lead in fashioning were vigorously attacked by political forces centered in the Sunbelt. Ronald Reagan and George Bush drew upon the support of this conservative movement in their successful campaigns for the presidency in 1980, 1984, and 1988. At the same time, however, the Federal Reserve and the U.S. Treasury emerged as channels through which at least one set of New York interests—those linked to the city's financial community—exercised considerable influence over national affairs. In the 1980s, national economic policies came to reflect the priorities of Wall Street more than they had during the postwar decades.[36] As a consequence, New York fared better economically during the 1980s than such New Deal bastions as Detroit or, for that matter, such bastions of Reaganism as Houston.

New York's financial community had benefited greatly from the liberal international order over which the United States presided during the postwar decades, but at the same time had been compelled to make substantial concessions to other interests incorporated into the nation's governing coalition. On the one hand, America's security umbrella and the Bretton Woods and GATT systems enabled the most important customers of New York's banks—the nation's major corporations—to expand abroad. As General Motors, General Electric, and IBM expanded their overseas operations, so too did First National City Bank, Chase Manhattan, and Morgan Guaranty. On the other hand, Wall Street faced substantial restrictions at home. Federal interest-rate ceilings, deposit insurance, and mortgage insurance channeled consumer savings into thrift institutions and residential mortgages and away from the New York money market. This benefited the S&L's, middle-class homeowners, the housing industry, and construction unions, at the expense of New York banks and their customers. The federal farm credit system diverted additional billions into rural banks and the agricultural sector. Restrictions on interstate banking prevented Wall Street from competing with regional commercial banks. Moreover, the Glass-Steagall Act deprived investment banks of access to the resources of commercial banks, thereby weakening Wall Street financiers relative to executives of the nation's major industrial corporations. In all, during the New Deal and postwar decades, Wall Street operated under the most stringent system of financial regulation in the Western world.[37]

Beyond this, to preserve a reasonably high level of employment and economic output (i.e., for the sake of labor and industry), the federal government during most of the postwar period pursued looser monetary and fiscal policies than the financial community would have preferred.[38] These economic policies exacerbated the balance-of-payments difficulties, pressures on the dollar, and inflationary pressures that the United States began to experience in the 1960s. (Other sources of the balance-of-payments problem included American military spending abroad, and, of course, the rebuilding of the European and Japanese economies.) Washington responded to these problems not with the orthodox solution of deflationary fiscal and monetary policies, but rather by placing controls on the export of dollars by major banks.[39] That is, the costs of adjustment were imposed not on labor, manufacturers, the military, or the beneficiaries of federal domestic spending programs, but rather primarily upon the New York City financial community.

To circumvent these restrictions, the major New York banks greatly increased their overseas operations.[40] The activities of American banks abroad helped foster the enormous growth of the Eurocurrency markets in the 1960s and 1970s. The burgeoning of the Eurocurrency markets, in turn, made it considerably more difficult for the U.S. and foreign governments to manage their economies.[41] This contributed to the dollar crises and double-digit inflation of the 1970s. To cope with those crises, President Carter in 1979 was all but compelled to appoint Paul Volcker—president of the New York Federal Reserve Bank and former Treasury undersecretary in the Nixon administration—to the chairmanship of the Federal Reserve.[42] Volcker was a symbol of monetary rectitude to the financial markets, and no one else was as likely to restore confidence in the dollar.

Under Volcker's leadership, the Fed undertook to demonstrate to the financial markets that it was totally committed to halting inflation. It drove interest rates to historically high levels and precipitated a recession in a presidential election year. As much as anything else, this combination of high interest rates, high unemployment, and lingering inflation—the "misery index"—was responsible for Ronald Reagan's landslide victory in 1980 and the Republican capture of the Senate that year. Thus, though motivated by economic rather than political considerations, Wall Street's overseas activities helped bring about the destruction of a regime that had opted to serve other interests at the financial community's expense.

After the 1980 elections, the Federal Reserve continued its tight money policies. In 1981–1982, it engineered the deepest recession since the Great Depression of the 1930s. This economic trauma was severe enough to overcome the inflationary pressures that had been building up in the economy for more than a decade. President Reagan lent crucial support to the Fed's campaign: Had the White House joined the Central Bank's critics as unemployment, farm foreclosures, and business bankruptcies increased, Volcker would not have been able to withstand the pressure to relent. The Federal Reserve's triumph over inflation convinced investors that it again was worthwhile to own financial assets and was the fundamental source of the great 1980s bull market in stocks and bonds.

The Reagan administration—in particular, the Treasury Department—undertook to strengthen the financial sector in a variety of other ways. Top officials in the department regarded finance as a leading sector of the American economy, and they also viewed the emergence of a "market for corporate control" on Wall Street as a way of compelling manufacturing industries to bolster their international competitiveness.[43] In 1984, the Treasury negotiated a pact with Japan (the yen-dollar agreement), opening that nation's financial markets to American institutions and liberating Japanese savings for investment in the United States, and it persuaded Congress to repeal the withholding tax on foreign holders of American government and corporate securities. The ensuing flood of foreign capital into U.S. bonds and stocks further boosted the financial markets.[44]

The regime that governed the United States after 1980 did not, however, simply represent the interests of New York's financial community. The coalition that supported the Reagan administration was quite heterogeneous, and there were sharp disputes over economic policy between what might be termed its Traditionalist and Supply-Side wings.[45] The Traditionalists were supported by the old Republican establishment, including Wall Street; they appealed primarily to the middle and upper classes and they gave first priority to the fight against inflation. The Supply-Siders were strongest in the Sunbelt; they sought to build a Republican majority by bringing working- and lower-middle-class voters into the GOP coalition; they placed greater priority upon cutting taxes, increasing defense spending, and promoting economic growth than on fighting inflation. Finally, though the Democrats lost effective control of Congress in the 1980 elections, they regained working majorities in the House in 1982 and Senate in 1986. In the 1980s, the Democrats came to speak for those interests most closely linked to the domestic state—especially racial minorities, unionized workers, and employees in the government and nonprofit sectors.

Although monetary policy in the 1980s was largely dominated by Traditionalists, fiscal policy reflected a more complex interaction among Traditionalists, Supply-Siders, and Democrats. The combination of monetary discipline, massive tax cuts, major increases in defense expenditures, and only limited reductions in domestic spending produced enormous budget and trade deficits. These deficits, however, were not entirely unwelcome by the administration.[46]

The budget and trade deficits of the 1980s must be regarded as integral parts of the Reaganite political order.[47] In the first place, they provided the administration with a politically beneficial means of financing its expenditures. Instead of taxing its supporters to cover the costs of government, the administration relied upon the Japanese to purchase Treasury bonds with profits accumulated from selling goods in the American market. Second, the twin deficits were weapons that the Reaganites used to attack the political forces, institutions, and practices that had sustained the hegemony of the Democrats for a half-century. The trade deficit gravely weakened organized labor, to the advantage of employers and detriment of the Democratic party. And the budget deficit placed restraints upon the ability of the Democrats to propose, and Congress to enact, new domestic spending programs for the benefit of the party's constituent groups.

As a result of these developments, a new balance emerged during the 1980s among major forces in American national politics. The Federal Reserve's triumph over the forces of inflation was a boon to the financial community. The Reaganite attack upon organized labor reduced costs and union restrictions on managerial discretion within the manufacturing sector. The administration's defense buildup channeled resources into the high technology sector and localities with military installations. Not least, tax cuts, trade deficits, and lower rates of inflation benefited most middle- and upper-class voters in their roles as taxpayers, consumers, savers, and investors. Together these groups comprised the Reagan-Bush coalition. The members of this coalition had also been incorporated into the postwar political order. However, the concessions they were compelled to make to organized labor and the clients of domestic social programs were less costly than those they formerly found it necessary to bear.

Equally noteworthy, recent years witnessed changes in the balance of power within the business community that worked to the advantage of New York. The first of these was a shift in the relative power of commercial and investment banks. Although New York remains America's premier financial center, the city's commercial banks are facing greater competition both in the United States and abroad.[48] This development has been counterbalanced, however, by trends towards "securitization" and "disintermediation" in the financial sector. Increasingly, corporations raise money not by borrowing from commercial banks but rather by issuing new types of securities developed by investment banks and sold to institutional investors. Regulatory authorities have not sought to impede this process lest borrowers and investors turn to foreign financial markets and institutions in their efforts to maximize returns and minimize risks. As a result, while over the past twenty years the major money center banks averaged only a 10 percent return on equity, the leading investment banks achieved returns ranging from 25 to 40 percent and their equity capital increased from a typical $10 million to $1 billion.[49]

The investment banks that underwrite, make markets in, and trade these new securities are overwhelmingly concentrated in New York. In fact, as the capital and skills required to operate successfully in volatile financial markets have risen, New York's hegemony in investment banking has increased. Seven firms dominated investment banking in the 1980s: Morgan Stanley, Salomon Brothers, Goldman, Sachs, First Boston, Merrill Lynch, Shearson Lehman, and Drexel Burnham. All were based in New York. In the crucial field of mergers and acquisitions, seventeen of the top nineteen firms had their headquarters in New York.[50]

The 1980s also witnessed a shift in the relative power of the financial and industrial sectors—as indicated by that decade's takeover boom on Wall Street. The sources of this development remain a matter of some controversy, but public policy clearly played an important role.[51] The combination of large budget deficits and tight monetary policies in the early 1980s increased real interest rates and raised the cost of financing the construction of new plants and equipment above the price of acquiring such assets on Wall Street. The easing of regulatory restrictions on the investments thrift institutions could make expanded the market for the high-yield bonds that financed many takeovers. And the Reagan administration's virtual abandonment of antitrust enforcement made possible the most extensive wave of corporate reorganizations since the merger movement of 1898–1904. Even if the 1990 prosecution of Michael Milken and collapse of Drexel Burnham turn out to mark the crest of this wave, the restructuring of corporate America by investment bankers, leveraged buyout firms, and arbitrageurs bespeaks a significant shift in the power of Wall Street financiers relative to corporate managements.

My argument that the New York financial community has come to exercise increasing influence in American national politics through the Federal Reserve and the Treasury raises an obvious question. In what way do these institutions "represent" the interests of Wall Street in the national political arena? This clearly is not true in any simple sense. The Federal Reserve under Paul Volcker and Alan Greenspan waged war on inflation to protect the long-term health of the economy, not simply the profits of New York banks, and victory in that war served the interests not only of Wall Street financiers but also of the consumers, savers, manufacturers, and workers who also had a stake in the economy's health. The Treasury negotiated the 1984 yen-dollar agreement not only because American banks and brokerage firms wanted to gain entry to the Japanese market but also because it wanted the Japanese to help finance the U.S. budget deficit.

Nonetheless, there was a mutually supportive relationship between the Federal Reserve–Treasury nexus and the New York financial community. On the one side, Wall Street served as the core of Paul Volcker's and Alan Greenspan's political constituency. President Reagan was compelled to reappoint Volcker in 1983, and to appoint a successor acceptable to him in 1987, for fear that otherwise the financial markets would collapse. More generally, banks helped defend the Federal Reserve system against efforts—such as the Hamilton-Dorgan bill of 1990—to curtail its autonomy. In a similar vein, the Treasury can count upon the support of the financial community in controversies concerning the trade-off between reducing unemployment and achieving price stability.

On the other side, the Federal Reserve's policies in the 1980s were especially beneficial to the largest financial institutions.[52] In this regard it is important to note that despite the Central Bank's announced conversion to the principles of monetarism in 1979, it subsequently presided over massive fluctuations in the money supply. It pursued very restrictive monetary policies in 1981–1982, but eased policy when confronted with the Penn Square and Mexican debt crises in mid-1982, and eased again in 1985–1986 to counter protectionist pressures in Congress. In addition, the Fed bailed out the nation's seventh largest bank, Continental Illinois, from imminent collapse in 1984, and it intervened aggressively to protect banks and securities firms on Wall Street in the aftermath of the October 19, 1987 break in the stock market.

Clearly, there was a strong case to be made for these adjustments: in each instance the Central Bank altered its course to protect the financial system from serious threats. Yet the Federal Reserve had not relented when its policies drove into bankruptcy hundreds of regional banks and thrift institutions, as well as thousands of firms in the agricultural, housing, energy, and manufacturing sectors. A major difference between these two sets of cases is that the financial markets regarded the Fed's adjustments in the former instances as bowing to necessity, whereas they would have regarded adjustments in the latter cases as bowing to political pressure. This is of great significance because the financial markets were the audience the Central Bank had to persuade when it set out to demonstrate that it was seriously committed to fighting inflation. It is in this sense that Wall Street's priorities gained increased influence over national policy in the 1980s through the Federal Reserve.

In a similar vein, the Treasury pursued exchange-rate policy in dialogue with the financial markets and the Fed. Through President Reagan's first term, the Treasury stood aside as the value of the dollar climbed to record levels. (Between January 1981 and January 1985, the trade-weighted dollar index rose by 60 percent in response to the decline in U.S. inflation and rise in real interest rates produced by tight monetary policies and huge budget deficits.) The strong dollar hurt American producers of tradeable goods, but benefited the financial sector by bolstering confidence in U.S. financial assets. In 1983–1984, however, growing deficits led interest rates to rise and the bond market to plummet. While continuing to ignore anguish in the manufacturing sector, the Treasury responded to distress in the government bond market by moving to attract additional foreign capital into U.S. financial markets—negotiating the May 1984 yen-dollar agreement and securing the repeal of withholding taxes on foreign owners of American securities. As two close observers of exchange-rate politics, I.M. Destler and C. Randall Hennings, remark:

> This was not, apparently, a conscious *political* strategy—we are not aware of anyone within the administration arguing, for example, that the interests of the tradeable-goods sector were to be given second priority to those of the interest-sensitive sector. Nevertheless, given the choices facing the administration in the middle of its first term, foreign borrowing was the path of least economic and political resistance. . . .[53]

During Reagan's second term, Treasury Secretary James Baker switched to a policy of actively managing exchange rates. To head off mounting protectionist pressures in Congress, Baker and the finance ministers and central bankers of the major industrial powers negotiated the September 1985 Plaza agreement to lower the dollar. By the spring of 1987, however, the bond market's concern about the inflationary impact of cheaper dollars led the Fed to begin tightening monetary policy. To forestall further tightening, Baker negotiated the Louvre agreement to stabilize the dollar. A statement by Baker castigating Germany for not fulfilling its commitments under the Louvre accord precipitated the October 1987 stock market break, but the stock market, the dollar, and the economy recovered and rose at a healthy pace through the balance of the decade.

As this account indicates, the Federal Reserve and the Treasury established policy during the 1980s in dialogue not only with the financial markets and one another, but also with the White House and Congress, and with the central bankers and finance ministers of the world's other leading industrial powers. Some of the policies pursued by Volcker and Baker imposed costs as well as conferred benefits on Wall Street—most dramatically in October 1987. That is, though they "represented" the financial community in the sense indicated above, Volcker and Baker determined how its interests were to be reconciled with those of other political forces. In this respect they resembled Martin Van Buren and Franklin Roosevelt—leaders who in earlier times established the terms on which metropolitan interests were integrated into the broader political and economic orders.

A major source of Wall Street's increased influence in American politics is the internationalization of financial markets. The growth of the Eurocurrency markets—in conjunction with financial deregulation and the development of new computer and communications technologies—has made it very easy to shift financial assets across national boundaries and among national currencies. This enables financial interests to protect themselves from public policies that threaten to undermine the value of their holdings and limits the ability of the federal government to impose burdens on them for the sake of other political forces. Policymakers thus were compelled to pay greater heed to financial interests in the 1980s than had been necessary during the New Deal and postwar decades. In other words, the internationalization of financial markets has both imposed limits on the power of American national state and increased the political leverage of the resources Wall Street controls.

Of course, Wall Street and New York City are not identical. It is true that the financial sector plays a major role in the city's economy and furnishes tax revenues to the municipal treasury that benefit the entire metropolis.[54] Moreover, Wall Street was a pillar of the regime, headed by Mayor Koch, that governed the city throughout the 1980s.[55] Nonetheless, there are millions of New Yorkers who have few ties to the financial community and derive few benefits from its enhanced national influence. The most obvious of these are the political forces that rallied behind David Dinkins's candidacy in the 1989 mayoral election: racial minorities, municipal employees, and organized labor. They participate in national politics, if at all, through older political channels.

The character of the institutions through which the city's financial elites have come to exercise influence nationally helps explain why the participation of New Yorkers in national politics has become fragmented in this way. When bankers and businessmen from the metropolis gained access to the national government through party organizations and executive institutions, mobilizing support locally enhanced their power in Washington. Therefore, business elites had an incentive to work out accommodations with other metropolitan interests. By contrast, the influence Wall Street exercises today through the Federal Reserve and the financial markets is not a function of the support it enjoys locally. Consequently, New York elites seeking to influence national politics have a smaller incentive today than formerly to strive for metropolitan unity.

Notes

1. Montgomery, David, *Beyond Equality* (New York: Alfred Knopf, 1967), p. 60.
2. Edsall, Thomas, *The New Politics of Inequality* (New York: W.W. Norton, 1984), chap. 2.
3. McPherson, James, *Battle Cry of Freedom* (New York: Oxford University Press, 1988), p. 334; Braestrup, Peter, *Big Story* (New Haven: Yale University Press, 1983).
4. Foner, Eric, *Reconstruction* (New York: Harper & Row, 1988), p. 216.
5. Gourevitch, Peter, *Politics in Hard Times* (Ithaca, NY: Cornell University Press, 1986), chap. 4.
6. It should be noted, however, that the patterns prevailing during each of these phases were layered over earlier ones; they did not completely supplant those previously established.
7. Ellis, Richard, *The Jeffersonian Crisis* (New York: W.W. Norton, 1971), chap. 17.
8. McCormick, Richard P., *The Presidential Game* (New York: Oxford University Press, 1982), chap. 4.
9. Wallace, Michael, "Changing Concepts of Party in the United States: New York, 1815–1825," *American Historical Review* 74 (December 1968): 453–491.
10. Remini, Robert, *Martin Van Buren and the Making of the Democratic Party* (New York: Columbia University Press, 1959), p. 142.
11. McGerr, Michael, *The Decline of Popular Politics* (New York: Oxford University Press, 1986), chaps. 2, 4, 6.
12. Bensel, Richard, *Sectionalism and American Political Development, 1880–1980* (Madison: University of Wisconsin Press, 1984).
13. McCormick, Richard L., "The Party Period and Public Policy: An Exploratory Hypothesis," *Journal of American History* 66 (September 1979): 279–298.
14. Bremer, William, *Depression Winters: New York Social Workers and the New Deal* (Philadelphia: Temple University Press, 1984), chap. 1.
15. Fraser, Steve, "The 'Labor Question,'" in Fraser, Steve, and Gary Gerstle, eds., *The Rise and Fall of the New Deal Order, 1930–1980* (Princeton: Princeton University Press, 1989), pp. 55–84.
16. Fraser, Steve, "Dress Rehearsal for the New Deal: Shop Floor Insurgents, Political Elites, and Industrial Democracy in the Amalgamated Clothing Workers," in Frisch, Michael, and Daniel Walkowitz, eds., *Working Class America* (Urbana: University of Illinois Press, 1983), pp. 212–255.

17. Berle, Adolph A., *Leaning Against the Dawn* (New York: The Twentieth Century Fund, 1969).
18. McJimsey, George, *Harry Hopkins* (Cambridge, MA: Harvard University Press, 1987).
19. Skocpol, Theda and John Ikenberry, "The Political Formation of the American Welfare State in Historical and Comparative Perspective," *Comparative Social Research* 6 (1983): 87–148.
20. Isaacson, Walter and Evan Thomas, *The Wise Men* (New York: Simon and Schuster, 1986).
21. Berkowitz, Edward and Kim McQuaid, *Creating the Welfare State*, 2nd ed. (New York: Praeger, 1988), p. 129; Shulzinger, Robert, *The Wise Men of Foreign Affairs: The History of the Council on Foreign Relations* (New York: Columbia University Press, 1984).
22. I owe this observation to Samuel Kernell.
23. Radosh, Ronald, *American Labor and U.S. Foreign Policy* (New York: Random House, 1969).
24. Collins, Robert, *The Business Response to Keynes, 1929–1964* (New York: Columbia University Press, 1981).
25. Katznelson, Ira, "Was the Great Society a Lost Opportunity?" in Fraser and Gerstle, eds., *The Rise and Fall of the New Deal Order*, pp. 185–211.
26. Amenta, Edwin and Theda Skocpol, "Redefining the New Deal: World War II and the Development of Social Provision in the United States," in Weir, Margaret, et al., eds., *The Politics of Social Policy in the United States* (Princeton: Princeton University Press, 1988), pp. 81–122.
27. Wilson, James Q., *Political Organizations* (New York: Basic Books, 1973), pp. 188f.
28. Branch, Taylor, *Parting the Waters* (New York: Simon and Schuster, 1988), pp. 209, 288, 348, 481.
29. Moynihan, Daniel P., *Maximum Feasible Misunderstanding* (New York: The Free Press, 1969), pp. 14–19; Polsby, Nelson, *Political Innovation in America* (New Haven: Yale University Press, 1984), p. 135.
30. Marris, Peter, and Martin Rein, *Dilemmas of Social Reform*, 2nd ed. (Chicago: Aldine, 1973), p. 20.
31. Moynihan, *Maximum Feasible Misunderstanding*, p. 42.
32. Marris and Rein, *Dilemmas of Social Reform*, p. 21.
33. See Piven, Frances Fox and Richard Cloward, *Regulating the Poor* (New York: Pantheon, 1971), pp. 260–261.
34. Lowry, W. McNeil, "The Past Twenty Years," in *The Performing Arts and American Society*, The American Assembly (Englewood Cliffs, NJ: Prentice-Hall, 1978), pp. 3–26.
35. Vogel, David, *Fluctuating Fortunes* (New York: Basic Books, 1989), p. 104.
36. This is not to say that the situation in the 1980s was unprecedented. During

the 1920s, the New York Federal Reserve Bank, which had close ties to the city's financial community, dominated U.S. domestic and international monetary policymaking. See Chernow, Ron, *The House of Morgan* (New York: Atlantic Monthly Press, 1990), pp. 181–182, 274–277; Kettl, Donald, *Leadership at the Fed* (New Haven: Yale University Press, 1986), pp. 30–34.

37. Hamilton, Adrian, *The Financial Revolution* (New York: The Free Press, 1986).
38. Orren, Karen, "Liberalism, Money, and the Situation of Organized Labor," in Greenstone, David, ed., *Public Values and Private Power in American Politics* (Chicago: University of Chicago Press, 1982), pp. 173–208.
39. Hawley, James, *Dollars and Borders* (Armonk, NY: M.E. Sharpe, 1987).
40. Aronson, Jonathan, *Money and Power: Banks and the World Monetary System* (Beverly Hills, CA: Sage Publications, 1977).
41. Strange, Susan, *Casino Capitalism* (Oxford: Basil Blackwell, 1986).
42. Wooley, John, *Monetary Politics* (Cambridge: Cambridge University Press, 1984), p. 55.
43. See, e.g., *New York Times*, 8 Nov. 1986, sect. A, p. 1; 12 Aug. 1987, sect. A, p. 23; *Economic Report of the President* (Washington, DC, 1985).
44. Destler, I.M. and C. Randall Henning, *Dollar Politics: Exchange Rate Policy-making in the United States* (Washington, DC: Institute for International Economics, 1989), pp. 28–29.
45. Ginsberg, Benjamin and Martin Shefter, "The Presidency and Social Forces: Creating a Republican Coalition," in Nelson, Michael, ed., *The Presidency and the Political System*, 3d ed. (Washington, DC: CQ Press, 1990).
46. Stockman, David, *The Triumph of Politics* (New York: Harper and Row, 1986).
47. Ginsberg, Benjamin, and Martin Shefter, *Politics by Other Means* (New York: Basic Books, 1990), chap. 5.
48. See Noyelle, Thierry, ed., *New York's Financial Markets: The Challenge of Globalization* (Boulder, CO: Westview Press, 1989).
49. Hayes, Samuel L., III and Philip M. Hubbard, *Investment Banking: A Tale of Three Cities* (Boston: Harvard Business School Press, 1990), p. 114.
50. Hayes and Hubbard, *Investment Banking*, chap. 5.
51. See, e.g., Brooks, John, *The Takeover Game* (New York: Twentieth Century Fund, 1987), chap. 8.
52. Greider, William, *Secrets of the Temple* (New York: Simon and Schuster, 1987).
53. Destler and Henning, *Dollar Politics*, p. 28.
54. Willis, Mark A., "New York's Economic Renaissance," in Salins, Peter, ed., *New York Unbound* (New York: Basil Blackwell, 1988), pp. 30–53.
55. Shefter, Martin, *Political Crisis/Fiscal Crisis: The Collapse and Revival of New York City* (New York: Basic Books, 1985), chap. 7.

6

Take Me Away from Manhattan: New York City and American Mass Culture, 1930–1990

James L. Baughman

"The most important single thing to say about Manhattan in relation to the rest of the United States is that it dominates what, for want of a better phrase, may be called American culture."

—John Gunther, *Inside U.S.A.* (1947)

"California sets the styles, Iowa follows."

—Lee Iacocca (1973)

"New York will remain a great city, but a much diminished one."

—Irving Kristol, "Why I Left" (1988)

In 1930, young Americans determined to succeed in the popular arts—songwriting, theater, or journalism—considered New York City their ultimate destination. The would-be film star or director had to go to California, the site of most motion picture production. But the ambitious journalist, playwright, or songwriter looked to New York.

The author wishes to thank Paul Boyer, Jack McLeod, Philip Ranlet, David Schuyler, Stephan J. Stroud, and members of the Center's Metropolitan Dominance Working Group for their comments and Andrew Feldman for his bibliographical assistance.

During the eighteenth and nineteenth centuries, America, unlike England and France, lacked a cultural capital. To Lord Bryce, writing in the late 1880s, no one American city had the "conjunction of the forces of rank, wealth, knowledge, [and] intellect." In Washington, the nation's political center, Bryce observed, "there are few men of letters, no artists, hardly any journalists."[1] It remained for the nation's largest commercial cities to compete for the greatest portion of the culture trade. In the eighteenth century, both New York and Philadelphia challenged Boston's cultural dominance. Despite a relative economic decline, Boston remained a powerful arbiter of culture through most of the nineteenth century.

In the late nineteenth century, however, New York began to pull ahead of its rival cities. Most prominent book publishers based their operations on Manhattan by the 1880s and most of the new, more aggressively "marketed" mass-circulation magazines came to the city in the following decade.[2] Popular periodicals still published in Boston and Philadelphia increasingly suffered from provincialism. Philadelphia's *Ladies Home Journal*, complained one reader in 1920, "triumphantly presented a non-existent world to unobservant readers."[3] The Chicago literary elite's goal of national cultural dominance came to nothing. The "Second City" remained the Second City.[4]

By the early twentieth century, producers of popular culture had little choice but to come to New York. "Since we have failed up to the present to develop genuine regional cultures," Lewis Mumford wrote in 1922, "those who do not wish to remain barbarians must become metropolitans. That means they must come to New York, or ape the ways that are fashionable in New York."[5]

Zenith of New York's Influence

New York's dominance increased even more during the 1920s. Aggressive new book publishers Alfred Knopf and Bennett Cerf based their operations in midtown New York. Two of the decade's most innovative and successful magazines, *The New Yorker* and *Time*, operated out of Manhattan. In the 1920s, too, New York became the center for major advertising agencies, vital to most periodicals and, in time, to radio networks. The term "Madison Avenue" gained currency in the decade as a synonym for the agents of persuasion.[6] *Time* co-founder Henry R. Luce tried to save money by moving his magazine's editorial offices to Cleveland in 1925. But he found it impossible to publish a newsweekly in a major metropolitan area other than New York, and *Time* returned to Manhattan after two years on Lake Erie.[7]

The major factor in *Time*'s move back was New York's position as the journalistic center of America. New York was the headquarters city of the two wire services, the Associated Press and the United Press, and every major newspaper chain had a New York daily. Red Smith, a young sportswriter for the *St. Louis Star,* regarded with awe the New York sportswriters he met during baseball spring training in 1929. "To a young reporter in the Midwest just breaking in," Smith's biographer wrote, "the New York writers were, Smith later said, 'god-like creatures.' And to be accepted by them, he said, was 'terribly important.'" Smith "found the vision of New York immensely appealing. He called it 'the capital.'"

> New York was the place where the best in his business went to make a name for themselves; (Ring) Lardner went there from Chicago, (Damon) Runyon from Denver, and Grantland Rice from Nashville. For the sportswriter in St. Louis, a dream was building. He wondered if one day there might be a spot for him on a daily in Manhattan.[8]

In the late 1920s, the nation's three best dailies, the *Times,* the *Herald Tribune,* and the *World,* were published in New York. In its cleverly packaged summaries of the week's news, *Time* shamelessly relied on the *Times.* No other newspaper in America so self-consciously aspired to the *Times*'s completeness. The *New York Times,* Elmer Davis wrote in his 1921 history of the paper, "approaches the character of a national newspaper more nearly than any other in America."[9]

As Davis himself admitted, competitors' emphasis on local news allowed the *Times* to stress national and international events. Elsewhere, dailies suffered from an overattentiveness to local happenings. Only a few, notably the *Chicago Daily News,* attempted to compete with the *Times* in the coverage of foreign affairs. Returning to Palo Alto in 1933, former President Hoover was horrified to discover the provincialism of northern California's dailies; he soon ordered the air delivery of thirty out-of-state papers.[10] Cities like Boston and Washington, that might have supported dailies modeled after the *Times,* were journalistic wastelands. In Washington in the 1920s and 1930s, the "cosmopolitan" consumers of national and international news regularly read a New York daily, as did their counterparts in Boston. "Nothing in Boston astonishes foreigners more than its press," Oswald Garrison Villard wrote.

"Nothing more clearly illustrates the passing of what was once the Athens of America."[11]

If New York was the nation's journalistic heart partly by default, the city's disproportionate concentration of popular music composition and performance in 1930 occurred by design. For more than a generation, most popular songwriters had worked in Manhattan. They had two patrons: sheet-music publishers located on "Tin Pan Alley," on Twenty-eighth Street between Fifth Avenue and Broadway,[12] and theatrical producers north on the Great White Way. Location similarly explained New York's appeal to musical performers. Manhattan—uptown and downtown in the 1920s—had the best nightlife of any American city. A band had succeeded by national standards only with an invitation to perform at a New York club. For African-American groups, the final stop was Harlem. Every town was an "apple," but there was only one "Big Apple."[13]

The newest communication technology of 1930, radio, appeared to reinforce New York's cultural dominance. A radio set boom began in 1924 and failed to abate with the Great Depression. In 1930 45.8 percent of all homes had one or more radios.[14] Unhappy with the uneven, if not crude, quality of much local programming, the majority of radio listeners began demanding that their stations carry far more polished programs—usually originating from New York—via a network "hook-up." When, in September 1928, the Federal Radio Commission attempted to limit network broadcasts to one hour an evening, a wave of protests flooded the commission's offices.[15] In December 1930, *Fortune* wrote of the new National Broadcasting Company, based in New York, "Giving pleasure (also instruction) to 13,478,600 families."[16] Within a few years, NBC moved its headquarters to the new "Radio City" complex in Rockefeller Center in midtown Manhattan, with its rival, the Columbia Broadcasting System, only a few blocks away. Because both radio "chains" relied heavily on advertisers to sponsor most programs, it made sense to base themselves near the major agencies.

The agencies assembled and the networks aired, originally from New York, the most popular radio fare. Powerful stations in larger cities initially produced local entertainment programs; in the early 1930s, a staff writer at WWJ in Detroit put out fifteen to eighteen dramatic scripts a week. But WWJ could not stave off its mother network. NBC programs, a WWJ executive recalled, "kept coming faster and faster and there was less and less time for local shows." The amount of NBC and CBS programming increased as vaudeville performers, out of work with the diffusion of the talking picture or attracted to higher salaries offered by advertisers, entered the newest medium beginning in 1933.[17] By

1943, some two-thirds of all radio stations had one or more network affiliations. The typical radio station, complained one critic, had become "a mere booster point for programs from afar."[18]

Technology at first strengthened New York's hold over network radio. Whenever possible, radio sought to broadcast programs live. Listeners, it was thought, expected no less. To the first generation of radio users, the magic of radio was the simultaneous broadcast; a vast national audience could hear the actual performance of a song or comic sketch. The networks' control over musical programming was all but assured by the American Society of Composers, Authors and Publishers (ASCAP), which then represented most sheet-music publishers and record manufacturers. Most individual stations could not afford the fee the Society demanded for the playing of an ASCAP song, whether by the town polka band or Duke Ellington; the networks, in contrast, could pick up the tab. Then, too, in a rare exercise of oversight, federal regulators insisted that a network or station indicate if a program was "prerecorded" in a manner some thought disdainful of the practice. Moreover, recorded transcriptions of broadcasts were, until the development of tape in the later 1940s, costly or of poor quality.[19]

Network radio in the early 1930s served all audiences. One of the most popular radio programs of the decade, *The Fire Chief,* which premiered in April 1932, was broadcast live from New York (at first at the New Amsterdam Theater). *The Fire Chief* always began with the same empty promise from the program's star, vaudeville refugee Ed Wynn, "I'm the chief," he assured his announcer, "tonight the program's going to be different."[20] More self-conscious listeners could receive instruction—from New York—on culture from William Lyon Phelps or Alexander Woollcott; the latter immodestly declared himself the nation's "taster-at-large."[21]

Another new communication technology of the early twentieth century, motion pictures, constituted the great exception to New York's cultural dominance. The governors of the "movie colony" had New York roots, and the New York–New Jersey area had been the site of the earliest motion picture production in America. But California's warm climate made possible year-round production; it also had a topography that made a wider variety of outdoor shots possible. Then, too, Los Angeles offered, compared to New York, cheap land for studios and lower labor costs; it was also farther from agents of the Edison Trust, that claimed a monopoly on motion picture production. And in Hollywood, the many Jewish entrepreneurs involved in movie-making could invent their own upper-class culture and escape the snobbery of the gentile aristocracies of the large eastern cities. "There was no real aristocracy in place," Neal Gabler wrote of Hollywood in the 1910s, "and few social impediments obstructing Jews." With them went some actors from the New York theater. By the mid-1910s, California had become the movie capital of the world.[22]

Yet, significantly, Hollywood was known as the movie "colony." The colony's "governors" took their orders from New York. A New York–based theater chain, Loew's Inc., owned the largest film-making concern, Metro-Goldwyn-Mayer. Other "moguls" in the early 1930s found themselves listening with respect to New York bankers. Several major studios, needing capital to expand their chain of theaters and to convert to sound film production, had borrowed heavily in the late 1920s. The Depression made lenders and borrowers anxious.[23] Much as they enjoyed being portrayed as omnipotent, the typical studio executive, like Monroe Stahr in Fitzgerald's *The Last Tycoon*, enjoyed at best limited autonomy.

Still, Hollywood in the 1930s began to chip away at New York's cultural empire. The coming of sound caused several studios, anxious to have a steady supply of music, to gobble up prominent New York music publishers. Warner Brothers alone bought three firms. "Some of Tin Pan Alley's historic and powerful publishing houses," remarked a historian of popular song, "became offshoots of the movie industry, subservient to the needs and demands of the screen."[24] Sound production also caused the studios to hire away Broadway writers while encouraging those who stayed to write plays with cinematic potential. Composers and actors, too, made the exodus to the other coast.[25] Most New York migrants shared a common discovery. Despite cracks to friends back east about the intellectual vacuousness of their new home, a majority preferred the climate and lifestyle of Southern California to the challenges to daily existence in Gotham. "I loved the air, I loved the sunshine, and going to the beach was so easy and then I had a car for the first time in my life," recalled one New York playwright of his time in Hollywood. "You don't know what it is to live in a city where the jackhammer wasn't going."[26]

The California temptation affected both Broadway and radio. Films had cut into Broadway's road show business in the 1920s and the talking picture proved an even more effective competitor to both the first-run and the road production.[27] By the mid-1930s, the radio networks began moving some of their program production to the movie colony. Director Cecil B. De Mille, intoning "from Hollywood" with every broadcast, took over the hosting of *Lux Radio Theater*, which began using scripts by writers in the film industry and not from Broadway. Hollywood stars participated in such programs.[28]

The film colony did not, however, gain independence in the 1930s. The networks did not relocate to Los Angeles. Manhattan-based advertising agencies retained strict controls over Hollywood-produced programs. In *The Hucksters* (1946), former advertising executive Frederic Wakeman described a special teletype connecting the West Coast studios to the New York agencies. Scripts, ideas for programs and guests, all had to be cleared with the agency handling the program for a sponsor. "The teletype," Wakeman wrote, "had created perhaps more occupational ulcers than straight whiskey or hastily eaten ham sandwiches."[29]

In the postwar years, New York appeared likely to continue to control the creation of America's mass culture. "The most important thing to say about Manhattan in relation to the rest of the United States is that it dominates what, for want of a better phrase, might be called American culture," John Gunther wrote in 1947.

> New York is the publishing center of the nation; it is the art, theater, musical, ballet, operatic center; it is the opinion center; it is the radio center; it is the style center. Hollywood? But Hollywood is nothing more than a suburb of the Bronx, both financially and from the point of view of talent. Politically, socially, in the world of ideas and in the whole world of entertainment, which is a great American industry needless to say, New York sets the tone and pace of the entire nation.[30]

To E.B. White, New York City remained the place that attracted the young and talented. New York, he wrote in 1951, "is always full of young worshipful beginners—young actors, young aspiring poets, ballerinas, painters, reporters, singers—each depending on his own brand of tonic to stay alive, each with his own stable of giants."[31]

Another home technology, television, appeared to reaffirm New York's central cultural role. New York–based corporations, including the two major radio chains, launched television networks in 1947. With an unprecedented enthusiasm over the next ten years, Americans purchased television sets; by 1958 83.2 percent of all households had one or more TV receivers.[32] And the first users of TV sets viewed programs likely to be produced in New York. Early in 1951 the *Charlotte* (N.C.) *News* reported the fears of the parents of a six-year-old boy who, with network TV available in the home, had begun talking "like a Yankee from Perth Amboy."[33]

Stations coveted network programming. In 1954, 90 percent of all stations had one or more network affiliations. TV stations preferred handing the risks and costs involved in producing TV shows to the national chains. In 1954 affiliates had asked NBC to offer the late-evening *Tonight Show* to spare themselves the expense of renting films or originating their own entertainment. As a West Virginia TV station president explained to the FCC in 1958, "The reason I am affiliated with NBC is to provide an outlet for NBC programs in the market—not to refuse to do so."[34]

The programs from New York varied in format from wrestling and boxing matches, roller derbys, original dramatic "anthologies," and variety programs with ex-vaudevillians like Ed Wynn and nightclub comics like Milton Berle as hosts. Before audiences at the Center Theater in Rockefeller Center, NBC produced a situation comedy about a shy high school science teacher, *Mr. Peepers*. Only at first, in the case of the anthologies, did Hollywood talent make the trip east. Early TV's heavy reliance on Broadway combined with live telecasting to give the newest medium a heavy theatrical flavor. "Every night," recalled a costume designer, "was opening night."[35]

Such was New York's prominence in television that the networks had to scramble for production sites. *Man Against Crime*, aired on three different networks between 1949 and 1956, was filmed beginning in the fall of 1952 in a facility that predated the movie industry's migration to California, the Thomas A. Edison Studios in the Bronx. "New York had been, up until now, the TV capital," wrote a *Saturday Evening Post* contributor early in 1952. "But in New York the whole industry is crying for studio space. Old theaters, the private dining rooms of hotels, abandoned churches and car barns are used for stages. One program started last summer originates in Philadelphia because no space whatever could be found in New York."[36]

Several factors explained New York's early role in TV program origination. Until the early 1950s, when AT&T completed installing the coaxial cables connecting all affiliates, it was not possible to originate a network program from Los Angeles or other midwestern and western cities. Then, too, network officials continued to believe that audiences preferred live programming. In June 1953, 81.5 percent of all network programming was live.[37] Even after the cable was laid, the time zone discriminated against the West Coast. A variety program produced in California for an 8 p.m. broadcast in New York would originate at 5 p.m. local time. Only after much bargaining did CBS allow Desi Arnaz and Lucille Ball, who adamantly refused to relocate to New York, to film their new situation comedy, *I Love Lucy*, in California.[38] Finally, the major Hollywood studios initially all but surrendered TV production to the New York networks. MGM, Warners, and other large film companies, correctly regarding television as a threat to demand for motion pictures, refused to supply the newest medium with programming.[39]

Losing Control

In a move that marked the end of New York's dominance of mass culture, Warners and other major film groups lifted their ban on TV program production in the mid-1950s. CBS had already been investing in West Coast studio facilities when, in 1954, the struggling third network, ABC, signed Walt Disney to a programming agreement. A year later Warner Brothers came to terms with ABC. By the late 1950s all three networks had increased their quota of filmed programs.[40] Two programming trends, first the western, then the detective drama, accelerated the shift to film.[41] These series replaced programs with a decidedly New York patina: the dramatic anthologies and comedy-variety programs hosted by Berle, Sid Caesar, and Jackie Gleason.[42] Television, *Printer's Ink* observed in August 1957, "is becoming an industry with New York showrooms and a West Coast plant."[43] All but ten of the ninety-six entertainment programs produced by the three networks in early 1965 originated from the Los Angeles area.[44]

For their part, the governors of the movie colony had little choice but to enter TV production. Partly in response to competition from television, the major studios had reduced their output of individual feature films while shooting more on location or overseas. They no longer needed large physical plants. Several smaller companies sold their studios outright to TV production firms like MCA and Desilu.[45] The major studios, pouring more resources into fewer films, aimed for a big money-maker or "blockbuster."[46] This left the surviving companies with underutilized production facilities and created a justification for TV program production. One summer day in 1959, some twenty-three TV shows—and no films—were in production on the Warners lot. Asked if Warners' deal with ABC would work, a studio official had replied, "It better . . . or else they'll have to turn the studio into a parking lot."[47]

The networks may well have always intended to turn over their programming to the studios. Frank Stanton, president of CBS, suggested as much to *Fortune* in 1951.[48] What had not been clear until the sale of old *I Love Lucy* episodes in 1955 was that "reruns" of popular filmed series could provide additional revenues unobtainable from a live show.[49] (Videotape did not come into common use until the 1960s.)

"Syndicated" reruns could be telecast by the networks and individual stations outside of evening prime time.

The continued diffusion of television may have hurt programming with a Gotham flavor. Among the last regions of the country to receive television signals in the 1950s were the less populated Plains states and southern rural regions whose viewers were least likely to enjoy (or comprehend) the humor of a big-city, Jewish comic. It is perhaps no coincidence, then, that certain performers like Berle could no longer compete for the great audience. Individual New York–based series like *Stanley* or *Car 54, Where are You?* would probably have enjoyed longer runs had they been first telecast in the early 1950s, when the TV audience had a more urban and Eastern bias. Conversely, performers appealing to the heartland, like Lawrence Welk, enjoyed greater appeal in the late 1950s.[50]

Perhaps nothing could have arrested Hollywood's eventual domination of TV program production. The very factors of climate and terrain that had made California a better place to shoot movies in 1910 made it a more sensible location for filming TV series in 1960. As one wag told a New York newspaper critic early in 1965, "It's difficult to shoot a Western in New York."[51] Then, too, with the mass suburbanization of America after 1945, California's geographically disperse, auto-driven culture more neatly fit the American stereotype than did New York's, which remained densely populated and subway-bound.[52]

Nor did New York have the movie colony's ample production facilities. When asked why *The Tonight Show* relocated to Burbank in 1972, Johnny Carson offered two reasons: wanting a house with a backyard and the relative convenience of putting together a program in California. "We found it much easier to work out here. Facilities are better. Studios are better. It's all in one building. If we want to do a sketch, all I have to do is call and say, 'I need a bathtub that comes through a wall,' and I've got it tomorrow. The facilities in New York are terrible."[53]

Nonetheless, New York remained a fixation for some program writers and producers, many of whom had ties to the city. A study of all TV detective series aired between 1949 and 1969 found that private eyes were most likely to operate out of New York.[54] Although only one TV program, *On Our Own*, was produced in New York in the fall 1977 season, the characters in ten network series, including *All in the Family*, *Kojak*, *Rhoda*, and *Barney Miller*, were Gotham-based.[55] Public television's most popular program in the 1970s, *Sesame Street*, was unmistakably located in a New York City neighborhood.

Yet there were still more blows to New York's cultural primacy. The 1950s saw a drastic decentralization in the production and distribution of popular music. This shift related closely to a sharp increase in the number of radio stations beginning in 1945; the number of outlets rose from 973 to 1945 to 2,867 in 1950. Most lacked a network affiliation or a network's attitude toward programming.[56] The new stations could also take advantage of new technologies that offered high quality sound broadcasts; listeners did not, after all, resent hearing a recording. A musical performance did not have to originate from a New York hotel ballroom. Stations also had more artists to choose from as Broadcast Music Inc. signed regional and minority artists ASCAP had spurned. Whereas the networks had refused to play certain songs (country music or rhythm and blues) thought indecent or outside the great white mainstream, many postwar radio outlets took risks that their operators hoped would appeal to audience subgroups heretofore ignored by CBS and NBC censors.[57] As a marketing strategy, this made perfect sense. Television had in effect robbed radio of the huge evening following of the 1930s and 1940s. No longer did so many stations carry network radio music, which had been carefully selected to appeal to the largest possible audience. Instead, outlets in smaller, rural markets aired country music; stations with large black followings carried rhythm and blues. In the early 1950s, "disc jockeys" at individual stations began playing R&B and its less racy white equivalent, rock 'n' roll, to appreciative adolescent listeners (teenagers were the least likely to watch television). By the late 1950s, individual station executives and disc jockeys in towns and cities across the country—not a few New York–based network executives—had created a far more diverse range of choices in music for consumers.[58]

At the same time, record companies had to relent and produce albums appealing to a larger and more diverse market. Heretofore preoccupied with the white middle-class audience, the album manufacturers and producers saw new rivals, based in cities like Detroit, Nashville, Los Angeles, and Memphis, boosting their share of total album sales by appealing to more specialized tastes.[59] As popular singers, even many country performers, migrated to Hollywood, most record companies quit Manhattan for Southern California. "The record companies had to come here because the action is here," the record columnist for *Daily Variety* observed in March 1978. "The deals are made sitting 'round the pool, not in offices in New York."[60]

New York's more prestigious newspapers initially suffered no such loss of cultural leadership. In the 1940s and 1950s, the *New York Times* remained the nation's most respected daily. Offered a position with the *Times* in 1954, Allen Drury eagerly accepted. "Unsolicited offers to work for the *Times* in Washington are both rare and rarely refused."[61] Such was the paper's overwhelming edge in daily journalism that few rejected employment at the *Times* in the next ten years. In the early 1960s, the paper's increasingly desperate local rival for the upper-middle-class reader, the *Herald Tribune,* began offering more news summaries, an "In the news this morning" column on page one, and a distinctive style of reportage, dubbed "the new journalism," that anticipated industry developments in the 1970s and 1980s.[62] Despite the *Herald Tribune*'s closing in 1966, however, the *Times* continued its unusual emphasis on national and international news. By then, the *Time*'s competitor for the national opinion leadership was the *Wall Street Journal,* also published in New York. Seeking to reach the country's financial and corporate elite, as well as information-hungry investors in stocks and bonds, the *Journal* established the first effective nationwide publication and distribution system and became the first true national daily. The paper's circulation rose from 100,000 in the late 1940s to 2 million by 1981. The paper's influence increased as well. In the 1970s, the *Journal*'s editorial page promoted supply-side economics to the corporate and Republican elite.[63]

The gap that had separated the *Times* from virtually all other dailies did begin to narrow in the 1970s. The *Washington Post* aggressively improved its national and international coverage and "scooped" the *Times* in handling the Watergate scandal of 1972–1974.[64] In the 1980s the nation's most influential TV critic no longer worked for the *Times* or *Herald Tribune,* as in the 1950s, but for the *Post.*[65] The *Los Angeles Times,* too, self-consciously took on the "other" American *Times* in setting national journalistic standards.[66] The *Los Angeles Times* and Knight-Ridder chain competed with the wire services, as well as the *New York Times,* in offering smaller dailies syndicated news analyses and features. Other big-city newspapers, including the *Chicago Tribune* and *Boston Globe,* that Villard and others had derided in the 1930s, enjoyed enhanced prestige in the 1970s and 1980s.[67] Ambitious journalists no longer had to look exclusively to West 43rd Street as the last step on the career ladder. If their aspirations were unconnected to a newspaper's reputation, they could hope, beginning in 1982, to labor at the nation's largest daily, *USA Today,* published in suburban Washington.

New York similarly lost some of its importance in periodical publishing. Popular mass-circulation magazines like the *Saturday Evening Post, Look,* and *Life* could not survive the diffusion of television. Some attributed the demise of *Life,* the last to survive as a weekly publication, to its being headquartered in New York City. By the late 1960s and early 1970s, *Life*'s editors had lost touch with their readers. New York City, a British journalist observed in 1973, "is a good place to judge New York from but a poor listening post for the rest of the States."[68] Nor did well-to-do periodical readers have to look to New York publications for guidance on the culture of consumption. By the early 1980s, some 120 "city" magazines, with their lists of local places to eat and shop extravagantly, permitted the more self-conscious well-to-do reader to think sophistication could be bought in Denver, Nashville, or Los Angeles, without taking cues from *The New Yorker*.[69]

Perhaps New York's cultural reign waned because Americans had lost their regional inferiority complexes. The seriousness with which some readers took city magazines offered one sign of a new regional identity, as did the expanded popularity of country music.[70] Californians, in particular, had reason for pride. Their state had passed New York in population in the 1960s; Californians by then had finally stopped dressing like easterners. For a band to play at a club in San Francisco or Los Angeles carried as much or more prestige as to perform at one in New York.[71]

Americans were less likely to need New York for cultural pointers. Perhaps the city's mass communicators had succeeded too well. Together the electronic and print media provided Americans with continuous contact with important trends or fads, and hence with the sensation of being "in the know." Less frequently did some, even in rural areas, feel out of touch with the world.[72] "I don't think there are any rubes left," Johnny Carson told *The New Yorker* as he prepared to move his program to California. "People are so much more sophisticated. They get live programs from all over the world, by satellite. So you're not going to impress them by broadcasting from New York. Those days are over."[73]

In television, New York continued to lose ground in the 1970s. Prizing geographical diversity, the planners of the Public Broadcasting System in 1966 and 1967 insisted that individual PBS stations, rather than a single public television authority, or the network's flagship station, WNET in New York, share in the creation of programming.[74] Three years later, the Federal Communications Commission moved more forcefully against New York–centered television. In the early 1960s, the three networks had wrested control over the selection and production of individual TV programs from advertisers. Although this new arrangement eliminated advertiser interference in programming, which had been roundly condemned by critics and regulators, it also created a conflict of interest for the networks. CBS, NBC, and ABC normally owned all or part of the programming they aired in the 1960s. Their executives were more likely to telecast a series in which their company held a financial stake. In 1970, the FCC ordered the networks to cease taking a proprietary interest in any commercial programming.[75]

Thereafter, the balance of power shifted between New York and California. Independent program producers like Norman Lear and Aaron Spelling had less difficulty selling—and suffered less interference in producing—a TV series. Mired in third place in 1981, NBC hired the head of one California-based production company, Grant Tinker, as president.[76] Tinker replaced Fred Silverman, who had tried to reestablish the older, network-dominant model of developing ideas for individual series and carefully supervising their production; the results for Silverman and NBC proved disastrous. He was no more successful than a *Life* editor in 1971 at predicting the nation's mass cultural appetite.[77] Gradually, the networks relaxed remaining controls—usually involving the policing of colorful language or sexual situations—over programming.[78] "We can stop worrying about the breakdown of standards in broadcasting," *Washington Post* TV critic Tom Shales wrote in October 1988, "because there are almost no standards left to break down."[79]

There were still more blows to New York television. A fourth TV network, Fox, began in the mid-1980s based in Hollywood.[80] The popularity of cable television in the 1970s and 1980s denied the networks—and eventually, network news programs—their once automatic hold over most of the great audience. In the 1970s, around 90 percent of the total TV audience viewed network programming in evening prime time; in the late 1980s, the networks' "share" had dropped to the high 60s. No longer were potential buyers willing to pay outrageous prices for top-market stations affiliated with a network.[81] Cable channels might originate from Nashville or Atlanta. One, Cable News Network, from Atlanta, competed directly with the network news divisions.[82] In response, early evening network news programs, led by CBS, tried to remove an East-Coast bias to their presentations.[83] Anchors hosted their newscasts from Texas and Iowa.[84] Cost-consciousness also dictated a geographic shift. Claiming it would save "in excess of $1 million," NBC late in 1988 moved *Sunday Today* from New York to Washington.[85]

Changes in network ownership in the mid-1980s, facilitated, ironically, by New York investment houses, had the effect of diminishing the broadcast chains' power. The purchase of ABC by Capital Cities in 1985 and RCA-NBC in 1986 were followed by sharp reductions in operating expenses. The new controlling shareholder of CBS, Laurence Tisch, sold off the company's book and music publishing divisions. In January 1988, the Sony Corporation purchased CBS Records.[86]

The merger mania affected other New York mass culture manufacturers. At Time Inc., pay cable operations, the fee-based transmission of Hollywood-made films, had increasingly diminished the importance of Manhattan-based periodical publishing[87] when the company combined with a cable and film-making giant, Warner Communications, in 1989. One analyst of the merger predicted that of the twenty-four members of the new Time-Warners board, only one would represent the magazine division.[88]

New York–based theater and book publishers traveled in opposite directions. As if to reassert their dominance of mass taste, New York publishing houses in the late 1970s gave more weight to the commercial prospects of potential manuscripts. Many authors went to regional houses and university presses willing to assume the financial risks associated with less profitable fiction and non-fiction.[89] New York theatrical producers suffered from a similar loss of nerve. More and more resources went into fewer and fewer shows. This blockbuster mentality dulled Broadway's creative edge. Critics looked with new respect at regional theater.[90] Yet producers were only partly at fault. In a trend that began in the 1960s, more and more composers, writers, and actors quit New York for Hollywood. Fewer sought to launch their careers on the stage. A 1985 obituary for the American musical spoke of "the dissolution of that community of composers, lyricists, book writers, performers and directors. New blood did not come in with another generation."[91]

New York in the 1990s

By the late twentieth century, technological, regulatory, economic, and demographic forces have ended New York's hegemony over American mass culture. Yet if New York no longer dominates mass culture, it is not about to become a Carthage of the popular arts. Despite the loss of talent and ever-spiraling costs of production, Manhattan is virtually certain to remain the home of the national theater. The city's two most respected dailies, the *Times* and the *Wall Street Journal*, maintain their national prestige and influence. An out-of-town rival might occasionally scoop the *Times;* none, however, enjoys the *Times*'s competitive advantage. As long as other dailies provide New Yorkers with the local news the *Times* ignores or downplays, the "newspaper of record" can devote more columns than any American daily to national and international reporting. And a national distribution system, developed in the 1980s, makes the *Times* available to opinion leaders in virtually all major American cities.[92]

In other cultural industries, however, New York has become largely an administrative center. The network news divisions are moving more of their operations to Washington, and only a few entertainment programs like *Late Night with David Letterman* and *Saturday Night Live* originate from the city.[93] Still, the continued concentration of the major advertising agencies in the city will keep the networks—or at least their brokers of time—from leaving Manhattan altogether. Madison Avenue will similarly keep at least some magazine publishers from departing.

The advertising industry is also becoming more decentralized. Television commercials are most often filmed in California. Agencies based in Los Angeles and San Francisco are competing successfully with Manhattan firms for national and international business. Many are considered more creative and closer to social trends and fads that California, and not New York, are setting for the nation. "California is, and has been, a trendsetter for the entire country," Hal Riney remarked in 1986.[94] President Reagan's reelection committee hired Riney's San Francisco firm, creators of the successful Bartles & Jaymes wine cooler campaign, to produce TV ads. Four years later George Bush's managers sought out a Milwaukee firm to make several of what proved to be Bush's most powerful television spots.

New York's prospects depend on the shape of the emerging world economy. The city's proximity to Western Europe may take on added significance if European economic unification in 1992 increases the demand for America's popular arts. On the other hand, if the Europeans impose further restrictions on the telecasting of American-made TV series and films, New York's position as a mass cultural administrative center will be impaired.[95] Should the Pacific Basin countries, as some forecasters suspect, prove a greater market for and investor in American mass culture than the Common Market states, Los Angeles will be the beneficiary.[96] Japanese car manufacturers, who beat out Volkswagen for shares of the domestic auto market, rely on California-based ad agencies or the New York firms' Los Angeles offices. They do not have to fly an additional five hours to Manhattan.[97] This trend has been reinforced by Sony's purchase of CBS Records in 1988 and of Columbia Pictures a year later.[98] "New York's going to remain a great city, but twenty years down the road things may change," a U.S. Bureau of Labor Statistics analyst remarked in March 1989. "Los Angeles has the raw physical energy, and if they harness it, it will become the true world city."[99]

Nevertheless, Los Angeles is not without problems that could prevent it from displacing New York as the mass cultural center. It is struggling with traffic congestion and rising housing costs. Although the well-to-do will, as always, find the means to finance comfortable residences, none will be able to escape the tyranny of backed up freeways. And only so much serious business can be transacted on a car-phone or by fax.[100]

Los Angeles's opportunities to overtake New York have also been frustrated by the rising cost of doing business in Southern California. In the late 1940s, as an economy move, the studios began to shoot more features on location; forty years later, parts of some TV series and many made-for-TV movies were no longer made in Hollywood. New York benefited from such on-the-scene shooting. Between 1983 and 1989, the number of feature films increased from sixty-two to 115.[101] Because of favorable foreign exchange rates in the late 1980s, Canada has emerged as a favored location for many films and TV series. Production in Canada enables companies to reduce their operating costs by one-third. In the most extreme example, *Electronic Media* reported in mid-1987, about 75 percent of the TV series produced by Stephen J. Cannell's company were shot in British Columbia and Alberta.[102] New air pollution controls threaten to add to Los Angeles' disadvantages as a production base and transform that city, like New York, into an administrative center.[103]

All told, the history of urban location and mass cultural production in America, a Hollywood agent might joke, has gone into syndication. As in the early nineteenth century, several cities now fight for the production or oversight of the popular arts. New York's hegemony may have been, in retrospect, a short-term phenomenon. In the 1880s, Lord Bryce had suggested that in time New York's domination of American culture would end. Bryce was less certain if one city would assume New York's position. As the population of the United States shifted westward, Bryce wrote, Chicago or a city in the Mississippi Valley might become America's Athens. Or perhaps the production of American culture would become decentralized and the nation would benefit. "It may be," he wrote, "that in the next age American cities will profit by their local independence to develop varieties greater than they now exhibit, and will evolve diverse types of literary and artistic production."[104]

Notes

1. Bryce, James, *The American Commonwealth*, vol. 2 (London: Macmillan, 1889), pp. 2:647–2:648. See also McKitrick, Eric L., "The City in History," Columbia University General Education Seminar, *Proceedings* 7 (Fall 1978): pp. 5–10.
2. Bryce, *The American Commonwealth*, 2:644–2:650; Bender, Thomas, *New*

York Intellect (Baltimore: Johns Hopkins University Press, 1987), pp. 173, 177, 178, 190, 207; Maier, Pauline, "Boston and New York in the Eighteenth Century," American Antiquarian Society *Proceedings* 91 (pt. 2, 1981): pp. 177–195; Shryock, Richard H., "Philadelphia and the Flowering of New England," *Pennsylvania Magazine of History and Biography* 64 (July 1940): pp. 305–313; Green, Martin, *The Problem of Boston: Some Readings in Cultural History* (New York: W. W. Norton, 1966); Harris, Neil, *Humbug: The Art of P.T. Barnum* (Boston: Little, Brown, 1973), pp. 19, 37–38; Baltzell, E. Digby, *Philadelphia Gentlemen: The Making of a National Upper Class* (Glencoe, IL: Free Press, 1958), pp. 150–151. On the "new" magazines, see Lichtenstein, Nelson, "Authorial Professionalism and the Literary Marketplace 1885–1900," *American Studies* 16 (Spring 1978): pp. 35–53.

3. Lukacs, John, *Philadelphia: Patricians and Philistines, 1900–1950* (New York: Farrar, Straus & Giroux, 1981), p. 172; Baltzell, *Philadelphia Gentlemen,* pp. 150–151, 154–157; Holder, Stephen, "The Death of the *Saturday Evening Post,* 1960–1969: A Popular Culture Phenomenon," in Nye, Russell B., ed., *New Dimensions in Popular Culture* (Bowling Green, OH: Bowling Green University Press, 1969), pp. 78–89. On the *Atlantic,* see Lichtenstein, "Authorial Professionalism."
4. Putnam, Samuel, "Chicago: An Obituary," *American Mercury* 8 (August 1926): pp. 417–425; Andrews, Clarence A., *Chicago in Story: A Literary History* (Iowa City: Midwest Heritage Publishing Co., 1982), pp. 145–146.
5. Mumford, Lewis, "The City," in Stearns, Harold E., ed., *Civilization in America; An Inquiry by Thirty Americans* (New York: Harcourt, Brace, 1922), p. 17.
6. Marchand, Roland, *Advertising the American Dream; Making Way for Modernity, 1920–1940* (Berkeley: University of California Press, 1985), pp. 6–7.
7. Elson, Robert T., *Time Inc.: The Intimate History of a Publishing Enterprise, 1923–1941* (New York: Atheneum, 1968), pp. 95–98, 101–102, 104–107; Busch, Noel F., *Briton Hadden* (New York: Farrar, Straus and Co., 1949), pp. 168–184.
8. Berkow, Ira, *Red: A Biography of Red Smith* (New York: Times Books), p. 41.
9. Davis, Elmer, *History of the New York Times, 1851–1921* (New York: The New York Times, 1921), p. 388. For a somewhat less fawning appraisal of the *Times* in the 1920s, see Bent, Silas, *Strange Bedfellows* (New York: Horace Liveright, 1928), ch. 15.
10. Smith, Richard Norton, *An Uncommon Man: The Triumph of Herbert Hoover* (New York: Simon and Schuster, 1984), p. 173.
11. Villard, Oswald Garrison, *The Disappearing Daily: Chapters in American Newspaper Evolution* (New York: Alfred A. Knopf, 1944), pp. 175–196. See also Young, Marguerite, "Ignoble Journalism in the Nation's Capital," *American Mercury* 34 (February 1935): pp. 239–243; Lyon, Louis M., *Newspaper Story: One Hundred Years of the Boston Globe* (Cambridge, MA: Harvard University Press, 1971), p. 317.

12. Ewen, David, *The Life and Death of Tin Pan Alley* (New York: Funk and Wagnalls, 1964); Rockwell, John, "New York's Music," in Wallock, Leonard, ed., *New York: Culture Capital of the World 1940–1965* (New York: Rizzoli, 1988), p. 218.
13. Erenberg, Lewis A., *Steppin' Out: New York City and the Transformation of American Culture, 1890–1930* (Westport, CT: Greenwood, 1981), pp. xii, 55.
14. Sterling, Christopher H. and John M. Kittross, *Stay Tuned: A Concise History of American Broadcasting* (Belmont, CA: Wadsworth, 1978), p. 533.
15. Federal Radio Commission, *Annual Report 1928*, p. 21; Smulyan, Susan, "The Rise of the Radio Network System: Technological and Cultural Influences on the Structure of American Broadcasting," *Prospects* 11 (1987): pp. 105–117, esp. p. 107.
16. "National Broadcasting Co., Inc.," *Fortune* 2 (December 1930), p. 70.
17. Barnouw, Erik, *A Tower in Babel* (New York: Oxford University Press, 1966), pp. 271, 273.
18. Siepmann, Charles A., *Radio's Second Chance* (Boston: Little, Brown, 1946), pp. 42–43, 48. See also Barber, Oren G., "Competition, Free Speech and FCC Radio Regulation," *George Washington Law Review* 12 (May 1943): pp. 34–53. On station-network affiliation, see "And Because They're Smart," *Fortune* 11 (June 1935), pp. 146, 148.
19. Waller, Judith C., *Radio: The Fifth Estate*, 2nd ed. (Boston: Houghton Mifflin, 1950), pp. 120–121; White, Llewellyn, *The American Radio* (Chicago: University of Chicago Press, 1947), pp. 48–49.
20. Wertheim, Arthur Frank, *Radio Comedy* (New York: Oxford University Press, 1979), pp. 94–96.
21. Rubin, Joan Shelley, "'Information, Please!': Culture and Expertise in the Interwar Period," *American Quarterly* 35 (Winter 1983): pp. 499–517.
22. Gabler, Neal, *An Empire of Their Own; How the Jews Invented Hollywood* (New York: Crown, 1988), p. 105; Sklar, Robert, *Movie-Made America; A Cultural History of American Movies* (New York: Random House, 1975), pp. 67–69; McLaughlin, Robert Guy, "Broadway and Hollywood: A History of Economic Interaction," Ph.D. dissertation, University of Wisconsin, 1970, pp. 45–53. Some film companies did maintain facilities in the New York area in the late 1920s, in part as a convenience to theater performers. *The Coconuts* (1929), starring the Marx Brothers, was filmed on Long Island. The leads were simultaneously doing a show on Broadway.
23. Vaughn, Stephen, "Morality and Entertainment: The Origins of the Motion Picture Production Code," *Journal of American History* 77 (June 1990): pp. 39–65; Gabler, *An Empire of Their Own*, pp. 132, 181.
24. Ewen, *Life and Death of Tin Pan Alley*, pp. 322–323; Sanjek, Russell, *American Popular Music and Its Business; The First Four Hundred Years*, vol. 3 (New York: Oxford University Press, 1988), pp. 3:47–3:56.
25. Marquis, Alice Goldfarb, *Hopes and Ashes: The Birth of Modern Times* (New

York: The Free Press, 1986), pp. 55–89; McLaughlin, "Broadway and Hollywood," pp. 109–114.

26. Jerome Chodorov quoted in Gabler, *An Empire of Their Own*, p. 323. See also Allen, Steve, "Nobody Told a Bad Joke Better," *New York Times Book Review* (4 December 1988), p. 14.
27. Poggi, Jack, *Theater in America: The Impact of Economic Forces 1870–1967* (Ithaca: Cornell University Press, 1968), pp. 33ff, 44, 74ff, 78, 81, 83–84; McLaughlin, "Broadway and Hollywood," pp. 21–24, 98–99, 105, 107.
28. Paley, William S., *As It Happened* (Garden City, NY: Doubleday, 1979, pp. 109ff; Reid, Louis R., "Amusement: Radio and the Movies," in Stearns, Harold E., ed., *America Now; An Inquiry into Civilization in the United States by 36 Americans* (New York: Scribner's, 1938), p. 10; McLaughlin, "Broadway and Hollywood," p. 146; Peck, Seymour, "When Movie Stars Took On the Bard," *New York Times*, 13 December 1981, 2:23–24; De Mille, Cecil B., *Autobiography* (Englewood Cliffs, NJ: Prentice-Hall, 1959), pp. 346–347; Hilmes, Michele, "Hollywood and Broadcasting: A History of Economic and Structural Interaction from Radio to Cable," Ph.D. dissertation, New York University, 1986, pp. 108–122. Beginning in 1937, AT&T made it possible to broadcast nationally from Hollywood at no extra cost. Wertheim, *Radio Comedy*, pp. 263–264.
29. Wakeman, Frederic, *The Hucksters* (New York: Rinehart & Co., 1946), pp. 157–158.
30. Gunther, John, *Inside U.S.A.* (New York: Harper & Bros., 1947), pp. 549–550.
31. White, E.B., *This Is New York* (1951), reprinted in *Essays of E. B. White* (New York: Harper & Row, 1977), p. 126.
32. Sterling and Kittross, *Stay Tuned*, p. 535.
33. Crosby, John, *New York Herald Tribune*, 25 February 1951.
34. Docket 12285, *Proc.*, pp. 2816, 2821–2822, FCC Records, General Services Administration, Accession Number 72A1986, vol. 8; Sterling, Christopher H. and Timothy R. Haight, *The Mass Media; Aspen Institute Guide to Communication Industry Trends* (New York: Praeger, 1978), p. 53.
35. Bill Jobe in Fireman, Judy, ed., *TV Book* (New York: Workman, 1977), p. 75; Wilk, Max, *The Golden Age of Television* (Dell, 1976), p. 75 and *passim.* See also Crosby, John, "It Was New and We Were Very Innocent," *TV Guide* (22 September 1973): pp. 5–8; Crosby, *New York Herald Tribune*, November 26, 1948; *Los Angeles Times*, January 4, 1972, p. 4:11.
36. MacKaye, Milton, "The Big Brawl: Hollywood vs. Television," *Saturday Evening Post* (2 February 1952), p. 102; Brooks, Tim, and Earle Marsh, *The Complete Directory to Prime Time Network TV Shows, 1946–Present* (New York: Ballantine, 1979), p. 373.
37. Baughman, James L., "Television in the 'Golden Age': An Entrepreneurial Experiment," *Historian* 47 (February 1985), pp. 182–183. Live telecast data

are from *Broadcasting Yearbook 1964* (Washington: Broadcasting Magazine, 1964), p. 26.

38. Andrews, Bart, *The Story of I Love Lucy* (New York: Popular Library, 1977), pp. 35–42.
39. Baughman, "Television in the 'Golden Age,'" pp. 184–185.
40. Anderson, R. Christopher, "Hollywood TV: The Emergence of Television Production at Warner Bros. Pictures and David O. Selznick Productions," Ph.D. dissertation, University of Texas, 1988; Boddy, William, "The Studios Move into Prime Time: Hollywood and the Television Industry in the 1950s," *Cinema Journal* 24 (Summer 1985): pp. 23–37; Baughman, James L., "ABC and the Destruction of American Television, 1953–1961," *Business and Economic History*, 2nd ser. 12 (1983): pp. 56–73; Tedlow, Richard S., and Henry Feingold, "Interview with Leonard Goldenson," *American Jewish History* 72 (September 1982), pp. 116–119. NBC emphasized live programming from New York until 1957, when it too looked west. See Bob Stahl, "Five Who Are Taking a Giant Step at NBC," *TV Guide* (10 October 1959), p. 10.
41. Two 1958–1959 police dramas, *Naked City* and *87 Precinct*, were filmed in New York. See Silverman, Fred, "An Analysis of ABC Television Network Programming from February 1953 to October 1959," M.A. thesis, Ohio State University, 1959, pp. 285, 299.
42. Gleason fared well in the ratings when he returned to TV in the 1960s, but he forced CBS to allow him to move his variety program from New York to Miami. Adler, Jerry, "The Fat Man's Last Laugh," *Time* (6 July 1987), p. 49.
43. *Printer's Ink* 260 (23 August 1957), p. 19. See also *New York Times*, 3 March 1957, p. 2:11; 14 July 1957, p. 2:9; Serling, Rod, "TV in the Can vs. TV in the Flesh," *New York Times Magazine* (24 March 1957): pp. 49, 52. On the anger over the anthologies' passing, see Baughman, James L., "The National Purpose and the Newest Medium: Liberal Critics of Television, 1958–1960," *Mid-America* 64 (April–July 1983), pp. 43–44; Boddy, William Francis, "From the 'Golden Age' to the 'Vast Wasteland': The Struggles over Market Power and Dramatic Formats in 1950s Television," Ph.D. dissertation, New York University, 1986, pp. 104–122, 155–157; and Aurthur, Robert Alan, "Creative Rating—Zero!" *TV Guide* (17 June 1961): pp. 26–29.
44. The ten New York–based programs were mostly game, musical and variety shows. *New York Times*, 30 March 1965.
45. Andrews, Bart, *Story of I Love Lucy*, pp. 193–194; Bernstein, Irving, *The Economics of Television Film Production and Distribution* (Hollywood: Screen Actors Guild, 1960), p. 34; Hentoff, Nat, "The Octopus of Show Biz," *Reporter* 25 (23 November 1961), p. 41.
46. Lincoln, Freeman, "The Comeback of the Movies," *Fortune* 51 (February 1955): pp. 127–131, et seq.

47. Whitney, Dwight, "The Producer Assembles His Products," *TV Guide* (31 October 1959), pp. 21–23. See also Smith, Richard Austin, "TV: The Light That Failed," *Fortune* 58 (December 1958), pp. 161, 162.
48. "TV's Time of Trouble," *Fortune* 44 (August 1951), p. 131.
49. *Sponsor* (26 December 1955), p. 2.
50. "Is There a Programming Crisis?" *Television Magazine* 14 (February 1957), p. 93; Silverman, "Analysis of ABC," p. 227. See also Shales, Tom, "That Crowd in Los Angeles Isn't the Same as in New York," *Milwaukee Journal TV Cable*, 14 July 1985, p. 2.
51. *New York Times*, 30 March 1965. The same story quotes Michael Dann, then of CBS, denying that it cost more to produce programs in New York than Los Angeles. By the late 1980s, most of the game shows had moved west.
52. Jackson, Kenneth T., *Crabgrass Frontier: The Suburbanization of the United States* (New York: Oxford University Press, 1985), chaps. 13–14.
53. White, Timothy, "Johnny Carson: The Rolling Stone Interview," *Rolling Stone* (22 March 1979), p. 53. City officials in the late 1950s and 1960s offered to assist in building a massive television center but could not persuade major program producers to commit themselves to keeping or relocating their operations in New York. See *New York Times*, 1 November 1965, 19 November 1965.
54. Of 63 network detective shows examined by Robert Larka, 23 series based the characters in New York, 15 in Los Angeles and 4 in San Francisco. See Larka, "Television's Private Eye: An Examination of Twenty Years of a Particular Genre, 1949–1969," Ph.D. dissertation, Ohio University, pp. 180–181. On the New York attitudes and roots of some in TV production in the 1970s, see Stein, Ben, *The View from Sunset Boulevard* (New York: Basic Books, 1979), chap. 10, and Cantor, Muriel G., *The Hollywood TV Producer; His World and His Audience* (New York: Basic Books, 1971), p. 236.
55. Based on the schedule and program descriptions in Brooks and Marsh, *Complete Directory to Prime Time*, passim and p. 458. Ten years later, two popular evening programs, *The Cosby Show* and *Kate & Allie*, were produced in Astoria, Queens. *Electronic Media* (16 November 1987), pp. 40, 50. Other network series in the 1987–1988 and 1988–1989 seasons, including *The Equalizer*, *Leg Work*, and *Tattinger's*, concerned New Yorkers, and their exterior shots were filmed in the city.
56. Stuart, Frederic, "Whatever Happened to Radio?" *Challenge* 11 (April 1963): pp. 4–7.
57. Peterson, Richard A. and David G. Berger, "Three Eras in the Manufacture of Popular Music Lyrics," in Denisoff, R. Serge, and Peterson, eds., *The Sounds of Social Change* (Chicago: Rand McNally, 1972), p. 289.
58. Macdonald, Dwight, "Profiles: A Caste, A Culture, A Market," *New Yorker* 34 (29 November 1958), pp. 95–98; Gillett, Charlie, *The Sound of the City; The Rise of Rock and Roll*, rev. ed. (New York: Pantheon, 1983), pp. 38–39,

351–353; Ward, Ed, Geoffrey Stokes, and Ken Tucker, *Rock of Ages: The Rolling Stone History of Rock & Roll* (Englewood Cliffs, NJ: Rolling Stone Press, 1986), pp. 69–71, 327ff. In the late 1950s, some stations began using "Format Radio" that compelled DJs to play only those songs listed on the weekly "Top 40" compilations of best-selling records. By the mid-1980s, some stations carried music preselected by syndicators like Satellite Music Network. See Ward, *Rock of Ages*, pp. 156–157; *Cleveland Plain Dealer*, 16 July 1984.

59. Peterson, Richard A. and David G. Berger, "Entrepreneurship in Organizations: Evidence from the Popular Music Industry," *Administrative Science Quarterly* 16 (March 1971), p. 102; Peterson, Richard A., and David G. Berger, "Cycles in Symbol Production: The Case of Popular Music," *American Sociological Review* 40 (April 1975), pp. 162–166; Gillett, *Sound of the City*, pp. 285, 324–326; Cramer, Edward M., "Music Biz Kissoff," *Variety*, 7 January 1976, p. 136; Macdonald, "Profiles," pp. 95–96; Belz, Carl, *The Story of Rock* (New York: Oxford University Press, 1972), p. 22; Ward, *Rock of Ages*, pp. 62–63, 72–82, 219–220, 234; Rockwell, "New York's Music," p. 229.
60. *The Trib* (New York), 27 March 1978, p. 25.
61. Drury, Allen, *Three Kids in a Cart; A Visit to Ike and Other Diversions* (Garden City, NY: Doubleday, 1965), p. 295.
62. Kluger, Richard, *The Paper: The Life and Death of the New York Herald Tribune* (New York: Knopf, 1986), pp. 608–615, 618, 634–637, 672–681, 703–709; Wolfe, Tom, "The Birth of 'The New Journalism': An Eyewitness Report," *New York* 5 (14 February 1972): pp. 30–45. *Esquire*, also based in New York, has also been credited with fostering the new journalism. See Harold Hayes's obituary, *New York Times*, 7 April 1989.
63. Wendt, Lloyd, *The Wall Street Journal* (Chicago: Rand McNally, 1982), esp. pp. 369ff, 416; Harden, Blaine, "The Editor Who Claims to Think Like the President," *Washington Post Magazine* (11 July 1982): pp. 13–19; Kuttner, Bob, "Up the Wall Street Journal," *New Republic* 190 (16 April 1984): pp. 15–21; Scharff, Edward E., *Worldly Power: The Making of the Wall Street Journal* (New York: Beaumont Books, 1986).
64. Roberts, Chalmers M., *The Washington Post: The First 100 Years* (Boston: Houghton Mifflin, 1977), chaps. 6–9.
65. Flanders, Judy, "A Case of Coziness: Tom Shales and CBS News," *Washington Journalism Review* 10 (September 1988): pp. 16–19, and *ibid*. 8 (February 1986), p. 25. A 1958 study for the Fund for the Republic ranked Jack Gould of the *Times* and John Crosby of the *Herald Tribune* as the nation's most powerful TV columnists. See paper, McGrady, Patrick, October 1958, Fund for Republic Papers, Box 63, Princeton University, and Morse, Leon, "Inside Jack Gould," *Television Magazine* 15 (November 1958): pp. 49–50; *Newsweek* (9 May 1966), p. 92.
66. The best recent history of the *Los Angeles Times* is Hart, Jack R., *The Informa-*

tion Empire: The Rise of the Los Angeles Times and the Times Mirror Corporation (Washington: University Press of America, 1981).

67. The *New York Times* was consistently ranked first in polls of newspaper publishers and journalism school faculty conducted in 1952, 1960, 1961, 1970, and remained first in a 1983 survey, conducted by Michael Emery. *Milwaukee Journal*, 15 June 1983. A year later, *Ad Week* ranked the *New York Times, Washington Post,* and *Los Angeles Times* the nation's best dailies. *Milwaukee Journal*, 26 April 1984.
68. Linklater, Magnus, "Death of *Life*," *Sunday Times* (of London) *Magazine* (11 February 1973), p. 45.
69. Fletcher, Alan D. and Bruce G. VandenBergh, "Numbers Grow, Problems Remain for City Magazines," *Journalism Quarterly* 59 (Summer 1982): pp. 313–317.
70. Peterson, Richard A. and Paul Di Maggio, "From Region to Class: The Changing Locus of Country Music: A Test of the Massification Hypothesis," *Social Forces* 53 (March 1975): pp. 496–506.
71. Nash, Gerald D., *The American West Transformed: The Impact of the Second World War* (Bloomington: Indiana University Press, 1985), sees this regional pride result from the West's growth during the 1940s. See also Marias, Augilera Julian, *America in the Fifties and Sixties* (University Park: Pennsylvania State University Press, 1972), pp. 204–207.
72. Suggestive in this regard is Linklater, "Death of *Life*," p. 46; Nash, *American West Transformed*, pp. 212–213; Hacker, Andrew, *New York Times Book Review* (November 9, 1975), p. 44, quoted in Murray, Lawrence L., "Complacency and Cooperation: The Film Industry Responds to the Challenge of Television," *Journal of Popular Film* 6 (no. 1, 1977), p. 50.
73. *New Yorker* 48 (11 March 1972), p. 31.
74. Baughman, James L., *Television's Guardians: The Federal Communications Commission and the Politics of Programming, 1958–1967* (Knoxville: University of Tennessee Press, 1985), p. 162; Report of Panel on Programming, June 20–21, 1966, p. 2; and White, Stephen, "Issues–June (1966) Meeting," Carnegie Commission on Educational Television, Box 2-1, State Historical Society of Wisconsin.
75. Federal Communications Commission, Office of Network Study, *Television Network Program Procurement*, Second Interim Report, 1965; Schuessler, Thomas L., "FCC Regulation of the Network Television Program Procurement Process: An Attempt to Regulate the Laws of Economics?" *Northwestern University Law Review* 73 (May–June 1978): pp. 227–306; Eck, Robert, "The Real Masters of Television," *Harper's* 234 (March 1967): pp. 45–52. Accepting the networks' plea of hard times, the FCC will allow the financial interest and syndication rules to expire in 1990. *New York Times*, 30 January 1989.
76. *New York Times*, 1 July 1981; Salmans, Sandra, "Tinker's Prime Time at NBC," *New York Times Magazine* (6 March 1986), pp. 24, 28, 72–74, 106.

Tinker, it should be noted, preferred living in California and eventually quit NBC after reversing the network's fortunes.

77. Bedell, Sally, *Up the Tube: Prime-Time TV and the Silverman Years* (New York: Viking, 1981), pp. 237–238.
78. *New York Times*, 20 August 1988; Clark, Kenneth R., "TV no-no's," *Chicago Tribune*, 16 December 1988, pp. 2:1, 3.
79. *Milwaukee Journal*, 1 November 1988. Protests of sexual explicitness caused the networks to reinstitute some controls. See *New York Times*, 25 July 1989.
80. *New York Times*, 5 October 1986, pp. 2:1, 26.
81. *Chicago Tribune*, 2 September 1987; *New York Times*, 14 November 1988. Observers attributed much of the fall 1988 decline to the effects of the writers' strike, which delayed the start of new programs. See *New York Times*, 5 December 1988, 16 January 1989; *Wall Street Journal*, 5 January 1989.
82. CNN originated from Atlanta, much as film production migrated to the West Coast, because of lower labor costs. See *New York Times*, 25 May 1980, pp. 3:1,4; 19 April 1987, pp. 3:8–9; Leiser, Ernest, "The Little Network That Could," *New York Times Magazine* (20 March 1988), pp. 36, 38.
83. Massing, Michael, "CBS: Sauterizing the News," *Columbia Journalism Review* 24 (March/April 1986), pp. 28, 30; Whitney, D. Charles, et al., "Geographic and Source Biases in Network Television News, 1982–1984," paper, Association for Education in Journalism and Mass Communication, annual convention, Memphis, August 1985.
84. Alter, Jonathan, "Anchors Away: At Home Abroad," *Newsweek* (10 March 1986), pp. 66–67.
85. *Chicago Tribune*, 25 December 1988, pp. 2:3.
86. *Electronic Media* (18 July 1985), pp. 1, 18; Boyer, Peter J., "Sony and CBS Records: What a Romance!" *New York Times Magazine* (18 January 1988), pp. 35–36, 38, 40–42, 44, 46, 49; *New York Times*, 25 October 1986, 15 January 1987.
87. By the late 1980s, the president and vice chairman of Time Inc., Nicholas J. Nichols, Jr. and Gerald M. Levin, had backgrounds in the corporation's video divisions. *New York Times*, 18 July 1986, 22 July 1988; *Wall Street Journal*, 18 July 1986. See also *New York Times*, 7 March 1983, 1 December 1985, 3:29; Bernstein, Lester, "Time Inc. Means Business," *New York Times Magazine* (26 February 1989), p. 24.
88. Bennet, James, "Time Out," *New Republic* 200 (24 April 1989), p. 22. See also "Warner's Ross Isn't Expected to Give Up Control," *Wall Street Journal*, 21 March 1989; Connor, Macaulay, "Backward Marches Time," *Spy* (October 1989), pp. 118–119. According to one forecast, periodicals would account for approximately 18 percent of Time-Warner's profits. *New York Times*, 6 March 1989.
89. Feldman, Gayle, "University Presses: A Changing Role," *Publishers Weekly*

(23 September 1988), p. 18; Summer, Bob, "University of Georgia Press Enjoys Its 50th Anniversary," *ibid.*, p. 24; Will Nixon, "University Presses: Highs & Lows," *ibid.* (22 September 1989), pp. 18–24; *Chicago Tribune*, 12 January 1982; Whiteside, Thomas, *The Blockbuster Complex: Conglomerates, Show Business, and Book Publishing* (Middletown, CT: Wesleyan University Press, 1981); Solotaroff, Ted, "The Literary-Industrial Complex," *New Republic* 196 (8 June 1987): pp. 28, 30–42, 44–45; Radway, Janice A., *Reading the Romance; Women, Patriarchy, and Popular Literature* (Chapel Hill: University of North Carolina Press, 1984), pp. 35ff; Prial, Frank J., "Stick This in Your Midsized Vuitton," *New York Times Book Review*, 28 August 1988, p. 11.

90. Alexander, Charles C., *Here the Country Lies: Nationalism and the Arts in Twentieth Century America* (Bloomington: Indiana University Press, 1980), pp. 263ff; Stone, Peter, "Give My Regards to Off Broadway and Beyond," *New York Times*, 21 June 1988; Gilman, Richard, "The City and the Theater," in Wallock, *New York: Culture Capital*, p. 210.
91. Marx, Robert, "The Glorious Era of the Broadway Musical Is Long Gone—and Economics Is Only One of the Reasons," *American Theatre* 2 (September 1985), p. 7.
92. This influence might be checked or even undone if or when the publishers of the *Washington Post* made their paper similarly available across the country. A weekly edition of the *Post* has been available since the mid-1980s. Direct competition with the *Times*, given the relatively small market for such dailies, however, would probably make both operations unprofitable.
93. Kristol, Irving, "Why I Left," *New Republic* 198 (11 April 1988), p. 24.
94. *New York Times*, 26 June 1988, p. 3:4; *Advertising Age* (20 October 1986), pp. S10, S12, S14.
95. "Buddy, Can You Spare a Reel?" *The Economist* 312 (19 August 1989), pp. 56–57.
96. Kotkin, Joel, "I Love L.A.," *Inc.* 11 (March 1989), p. 96; Lueck, Thomas J., "New York City Is Challenged as Giant of Global Economy," *New York Times*, 27 June 1988; Lockwood, Charles, and Christopher Leinberger, "Los Angeles Comes of Age," *Atlantic* 261 (January 1988), pp. 39–40.
97. In 1989, California agencies handled the accounts for American Honda and Nissan. The Los Angeles offices of two New York agencies handled the American Isuzu and Toyota accounts. *Standard Directory of Advertisers 1989* (Wilmette, IL: National Register Publishing Co., 1989).
98. "Japan Goes Hollywood," *Newsweek* (9 October 1989), pp. 62–67.
99. Kotkin, "I Love L.A.," p. 96.
100. Lockwood and Leinberger, "Los Angeles Comes of Age," pp. 46–54; "Spilling into California's Centre," *The Economist* 312 (12 August 1989), pp. 19–20. Traffic snarls isolate the novelist living in the Los Angeles area, in See, Carolyn, "To Live and Write in L.A.," *Washington Post Book World*, 7 January 1990, p. 15.

101. Dullea, Georgia, "Glitter of Hollywood on Streets of New York," *New York Times*, 29 January 1990, p. B1.
102. *Electronic Media* (22 June 1987), pp. 1, 31; Silverman, David, "Chicago and Illinois Left on Cutting Room Floor," *Chicago Tribune*, 14 June 1988; Jowett, Garth, *Film: The Democratic Art* (Boston: Little, Brown, 1976), pp. 431–433.
103. Weisman, Alan, "L.A. Fights for Breath," *New York Times Magazine* (30 July 1989), pp. 15–17, 30.
104. Bryce, *The American Commonwealth*, 2:647, 2:649. See also Lindberg, Tod, "New York Down, Washington Up," *Commentary* 81 (January 1986), p. 42.

7

New York Culture: Ascendant or Subsident?

Vera L. Zolberg

Long preeminent as the site of corporate headquarters, banking, certain kinds of manufacture, and as a cultural center, New York City benefited from the dominant international position of the United States after World War II to become the art center of the world. In recent years, however, the emergence of new economic rivals has challenged the standing both of America in the world and of New York within the United States. In the face of this challenge, is it possible for the city to maintain its cultural importance?

This chapter analyzes New York City's influence on high culture in America by focusing on two institutions of exceptional stability—art museums and symphony orchestras—and the art forms they incorporated.[1] After discussing some significant differences between these institutions, it analyzes the rise of New York's influence on modern art and symphonic music in America, the city's role in the growth of foundation and government support for the arts, and New York's contemporary cultural standing.

I greatly appreciate the helpful comments on an earlier version of this chapter by Thomas Bender, Janet Abu-Lughod and Arthur Vidich. In particular, I wish to acknowledge the valuable advice offered by Paul DiMaggio, many of whose ideas I have incorporated, as noted.

Art Museums and Symphony Orchestras

Both art museums and symphony orchestras are expected to meet the standard of disinterestedness that serves as the rationale for sheltering nonprofit cultural institutions from commercial pressures. Nonetheless, these institutions cannot be understood apart from market forces, political pressures, and the interests of the actors involved in their creation and maintenance. These forces have differing impacts, however, upon symphony orchestras and museums by virtue of differences in the very structure of music and visual arts.

Whereas paintings and sculpture are concrete objects, capable of being bought and sold, the performance of music is ephemeral. That is, before the technological developments which made reproduction of musical performance possible, only actual attendance at concerts or active participation in performances provided access to symphonic music. Moreover, unlike art museums, where a variety of works can be displayed simultaneously, permitting members of the public to select what they want to look at, members of an orchestral audience have no option but to hear a single work at a time.

Not only reception, but patronage, too, is affected by structural differences between music and painting. Although assumed to be altruistic, collectors who donate works to museums can obtain not only symbolic gratification (as when their collection is displayed in special rooms marked with their names), but also material benefits. As a result of the legitimacy that art museums confer on works and artists, paintings by the same artist that donors *retain* in their personal collections increase in value. This provides private collectors with a powerful incentive to serve as patrons to museums.[2]

Music does not have the same potential for investment as paintings. With the important exception of individuals in the music industry—instrument manufacturers, music publishers, impresarios, and performers—patrons of music gain largely symbolic rewards.[3] This difference between paintings and music helps explain the contrasting directions of institutionalization that art museums and symphony orchestras followed.

Art museums tended to be institutionalized earlier than orchestras. New York elites led those of other major American cities in creating the mixture of public and private financing that served as a model elsewhere in the nation. They established the Metropolitan Museum of Art through a celebrated "deal" between its founders (mostly members of the Union League Club) and the political boss, William M. Tweed. According to its terms, the city paid for the museum's construction in

Central Park and undertook its maintenance. In exchange for providing the opportunity such a major construction enterprise afforded the Tweed machine to inflate costs for their own and their cronies' benefit, the trustees retained ownership and substantial control of the collections. This arrangement was an innovation in municipality-elite relations that civic leaders of other cities (Boston is the major exception) followed in varying degrees.[4]

In the mid-nineteenth century symphonic music depended not so much on wealthy patrons, but on players who were mostly European and who catered to a public composed chiefly of Germanic immigrants. They built an audience for "serious" music and played new works, some of which have been accepted into the canon of high art (Wagner, Brahms, Beethoven). Symphony concerts, as opposed to the heterogeneous entertainments with their promiscuous audience contacts of earlier decades, achieved a reputation for seriousness through their increasingly uncompromising repertoire. The difficulty of the music enhanced its legitimacy for assuming a central position in the framing of an elite culture during the late nineteenth century.[5] Whatever the national origin of particular works of symphonic music, they were defined as of universal or transcendant value. With the gradual elimination of crowd-pleasing elements, this music was made accessible to the white, Anglo-Saxon, college-educated elites, who became convinced that they should finance the orchestras that performed it in return for considerable authority over them.

Despite the pleas of critics and musicians acquainted with the European practice of state, royal, or other patronage, only in rare circumstances was federal subsidy given to music, nor did most American municipal governments support orchestras as they did museums. The elites who might have been expected to be their allies in persuading governments to subsidize orchestras appear to have seen this as a threat to their control. They tried as much as possible to pay the costs of running symphony orchestras themselves, or in alliance with instrument-making firms. As a result, the auditoriums that were specially built for symphony orchestras in the late nineteenth century tended to be financed by private rather than by city funds.

In relation to artistic innovation, symphony orchestras and museums followed opposite trajectories. During much of the nineteenth century, symphony orchestras and opera companies competed with one another by introducing new works and star performers, especially from Europe. As the costs of rehearsal time and performances rose, however, the introduction of new works that might fail to draw the public became too speculative and orchestras changed their strategy. The symphony orchestra became a museum of conventional elite taste. By contrast, art museums initially displayed antiquities and old master works, even though often of dubious authenticity. They rejected works of contemporary artists, especially living Americans working in new styles. The Metropolitan Museum of Art was a leading example of this practice, becoming the creature of its most conservative collector-trustees. Those few modern paintings that had somehow been acquired were hidden away. This pattern changed in the twentieth century, with New York elites leading the way through their access to national policy.[6]

New York and Modern Painting: Institutionalizing the New

Although many people of wealth collected works in established art styles, a few, belonging to status groups of relatively new wealth, sought and actively promoted new canons of artistic taste. Enlisting the support of political figures at the state and national levels, New York businessmen, who normally opposed government interference in their affairs, lobbied for changes in inheritance laws, taxes, and tariff laws in the interest of directly or indirectly subsidizing art collecting and the museums in which some of their collected works came to rest. In this way, John Quinn, a leading New York lawyer who specialized in defending trusts and monopolistic firms, successfully lobbied Congress in 1909 to make the importation of *old* art duty free. As a result, J.P. Morgan was able to import his enormous art collection from England. In his own interest as a collector, Quinn in 1913 achieved the same advantage for collectors of contemporary art.[7]

An ambitious provincial from a small town in Ohio, Quinn, through his congressional lobbying, made himself indispensable to wealthy New Yorkers and ended up in the elite circles to which he aspired. Although he worked for established elites, most of them connected to the Metropolitan Museum of Art, Quinn was also a patron of modern art and collaborated with the photographer Alfred Stieglitz, whose gallery and publications exposed New York artists and collectors to European modernists and the primitive art of Africa and Oceania. Quinn was a key player in the construction of modernism in art through his organization of the Armory Show of 1913, an artistic event that launched Post-Impressionism in America. Thereafter, through the combined efforts of patrons, dealers, writers, and artists, modern Euorpean art was shown regularly in New York, and the internationalism of modernism became central. Coverage by art critics in the little magazines which flourished in that period, most of them staffed by aspiring literary intellectuals, also drawn to New York from the "provinces," brought these currents to the attention of new publics.[8]

With a large heterogeneous elite, an infrastructure of cultural institutions and commercial culture, and close connections with Europe, New York City became one of the few cities in the world in which a great variety of modern art trends could be seen and works bought. Kathryn Dreier's "Société Anonyme" (an exhibition entity which she ran with Marcel Duchamp) focused on European abstraction and what later came to be called conceptual art. American modern artists fared less well than Europeans, since neither Quinn nor Stieglitz (in spite of having married one, Georgia O'Keeffe, and promoting several others) was greatly impressed by most of them. But Gertrude Vanderbilt Whitney, who exhibited the work of American modernists in her Studio Gallery, became the champion of American modernists.

Beyond the activities of patrons and collectors, New York's world of bohemian subcultures was attractive to artists fleeing the stodgy environments of Boston or Philadelphia. New York also provided opportunities for employment in teaching at the numerous art schools that had been located there, and in "satellite trades," such as designing and painting stage sets; illustrating books, magazines, greeting cards, and posters; creating book bindings, toys, women's fashions; interior decoration; and in advertising.[9] Yet very few established museums made modern art part of their permanent collections. It was largely because of this rejection, in the view of several scholars, that during the 1920s and 1930s the majority of American avant-garde artists gave up abstraction as a style.[10]

The reluctance of the establishment Metropolitan Museum of Art to consider accepting contemporary works into their collection led collectors of modern art to adopt the strategy of creating alternative institutions. They founded the Museum of Modern Art (MoMA) in 1929, the Whitney Museum of American Art in 1931, and the Guggenheim Museum in 1939. New York was not the only American city in which modern collections began to go on public display (others were the Phillips Collection in Washington, D.C., and the Barnes Collection in Merion, Pennsylvania), but the three museums in New York became the most prominent in the United States, expansive in their willingness to encompass new works and innovative in display techniques and the kinds of objects they exhibited. Pioneers in and proselytizers for modern art, they started on a small scale, occupying temporary (sometimes borrowed) quarters for a considerable time before erecting more permanent buildings. Beyond serving as loci of elite display, as did older museums, they committed themselves to expanding their public. The MoMA in particular initiated an ambitious loan program and informative lectures for other museums and schools throughout the country.[11]

Since the core of a museum's holdings depended upon what its patrons collected, each became the representative of a relatively coherent set of styles. The Museum of Modern Art had the greatest breadth, inspired by the Quinn works, many of which it eventually obtained: Paris-based Fauves, Cubists, and their immediate ancestors (Cézanne, Van Gogh, Gaugin, Impressionists, and Neo-Impressionists), German Expressionists, Italian Futurists, Russian Modernists, and Surrealists. Solomon Guggenheim's collection, largely composed of German and Russian abstraction, was first introduced to Americans curious about modern art in a tour of the South during the 1930s, before coming to rest in New York City in 1939 as the Museum of Non-Objective Art. Only the Whitney, successor to the Gertrude Whitney's Studio Gallery, devoted itself exclusively to American artists, few of whose works were shown in the other museums. Indeed, in 1940 a group of American artists picketed the Museum of Modern Art to protest what they took to be their exclusion.[12]

Although they differed in taste and occasionally came into conflict, these institutions were not entirely estranged from one another. At times, both the MoMA and the Whitney acted in concert, and even jointly with the Metropolitan. Certain trustees served simultaneously or consecutively on their boards (Nelson Rockefeller, for example, on the MoMA and the Metropolitan). They negotiated accords providing that older works from the MoMA or the Whitney would eventually be offered for purchase or exchange to the Metropolitan. These ties did not bind for long, nor did they extend to the Guggenheim Museum, even if at least one member of the Guggenheim family was a generous donor to the MoMA.[13] But despite some dissension and taste differences, the new museums shared the goal of providing modern art with respectable institutional venues in New York City, giving it a base from which to appeal to potential art lovers. They succeeded in simultaneously establishing the validity of their collections, and of bestowing the title of *art* on the objects which they exhibited.

Whereas the Metropolitan Museum collected and displayed art that was already sacralized, the modern museums had to create legitimacy for the controversial styles that they showed (Picasso's Cubist paintings at the MoMA, Kandinsky's abstractions at the Guggenheim), as well as photographs, architectural drawings, or the "found objects" of Duchamp and other Dadaists.[14] United in pursuing the goal of institutionalizing modernism, the modern art museum, itself a challenge to the academy, came to be viewed as a veritable academy for the "tradition of the new."

The triumph of modernism can be understood aesthetically as the recognition or attribution of excellence to previously poorly regarded art; symbolically, as the association of elite-based aura with these works; and ideologically and politically. It is ideology and power which are central to Serge Guilbaut's interpretation of the hegemony of Abstract Expression—and New York's usurpation of Parisian dominance of the world market in modern art. In his controversial book, *How New York Stole the Idea of Modern Art,* Guilbaut attributes New York's dominance to the State Department's promotion of certain kinds of abstract art, that of New York Abstract Expressionists. He interprets this as a way of contrasting the fruits of liberty with Soviet iron control over art. By exhibiting this difficult work the State Department supported the ideal of America as the bulwark of democracy, where the individual artist could attain the Romantic ideal of spontaneity and freedom.

Guilbaut argues plausibly that because it is capable of being interpreted in a variety of ways, abstract art lends itself to multiple ends. He adduces evidence linking United States Cold War policy to the State Department's support for exhibitions abroad of abstract art. But he assumes more concentration of efforts among art world gatekeepers and political actors than was the case in that highly competitive world; takes account neither of the stagnation of French art over the previous decades nor the prior "usurpation" by London of France's control over the international art auction market; nor explains why American politicians who had labeled modern art "Bolshevik" subsequently supported it.[15]

Guilbaut also does not recognize the importance of artistic changes in New York City in particular, and the United States more generally. Whereas during World War I the presence of émigré avant-gardists such as Duchamp and Picabia had made New York a cosmopolitan art center, once the war ended the artistic center of gravity reverted to Paris. During World War II, however, newly arriving émigré artists found a larger, more active set of American artists, involved in both political and cultural activities, and made more confident by the support they had been receiving from the federal government under New Deal programs. For the first time an indigenous, self-conscious, and original school of avant-garde art, claiming a universal rather than local content, such as that pervading the works of "American scene" painters, emanated from American artists in New York. Whereas locally oriented art tended to be only of marginal interest to the emergent modern art world, the new abstract art that was seen engaging conversation with art history and

European contemporary art gained in stature. Furthermore, even though New York's established museums in the 1940s were still mostly strongholds of conservative taste, the new ones augmented artistic life by their openness to innovative ideas.

Especially influential in this regard was the Museum of Modern Art. As one of the leading New York art dealers, Lawrence Rubin, stated, "Only by going to museums can any student or collector learn what good painting is, and in New York we are very lucky to have the world's most important teaching instrument for modern art, The Museum of Modern Art."[16] The MoMA played an important role in shaping taste for modern art among collectors, acquainting artists with novel art styles and conceptions, and displaying Abstract Expressionism from its earliest days on the New York scene.

Moreover, in the cultural expansiveness of the post–World War II era, the number of New York galleries handling modern art increased from twenty to 300; serious collectors of modern art went from perhaps a dozen to the thousands; and exhibitions by painters rose by 50 percent. Outside New York, new public, corporate, or college museums were created; and according to some estimates, the number of people calling themselves artists grew from 600,000 in 1970 to over a million by 1980. Those who identified themselves as painters and sculptors alone increased from 86,849 in 1970 to 153,162 in 1980.[17] Art "movements" proliferated in the period from the 1940s to 1980, succeeding one another in rapid succession in new, radically different styles.[18]

The modern museums, however, had become relatively less open to new art than they had been to Abstract Expressionist works. Although the Whitney exhibited samples of most of the styles in their Biennials, it acquired them selectively for its permanent collection; the Guggenheim collected even fewer.[19] To exhibit and sell their work, artists turned to new galleries and dealers, especially in out-of-the-way, low-rent neighborhoods, such as SoHo and the East Village, and to regional museums, and corporate collections. If the force of New York's domination of the modern art world can be attributed to its role in attracting and giving recognition to innovations, then this dispersion poses a challenge to the city's standing in the visual arts.[20]

The music world developed differently. American composers of new music in experimental, difficult to grasp modes had little to offer any but the most altruistic patrons, since their works were not collectibles that might grow in value. Rejection by established orchestras left them with little choice but to compose for small ensembles and to teach and perform in universities, some of them in New York. Funds offered by private patrons were scanty, but eventually American composers were able to have access to the funds made available by government agencies and foundations. Because of the nature of the music world, they faced acute need.

New York and Symphonic Music: Institutionalizing the Old

In the United States, symphony orchestras depend on boards of trustees and donors to cover their recurrent deficits. Beyond their patronage, performance of even the most established classical music is based on entrepreneurship in concert bookings, music publishing, and audience development. The connection with the music business is particularly salient in the history of the New York Philharmonic Symphony Orchestra.

Of all the impresarios and musicians who have played active roles in developing New York City as a classical music center, Arthur Judson was perhaps the most important. Judson, like John Quinn, was born in the Midwest, and he began his career there managing performing artists and running a leading professional and business publication, *Musical America*. He became manager of the Philadelphia Orchestra in 1915, and continued to hold that position even after moving to New York in 1934 to manage the Philharmonic more directly. Judson made New York the bookings center for national concert and opera tours. From his base in New York, he advised other orchestras, as well, eventually, as the American Symphony Orchestra League, the professional association and lobbying arm of the nation's symphony orchestras. Finally, and most importantly, Judson brought the communications revolution of radio to the world of classical music.[21]

Through his own agency, Judson booked radio performances of classical music, and eventually became a major force and stockholder, second only to William Paley, of the Columbia Broadcasting System. As a result of Judson's and Paley's influence, the New York Philharmonic became in 1922 the first American orchestra to broadcast regularly on local stations, and the Philadelphia Orchestra the first to broadcast nationally in 1930. Judson gained control of concert bookings nationally by merging New York's independent booking agencies into the Columbia Concerts Corporation and its audience-building arm, Community Concerts. He extended his control to the touring and guest appearances of virtually every major conductor and performer. With his own funds and the financial backing of CBS, he brought about regularity in engagements, payments to performers, and audience development by subscription. Eventually the National Broadcasting Company organized a competing organization, National Concert and Artists Corporation (NCAC), but rather than fight each other openly, the two giants, through gentlemen's agreements, divided up circuits so as not to infringe on each other's territory. At their height, the two agencies controlled live classical music for 2,000 American towns!

Not only conductors and orchestras, but opera companies and most of their solo artists came to be incorporated into the circuits of New York's booking agencies. These agencies also arranged a major share of recording contracts. Judson and Paley controlled Columbia Records in competition with their most prominent rival, David Sarnoff of NBC and RCA Victor.[22] To the extent that American classical musicians were regularly employed, it was largely through the commercial paternalism practiced by Judson, his associates, and his business rivals. The cost of this system to individual artists and most orchestras, in addition to substantial fees, was that they had to perform increasingly standardized repertoires. It also made it more difficult for aspiring musicians to break into the field. Except during the New Deal, when alternative funding from federal sources became available, performers were at their mercy. These monopolistic arrangements began to fray when antitrust actions in 1940 and 1952 put an end to them and enabled a number of new management agencies to open localities to other talent.[23]

New York's position as the nation's communications capital also had enabled Arturo Toscanini, as conductor of the New York Philharmonic Orchestra (1926–1936) and then of a symphony orchestra created for him by NBC (1937–1954), to shape the audience for, and interpretations of, symphonic music in the United States. But despite his celebrity, Toscanini and his orchestras increasingly became pawns in the business world of musical monopoly. Originally Toscanini had been the standard bearer for Judson's New York Philharmonic and performed on CBS radio as well as in leading European opera houses and auditoriums. But eventually he became the property of Sarnoff's NBC and RCA Victor Records.[24]

The growing market for classical records made it advantageous for orchestras to appeal to the widest possible audience, thereby excluding new, difficult music from their repertoires. Nevertheless, although concern for audience-building made symphony orchestras unreceptive to new music, a wealth of other New York institutions made the metropolis the center of avant-garde music in the United States. Modern composers sought alternative venues for performance in music schools or music departments in universities, settlement houses, off-Broadway and Broadway theater, jazz clubs, churches, lofts, and museums. The cross-over possibilities for composers in New York included not only unconventional forms of music (electronic music, popular, and ethnic music), but also other art forms, such as poetry, dance, and painting.[25]

In the 1960s, in the face of increasing demands by musicians for union membership, better working conditions, and an end to managerial arbitrariness, despite opposition by many orchestra trustees to external interference with their control, they had to give in. Orchestra managers were obliged to seek and take advantage of the new sources of support that became available from foundations, the federal government, and corporations. To a large extent the New York cultural institutions played a major role in fashioning these forms of support.

New York and the Growth of Foundation and Government Support

Starting in the late 1950s several New York–based foundations initiated or enlarged their cultural patronage.[26] The Rockefeller Foundation increased its donations to universities and individual creative artists, but its major support went to the Lincoln Center complex, which served as a model for performing arts centers that subsequently were established in other major cities, such as Los Angeles and Washington. At the same time, the Rockefeller Brothers Fund helped promote international cultural exchanges.

The massive entry of the Ford Foundation into the support of arts organizations and individual artists throughout the United States had an immediate impact on cultural life. Through W. McNeil Lowry, who headed its arts and humanities program, the Ford Foundation sought to foster performance arts that surpassed mere commercial entertainment. It launched one of its most striking programs in 1966 by making grants to sixty-one symphony orchestras.[27] With a national orientation and ample means—Lowry controlled a budget of $80 million in 1966 alone—the Ford Foundation helped transform performed art in America from a system dominated by a center surrounded by a wasteland to one characterized by a set of lively regional competitors.[28]

With help from New York political and philanthropic leaders, the city's private foundations also lobbied the national government to provide federal funding for the arts. A precedent had been set by Governor Nelson Rockefeller, himself an important art collector and a force in cultural institutions, who in 1960 secured an appropriation of $50,000 to pay for the assessment of New York State's cultural resources, promote touring companies, and support individual artists. Local arts organizations were required to match New York State Council for the Arts grants with private funds, a procedure that was adopted by other state agencies, and subsequently became the practice of the National Endowment for the Arts.[29] New York Senator Jacob Javits and Congressman (later New York's mayor) John Lindsay played major roles in securing federal support for the arts. The practice of allocating grants through decisions by panels of professional artists and musicians, which was initiated, became a standard mode of operating.[30]

In general, proponents of government funding for the arts were aided by the decades of live symphonic music featured on radio and the weekly broadcasts of the Metropolitan Opera, which brought classical music before a larger audience than ever before. The heritage of Arthur Judson and David Sarnoff in harnessing communications innovations to high art helped persuade the public that symphonic and operatic music deserved public funding. But New York's influence went beyond creating a favorable public climate for culture. Indeed, other regions have tended to resent New York's influence. To meet the objections of states distant from New York and other major cultural centers, the 1965 legislation creating the National Endowment for the Arts (NEA) adopted the principle of "federal-state partnership" under which grants were given to each state to establish state arts agencies. Although this practice was supposed to permit the rest of the states to have a voice in the creation and selection of the arts, until recently it could be argued that the NEA serves as a channel through which the perspective of New York's cultural establishment continues to influence the arts nationally.

The NEA's first director was a New Yorker, Roger Stevens, and, more importantly, its key organization builder was Nancy Hanks, former aide to Nelson Rockefeller and closely associated with the Rockefeller philanthropies. It is true that non–New Yorkers have headed the NEA since 1980, but until recently the only member of the endowment's leadership team with a strong arts background was Deputy Chairman Hugh Southern, a respected member of the New York arts community. It also may be that the panel system the NEA employs in evaluating grant applications serves as a channel of New York influence. It can be hypothesized that panelists who have New York backgrounds, or who hew to definitions of artistic excellence prevalent in the city, are in a position to impose these standards on arts organizations that previously would have lacked much contact with the metropolis and thus had been more likely to develop along idiosyncratic paths.[31] However, currently under debate, the panel system is likely to move from the control of New York–oriented professionals to greater input by lay members. In fact, the political reorientation of NEA leadership in recent years may weaken New York City's impact on national cultural policies.[32]

The infusion of government support has fostered the dissemination of high culture throughout the nation, and has even increased the performance of experimental works.[33] This was an important change from the days of the Judson system, of New York–based commercial control over musical performance that had enforced a rather uniform, middlebrow product. Although most orchestras still conform to the standard repertoire, a few have used government and foundation support to perform contemporary (and difficult) works, even at the risk of losing some of their audience.[34] At the same time, universities, both in New York City and elsewhere, have supported composers working in very experimental modes.[35]

With the rise of foundation and government support, Americans now have more access to culture than ever before. Equally important in producing this outcome are corporate support and the *business* of the arts. Together these forces have changed the cultural geography of the nation, and may threaten New York City's dominance.

New York's Contemporary Cultural Standing

In recent years, New York City has faced strong competition from other localities for manufacturing plants and corporate headquarters. Does a similar pattern show up with regard to art and music? Are the artists—who are the creators of art and music—still being drawn to New York City? Are the marketing forces for their works—galleries, auction houses, impresarios, booking agencies—still centered in the city? Are museums and performance art venues open to their innovations? Answering these questions requires that we look at where artists live; the character and importance of the arts business; and the nature of cultural institutions.

Where Artists Live

Whether or not artists are a necessity for a cultured city, the city seems to have been a necessity for artists. In the United States artists tend to be more urban than the population as a whole and they prefer living in the city's heart rather than its suburbs. Historically, painters have been somewhat more concentrated than musicians, who locate themselves in proximity to performance locales, some of which are in warm resort areas. Actors usually live either near the theater center of New York or the television and movie studios of Hollywood. But according to the studies of James Heilbrun, this pattern seems to have changed recently. He found that whereas performing artists were becoming relatively more concentrated, painters and sculptors were becoming less so.[36]

Nevertheless, they are not scattering all around the country. By 1980 only the West Coast effectively competed with New York for artists: nearly one out of ten lived in New York (102,954), but Los Angeles had reached second place (77,768). These are the only metropolitan areas in which artists, in the broad sense used by the United States Census Bureau, exceed 2 percent of the civilian labor force.[37] Somewhat like the siting of corporate offices, as Heilbrun shows, metropolitan areas that are densely populated, with a high proportion of employment in the service sector, a previously established high level of arts activity, and either a Northeast or West Coast location have lost smaller proportions of artists than those with less density, more manufacturing, a low level of arts activity, and location in the South or Midwest.[38]

The Art Business

Just as the New York metropolitan region has more artists in residence than other areas, it also leads in the concentration of dealerships—209. In contrast, the 205 art dealers in California are distributed among Los Angeles–Long Beach, San Francisco–Oakland, San Diego, and other cities. Moreover, New York's metropolitan area by itself accounted for nearly three times the total value of sales in Los Angeles–Long Beach and San Francisco–Oakland combined. Compared to the Los Angeles metropolitan area, New York accounted for nearly five times as much in sales. The economist, Leslie Singer, has shown that despite premature overexposure of too many artists, "other things equal, the path to a museum show is shorter for artists entering through a New York gallery."[39]

As intermediaries between artists and collectors, art dealers see no need to locate near artists. But they must be convenient to collectors, many of them foreign, and to corporate buyers who are drawn to New York. As Diana Crane shows, "the New York art world retained its status as the ultimate arbiter of artistic success." She attributes this to the dominance of a few (eleven) galleries which controlled access to the auction market, and show no sign of losing that control in spite of the growth of regional art museums and art collecting by corporations.[40]

It is important to recognize that regional museums, corporate collectors, dealers, and galleries do not seek the same kinds of art as do their counterparts in the New York City area. Rosanne Martorella's study of corporate collecting, which amounted to an estimated $40 million in 1986, indicates that corporations exhibit different "taste cultures" that correspond to regional location, size, and clientele. Large firms with international clients collect works of internationally known artists from their clients' countries, or internationally known Americans, mostly in avant-garde styles; smaller local firms prefer works by regional artists. The major northeastern corporations are the clients of the leading SoHo and Upper East Side galleries. Regionally oriented firms, by contrast, have little to do with the New York art world, and the styles they collect are marginal to international trends. If they compete at all, it is with local or regional museums. Thus in painting, despite competition from other regions of the United States, as well as from Europe, great reputations are still made in New York.

New York's preeminence persists for classical music as well, and for similar reasons. The fact is that New York City retains its centrality for the business and management of important music bookings and recording contracts.[41]

The Significance of Location for Cultural Institutions

Although New York City's importance in the arts persists, the effect of spatial location on cultural activities is less clear today than in the past. As early as 1969, Sotheby's in London dealt with an increasingly global market by sending important works for auction not only to New York but also to Los Angeles and Houston where probable buyers might see them, before selling them in London. In the 1970s, Geneva, Zurich, and (as the yen rose in value) Tokyo were added to the tour. Still, despite the relative increase in importance of other nations' economies, art sales were frequently concluded in New York.

Although radically divergent art styles seem to be nearly as common as seasonal changes in fashion, museums change only slowly. Their collections may be loaned, but they are rarely sold. Their creative and managerial talent and expertise travel, but they are not as portable as ordinary goods and services. Moreover, in the very process of competing, museums are drawn into cooperative relationships with one another—for example, in organizing traveling exhibitions. In seeking to secure prestigious exhibitions, museums have two resources with which to bargain: their own collections and the connections of their trustees, curators, and administrators to other museums in the United States and abroad. Eliminating competitors may be rational in certain economic or political domains, but it is not the way the world of culture functions.

On the contrary, the very standing of cultural institutions depends on the existence of friendly rivals.

As modern art museums are founded in other cities, as works of modern European artists compete for exhibition and sale in the United States, and as previously conservative museums acquire modern art, the dominance of New York as the creator of value in contemporary art has become diffused. But with the founding of the New Museum of Contemporary Art and a number of alternative museums, the pattern of creating new museums when old ones hesitate to accept unfamiliar art continues unabated in New York as well. Virtually all art, including non-Western as well as European art, whose creators and supporters aspire both to a place in art history and to worldwide sales, comes to New York.[42]

When it comes to music and other performing arts, despite the rise of regional orchestras, theaters, and dance companies, New York continues to exert a pervasive influence in the United States and abroad. New York's Philharmonic Symphony is comparable in size, quality, salaries, audience, and revenues to other leading orchestras, such as Boston's and Philadelphia's.[43] Symphony orchestras have become international institutions, vying for the same soloists, players, and conductors, touring in one another's home cities, and signing contracts with transnational record companies. The stakes are at least as high as they were in the days when Judson and Sarnoff were fighting for total control over the classical music business. Presently, multinationals play an important role in classical recordings, but the technological innovations that have changed the structure of the recording industry have reduced the dominance of the top few firms.[44] As Japanese and Korean manufacturers of musical instruments have grown in importance, like their predecessors, they are increasingly involving themselves in music patronage and support of new musicians, including those from their own countries.

New York may be less likely to be the originator of Broadway productions than was previously the case, but although some regional theaters produce original works, most plays start on Broadway, off-Broadway, or off-off-Broadway. Even when productions are imported from England, a New York run is vital for the success of tours, recordings, and other tie-ins.[45] Therefore, despite cultural developments in other regions of the United States and in other countries, New York continues, as Richard Gilman puts it, to be "the theatrical judge for the nation . . . where *big* reputations are made, or at least confirmed."[46] The same may be said for other art forms whose practitioners continue to depend for world class standing on New York's critics.

This overview suggests that within the United States, New York continues to lead in the creation of new works of art and music, in the exhibition and performance of works created everywhere, in accumulated collections, and influence on arts industries. But what may once have been a cultural system of dominance has become a multicentric network, functioning through relatively stable interactions with other major centers. A lodestone for artists and musicians, individual and corporate collectors, and culture consumers, with its dense and varied cultural infrastructure, New York City remains a major player in the realm of culture, both in the United States and throughout the world.

Notes

1. Space constraints have led me to exclude from consideration those art forms that seek to make a profit, such as theater, dance, jazz, and commercial art, even if some of them are now subsidized as not-for-profit art forms.
2. See my argument in "Displayed Art and Performed Music: Selective Innovation and the Structure of Artistic Media" in *Sociological Quarterly* 21 (Spring 1980): 219–231.
3. In nineteenth-century New York and other cities, instrument makers supported concerts, constructed concert halls (e.g., Steinway and Aeolian halls), and organized concert tours by virtuoso musicians who endorsed their products. Concerning New York's importance in manufacturing instruments, see Lampard, Eric E., "The New York Metropolis in Transformation: History and Prospect. A Study in Historical Particularity" in Ewers, Hans-Jurgen, et al., eds., *The Future of the Metropolis* (New York: Walter de Gruyter and Co., 1986), p. 99, ft. 29.
4. For an account of the deal with the redoubtable "Boss" Tweed, see Coleman, Laurence Vail, *The Museum in America* (Washington, DC: American Association of Museums, 1939), 3 vols.; and Tomkins, Calvin, *Merchants and Masterpieces: The Story of the Metropolitan Museum of Art* (New York: E.P. Dutton, 1973), pp. 40–41.
5. See DiMaggio, Paul J., "Cultural Entrepreneurship in Nineteenth-Century Boston" in *Media, Culture and Society* 4 (1982): 33–50 and Sablosky, Irving L., *American Music* (Chicago: University of Chicago Press, 1969). Although the New York Philharmonic Symphony (originally two separate orchestras) was founded before the Metropolitan Museum of Art, it depended on ticket sales.
6. Zolberg, "Displayed Art and Performed Music."
7. For an analysis of this process, see Zolberg, Vera L., "New Art, New Patrons: Coincidence or Causality in the Twentieth-Century Avant-Garde" in Bulkova, Maya and Tatyana Mineva, *Contributions to the Sociology of the Arts* (Sofia, Bulgaria: Institute for Culture, 1983), pp. 309–335. J.P. Morgan, who

lived in England for many years, spent an estimated £10 million on art between 1900 and his death in 1913 alone. England's imposition of death duties induced him to move his collection to New York. For details, see Faith, Nicholas, *The Revolution in the Art Market* (London: Hodden and Stoughton, 1985), p. 28. Morgan's view of New York as an extension of Europe is noted in chapter 4 of this book by James R. Kurth.

8. Zolberg, "New Art, New Patrons"; Goodrich, Lloyd, *The Decade of the Armory Show* (New York: Whitney Museum of American Art, 1963); and Westheim, Arthur Frank, *The New York Little Renaissance: Iconoclasm, Modernism and Nationalism in American Culture, 1908–1917* (New York: New York University Press, 1976).
9. Morgan, H. Wayne, *New Muses: Art in American Culture, 1865–1920* (Norman, OK: University of Oklahoma Press, 1978), pp. 23–24, shows how New York's commercial possibilities permitted artists, however precariously, to support themselves. Advertising became increasingly important in the early decades of the twentieth century. As late as 1926, New York's advertising agencies were still challenged by rivals in Chicago and Philadelphia (where two of the three largest firms were headquartered), but out-of-town agencies soon established branch offices in the city. As Roland Marchand observes, "Madison Avenue" became a metaphor for advertising expertise in uptown Manhattan. During that decade corporate mergers brought more companies under Wall Street influence, and along with the advent of radio and the growth of national magazines, this served to centralize national advertising in New York City. See his *Advertising the American Dream: Making Way for Modernity, 1920–1940* (Berkeley: University of California Press, 1985), pp. 6–7.
10. On this subject, see Goodrich, *The Decade of the Armory Show*, p. 40; Ashton, Dore, *The New York School: A Cultural Reckoning* (New York: Viking Press, 1973); and Rose, Barbara, *American Art Since 1900: A Critical History* (New York: Praeger, 1973), pp. 112–113. A shift away from abstractionism is noticeable among a large number of European painters as well. See Kramer, Hilton, "MoMA, How Could You? The Forgetful Museum" in *New York Observer*, April 13, 1992, p. 1.
11. For the history of its first half-century, see Lynes, Russell, *Good Old Modern: An Intimate Portrait of the Museum of Modern Art* (New York: Atheneum, 1973), especially p. 168.
12. This event is covered by Rose, *American Art Since 1900*, p. 148.
13. Lynes, *Good Old Modern*, p. 439.
14. The MoMA led other museums by incorporating into its collection movies and industrial design in addition to painting and sculpture. This is not to say that museums of design had not existed before (the Musée des Arts Décoratifs in France, or the Victoria and Albert in England, for example). The difference is that the conception of art itself had been exploded by the avant-garde experiments of artists such as Marcel Duchamp, and the

rethinking of art by movements such as the Bauhaus. By the time Alfred Barr included a 35-cent Woolworth's potato peeler in a design show, the aesthetic idea had come to permeate the ordinary, not only handcrafts, following William Morris, but industrial mass-produced items as well.

15. See Guilbaut, Serge, *How New York Stole the Idea of Modern Art* (Chicago: University of Chicago Press, 1983). For the analysis of the shift of the auction market, see Faith, *The Revolution in the Art Market*, p. 65.
16. Rubin joined Armand Hammer's Knoedler & Co., of which he became president and director in 1977. His statement is cited in De Coppet, Laura, and Alan Jones, *The Art Dealers* (New York: Clarkson N. Potter, 1984), p. 78.
17. Gross estimates are suggested in Crane, Diana, *The Transformation of the Avant-Garde: The New York Art World*, 1940–1985 (Chicago: University of Chicago Press, 1987), pp. 3–6. For greater detail, see NEA, "Where Artists Live: 1970," Research Div. Rept. #5. Washington, DC: 1977. It should be noted that the category "artist," employed by the NEA, is extremely heterogeneous: authors, designers, musicians/composers, actors/directors, painters/sculptors, craft artists, artist printmakers, photographers, dancers, unspecified performers, radio/TV and other announcers, architects and teachers of art, drama, and music in higher education (NEA, Res. Div. Note #5, Sept. 5, 1983). In the early 1960s, in an attempt to estimate only "fine artists," Hall Winslow arrived at a figure somewhere between 7,500 and 15,000, of whom two-thirds lived in New York. See Winslow, Hall, *Artists in the Metropolis* (Brooklyn: Pratt Institute, 1964), p. 14. James Heilbrun, working from NEA data sets, found that the numbers of just painters and sculptors had increased by 56 percent, as against 60 percent growth of artists overall; see Heilbrun, James, "Growth and Geographic Distribution of the Arts in the U.S." Paper presented at Conference on Cultural Economics and Planning, Avignon, May 1986.
18. The most prominent styles noted by Diana Crane in *The Transformation of the Avant-Garde* are Pop, Minimalism, Figurative Realism, Photorealism, Pattern, and Neo-Expressionism. Several others of varying importance may be added: Op Art; other visual forms not intended for museums (Christo's wrappings, and other site-specific or ephemeral forms such as "happenings"), many of which had museum or sales potential in the form of drawings or photographs.
19. The Jewish Museum, which did not have a substantial collection of modern art, and the Guggenheim were instrumental in launching Minimalist and Pop art, according to Crane in *The Transformation of the Avant-Garde*, p. 119.
20. On the development of SoHo as an art center, see Zukin, Sharon, *Loft Living: Culture and Capital in Urban Change* (New Brunswick, NJ: Rutgers University Press, 1987).
21. As James L. Baughman notes in chapter 6, radio rapidly became the dominant mass medium for music in the early 1920s.
22. For a detailed analysis of this celebrated rivalry, see Horowitz, Joseph, *Un-*

derstanding Toscanini: How He Became an American Culture-God and Helped Create a New Audience for Old Music (New York: Alfred A. Knopf, 1987).

23. Hart, Philip, *Orpheus in the New World, The Symphony Orchestra As an American Cultural Institution* (New York: W.W. Norton, 1973), pp. 96–113. Hart points out that, although it gave many greater opportunity, the transformation created greater uncertainty for performers.
24. Significantly, once Toscanini left the Philharmonic, Judson replaced him with the younger, less demanding, more manipulable John Barbirolli. Similarly, after the dominant personality of Leopold Stokowski was gone from the Philadelphia Orchestra, Judson selected as his successor Eugene Ormandy, who was much easier to manage. For an analysis of the decline of innovativeness in the Philadelphia Orchestra, see Arian, Edward, *Bach, Beethoven, and Bureaucracy: The Case of the Philadelphia Orchestra* (Tuscaloosa, AL: University of Alabama Press, 1971).
25. For an overview of these developments, see Wallock, Leonard, ed., *New York: Cultural Capital of the World, 1940–1965* (New York: Rizzoli, 1988). Particularly informative chapters in this collection are Wallock's Introduction, Dore Ashton's "The City and the Visual Arts," Lynn Garafola's "Toward an American Dance: Dance in the City," and John Rockwell's "New York's Music."
26. DiMaggio shows that the Carnegie Foundation had been the leading patron of the arts for well over two decades, but virtually stopped those activities in 1943. See his "Support for the Arts from Independent Foundations" in DiMaggio, Paul J., ed., *Nonprofit Enterprise in the Arts: Studies in Mission and Constraint* (New York: Oxford University Press, 1986), p. 116.
27. DiMaggio, *Ibid.*, p. 117.
28. See Ross, Laura, ed., *Theatre Profile 7: The Illustrated Guide to America's Nonprofit Professional Theatres* (New York: Theatre Communications Group, 1986), pp. 24–27. According to Ross, pp. ix, 27, 34, before the Ford Foundation's program, only four regional nonprofit theaters existed, whereas by 1987 at least 199 theaters had come into being across the country. Of the $60 million for theater, one-third went to eight troupes: two in New York, two in Los Angeles, and one each in Minnesota, Louisiana, Oklahoma, and Connecticut.
29. Netzer, Dick, *The Subsidized Muse: Public Support for the Arts in the United States* (New York: Cambridge University Press, 1978), p. 80.
30. Biddle, Livingston, *Our Government and the Arts: A Perspective from Inside* (New York: American Council for the Arts, 1988).
31. I owe the hypotheses in this paragraph and some of the language to a personal communication from Paul DiMaggio.
32. The proposal to include more lay members on the panels is found in the recommendations of the Independent Commission, "A Report to Congress on the National Endowment for the Arts." Washington, D.C.: Sept. 1990,

pp. 74–75. President Bush's appointment of John E. Frohnmeyer from Oregon to head the NEA was considered an attempt to exercise greater control over the sexual and religious content in federally supported art. A moderate, Frohnmeyer was later dismissed and replaced by an acting head from Buffalo, who immediately overrode the strong recommendations of a peer panel because of alleged sexual content (see "Arts Panel Protests the Denial of 2 Grants" in *The New York Times*, May 16, 1992, p. 11).

33. In the case of dance, for example, the NEA gave a substantial grant to New York's Joffrey dance company, matched by the Washington State Arts Commission, for a summer residency in Seattle-Tacoma, and supported Martha Graham's national tour. Whereas the dance audience of the nation in the 1960s was approximately 1 million, mostly in New York, two decades later, Livingston Biddle estimates it at 15 million, mostly outside of New York. Comparable growth in opera throughout the country has resulted from federal and foundation funding. See Biddle, *Our Government and the Arts*, p. 244.
34. Opera companies also have benefited. When the Ford Foundation helped fund the New York City Opera in 1957, it provided money to commission contemporary operas. See Sablosky, *American Music*, p. 182. The NEA added an opera component in 1972 and established a separate opera-musical theater program in 1978.
35. Rockwell, "New York's Music," pp. 224–225.
36. Heilbrun, "Growth and Geographic Distribution of the Arts," 1986; and his "The Distribution of Arts Activity among U.S. Metropolitan Areas." Paper presented at Fifth International Conference on Cultural Economics, Ottawa, Canada, September, 1988.
37. See ft. 17 for the census definition. Nearly 20 percent of all *employed* artists lived in the metropolitan areas of New York or Los Angeles, but this varied with the art form. Actors were the most localized (New York and California) and the most urban (95 percent); painters (including commercial artists and restorers) resided largely in three metropolitan areas (New York, Chicago, and Los Angeles). Musicians and composers (undifferentiated among popular and classical) were more dispersed, with California slightly ahead of New York. See NEA 1978; NEA 1983; and Winslow, *Artists in the Metropolis*, p. 98.
38. Heilbrun, "Growth and Geographic Distribution of the Arts," 1986.
39. NEA. Research Division Note #19 (Jan. 7, 1987) on Retail Art Dealers. See Singer, Leslie P., "Odds on Probability of Selecting Winners Among Gallery Artists: A Multiple Logit Analysis" (forthcoming in the *Journal of Cultural Economics*).
40. Crane, *The Transformation of the Avant-Garde*, p. 136.
41. Its impact pervades not only classical music, but most varieties of performed arts. Existing management infrastructure of Tin Pan Alley days has gener-

ally become adapted to the new music forms of rock and soul songwriters, and classical music management continues to influence performed music by American and European artists and ensembles; Rockwell, "New York's Music," pp. 232, 235.

42. For an important example of innovation and reformulation of African art, see Vogel, Susan, ed., *Africa Explores: 20th Century African Art* (New York: Center for African Art and Munich: Prestel-Verlag, 1991).
43. Based on reporting by the American Symphony Orchestra League, 1980–1981, in *The New York Times*, Nov. 2, 1988.
44. Murph, A. Franklin, "The Classical Record Industry in the United States," in *The Journal of Cultural Economics* 8 (June 1984): 81–89. Murph points out that the two companies, Victor (since 1929, RCA) and Columbia (now CBS), were able to dominate the classical record industry because of the complexity and expense of the recording process itself. Tape recording opened the way to less heavily capitalized firms, so that by 1954 there were 200 companies both in classical and popular recording in the United States alone. Because the big two controlled contracts, independents did most of their recordings in Europe, where fees were lower, thereafter peddling their tapes to one of the United States companies for manufacturing the records. LP technology led to the export of European records to the United States. The four companies that now dominate the industry (Polygram, Capital EMI, RCA, and Columbia—now Sony), however, did not control as great a percentage of the field as the pre-1950 giants. Even the distribution bottleneck of classical recordings is being overcome by development of nationwide mail-order services. The impact of technological innovations such as CD's and digital tape is still uncertain.
45. According to the study of the Commission for Cultural Affairs of the City of New York, in the two years between 1974 and 1976 alone, twenty-eight New York performing arts organizations toured 501 cities, and eleven toured 110 cities in 41 countries. See "New York as a National Cultural Resource: A Report to the American People," n.d.
46. See Wallock, *New York: Cultural Capital of the World*, p. 210.

8

The National Influence of Jewish New York

Nathan Glazer

New York stands apart from the other great capitals—London, Paris, Tokyo, and add as many more as you wish—in that its population diverges sharply from the nation of which it is the largest and chief city. If New York is seen by the hinterland as something of a "comprador" city, perched on the country's eastern perimeter and diverging from it in culture, politics, and economics, this is not simply because New York is a cosmopolitan city that arouses the suspicion of provincials and a financial center that is viewed warily by those who grow or process material things. All this is the case with New York City, and in varying degrees other great capitals. But there is something more.

New York is a Jewish city. An ethno-religious group that comprises at best 2.5 percent of the American population has made up a quarter or more of the population of New York for the better part of this century. The issue of course is not simply that New York is ethnically unrepresentative. It is that a marked distinctiveness in political orientations, occupational pursuits, and cultural tastes distinguishes American Jews from their fellow Americans. When this Jewish distinctiveness reaches the concentration that it does in New York, a "spin"—to use a term current in today's political wars—is placed on the way New York influences the nation's politics, economy, and culture.

In politics, the influence of New York City Jews has been and remains markedly liberal, despite the unpopularity into which that term has fallen. In the economy, the distinctive Jewish role has been in the areas of the new. Initially this meant the fringes of the economy—as in merchandising, or Hollywood. But in the postwar world such areas of Jewish investment as entertainment became as large as the steel industry and were generally more prosperous. Jews also played a remarkably prominent role in developing the new financial mechanisms and practices—such as leveraged buy-outs—that restructured the largest companies in the United States in the 1980s and transformed the American economy. In culture, the distinctive role of Jews has been as advocates of the avant-garde, whatever that avant-garde happened to be at any time. The term may have a rather arrière-garde sound today, but there is always a fringe of experimentation in the arts, music, writing, criticism, academic culture—and Jews are to be found prominently there.

The interplay among these roles is complex, but all three areas have been characterized by substantial Jewish influence in New York, and through that on the nation, during the postwar period. I am not arguing that this influence has been uniform in all three areas throughout the postwar period, nor is there any guarantee that it will continue in the future. Indeed, I believe one can detect both in politics and in culture a passing of the zenith of Jewish influence. These are large assertions, scarcely to be proved, but at least they can be argued with some data and set on the table for further discussion.

From Prewar Marginality to Postwar Influence

Until the 1950s Jews had modest influence in New York City, let alone the nation. East European Jews entered a society in which anti-Semitism had become endemic in the upper classes. This scarcely mattered to the immigrants, who had a ways to go before they could be affected by the anti-Semitism that limited Jews in elite colleges, corporate business, law firms, hospitals, and elite residential areas and clubs. It did, however, bother well-to-do German Jews, who in the early twentieth century formed the American Jewish Committee to protect Jewish interests, domestic and foreign.

The East European immigrants who swelled the Jewish population of New York from 60,000 in 1880 to almost 2 million in the 1930s were for the most part workers and operators of small businesses. Their children avidly pursued higher education. They became a majority of the students in the free City College in the first decade of the twentieth century.[1] By the second decade, the number of East European Jews seeking and gaining admission to New York City's two major private universities, Columbia and New York University, already alarmed them.[2] Much in the history of these institutions in the 1920s, 1930s, and 1940s can only be understood in the context of an effort to "repel the invasion," to use Harold Wechsler's term. In various ways Jewish admissions were limited in the elite undergraduate colleges, and in particular in the medical schools. Jews could not fight this discrimination effectively until the late 1940s.

In the 1930s, there was an endemic anti-Semitism which reached all the way from the city's social peaks to its abysses, and anti-Semitic demagoguery and discriminatory practices flourished.[3] Concern over anti-Semitism was such that in 1936 the editors of *Fortune* devoted a special issue to the Jews, and in particular to charges of their inordinate economic power. They found Jews totally absent from commercial banking and insurance, automobiles, steel, petroleum, chemicals production, advertising, and journalism. Twenty-five years later the situation had not changed markedly. As I observed in *Beyond the Melting Pot:*

> In the great banks, insurance companies, public utilities, railroad and corporation head offices that are located in New York, and in the Wall Street law firms, few Jews are to be found. . . . An American Jewish Committee study of graduates of the Harvard Business School shows that the non-Jewish graduates outnumber Jewish graduates in executive positions in the leading American corporations by better than 30 to 1. John Slawson, the head of the Committee, has asserted, 'Jews constitute less than one-half of 1 percent of the total executive personnel in leading American industrial companies.' This he compared to the fact that Jews form about 8 per cent of the college-trained in the country. The Anti-Defamation League has studied employees making more than $10,000 a year. . . . in seven insurance companies. While 5.4 per cent were Jewish, they were mostly engaged not in the home offices but in sales jobs. . . . Even the small number of Jews employed in home offices tend to be technicians—actuaries, physicians, attorneys, accountants. The Anti-Defamation League has also studied . . . eight of the largest banks in the city. Of 844 vice presidents and above, only 30 are Jews. . . . Four of the banks did not have a single Jewish officer. Of the top ten social clubs in the city in 1959, only one had Jewish members.[4]

In city politics, of course, Jewish weight was greater: that after all is based on voting population, as well as numbers of lawyers and financial backing. But in the 1930s and 1940s the Jewish community was split among Democrats, Republicans (the dominant allegiance of the German Jews), Socialists and their heirs (American Labor party and Liberal party), and Communists. Much Jewish political energy went into small radical parties and the building of the Jewish trades unions. It is a startling fact that in this city of huge Jewish population the first Jewish mayor did not take office until 1973. Fiorello La Guardia was half-Jewish, and the Jews of New York City knew it, but neither his mother, a Trieste Jew, nor he, raised in army camps where his bandmaster father served, were representative of the Jewish community. (Nor of the Italian community: he was Protestant.) Until La Guardia became mayor in 1934, and began to use in much larger measure criteria of competence and job experience rather than party loyalty in making appointments, Jews received less than 10 percent of major mayoral appointments.[5]

While Jews were elected to Congress from majority Jewish districts, Jewish political influence scarcely matched their numbers. In New York State, it took a fierce battle to get a law enacted in 1948 banning discrimination on grounds of religion in higher education.[6] Preceding and during the war, Jewish politicians and organizations scarcely dared to make much noise about the exclusion of persecuted Jews from the United States by the immigration laws. This tragic episode has been studied in detail by many, and it is clear that Jewish influence was minimal.[7] In the varied fields of culture the Jewish role was hardly evident. Publishing was almost entirely non-Jewish in the 1930s and 1940s. The figures who were later to be summed up as the "New York intellectuals" were for the most part unemployed radicals, and had been heard of by nobody. Lionel Trilling and Sidney Hook stood out in the group as having academic jobs but scarcely secure ones.[8]

The Jewish role in New York City's elite cultural life was also limited. The opera had a major German-Jewish banker patron, but Jewish trustees were scarce or absent from the symphony orchestra, the Metropolitan Museum of Art, the board of Columbia University, and other institutions. As was characteristic for a rising proletarian group, they played a much larger role in the popular theater, popular music ("Tin Pan Alley"), and boxing—the amusements of the masses. There was a time in the 1930s when most of the holders of "world" boxing championships in the various weight classes were Jews. In the field of commercial popular music—music for radio, Broadway musicals, and Hollywood—Jews were preeminent. Some of these Jewish songwriters and composers are now part of the history of American popular music: George Gershwin, Jerome Kern, Irving Berlin, Oscar Hammerstein, Richard Rodgers, Lorenz Hart.

Despite the outcry by influential demagogues such as Father Coughlin over Jewish influence in Wall Street, the economy and popular culture during the 1930s, Jewish influence then and during World War II was minimal. Despite the presence of some important German-Jewish banking firms—Kuhn Loeb, Lehman Brothers—Jews played a decidedly minor role in investment banking. There were only three areas in the economy where Jewish influence was marked: clothing manufacturing, department stores, and entertainment.[9] These areas of influence were hardly the heights of the economy.

One can, of course, think of individual Jews who wielded substantial national or local influence before the 1950s: Justices Louis D. Brandeis and Felix Frankfurter, Governor Herbert Lehman, Walter Lippmann, and Robert Moses, and some advisers of President Roosevelt. In contrast with what was to happen in the post–World War II world, however, this seems minor. One may also note that Lippmann and Moses did not acknowledge their Jewish origins, and that Brandeis was almost furtive in his involvement in Jewish affairs. Finally, all were German Jews—from a community that was a very small part of the Jewish population. The overwhelming majority of Jews, the immigrants from Eastern Europe, had no sense of wielding substantial power, and regarded themselves as an aggrieved minority. In view of the extent of anti-Semitism, they had considerable justification for doing so.

Although Jewish numbers in New York did not translate into major influence in the city, let alone the nation, in the 1930s and 1940s, this was all to change with great rapidity in the postwar world. Anti-Semitism, which had for so long been a norm of opinion, expression, and practice among the upper and upper-middle classes, and epidemic in the institutions they controlled, rapidly became unfashionable. The Jewish advantage in education became a significant basis for advancement in the professions and higher education, particularly with the enormous expansion of colleges and universities in the 1950s and 1960s. Laws against discrimination in education, employment, and housing in New York assisted in this rapid change.

There was a rise of Jewish influence, on the basis of advanced education, increasing income, increasing acceptability within a variety of institutions, but our thesis is that this was not simply influence by persons who happened to be Jews: In each key area of influence a distinctive weight was brought to bear, a distinctive twist. There was not only influence by individual Jews, but rather influence that bore distinctive characteristics flowing from a Jewish experience that marked Jews off from their fellow Americans.

Demography

New York's Jewish population goes back almost to New Amsterdam's beginnings in the seventeenth century, but was hardly major until the twentieth century. Jews were perhaps 5 percent of the city population in 1880 on the eve of the mass East European Jewish immigration. This 5 percent was in small part Sephardic (Spanish and Portuguese Jews, by way of the Netherlands, Brazil, England, and other countries), in great part German in origin. The great migration from the Czarist Russian Empire, eastern parts of the Austro-Hungarian Empire, and from Romania, began in the 1880s. New York's Jews were 10 percent of the population in 1890. By 1900 New York City was 17 percent Jewish, by 1915 more than a quarter Jewish.[10]

Jews were the largest single ethnic-religious element of New York City's population between the 1920s and the 1960s. As the black and Puerto Rican elements in New York City's population rose in the 1940s and 1950s, Jews declined as a proportion of New York City's population, but remained the largest single component of the white non-Hispanic population: 30 percent in 1940, and 31 percent in 1955. Even as the white population hemorrhaged to the suburbs and immigrants poured into New York, Jews still, in 1981, made up 31 percent of the city's non-Hispanic white population.[11]

It was not only that there were so many Jews in New York City that led to the identification of the city with Jews during the early decades of the twentieth century: it was also the fact there were relatively few Jews anywhere else. New York City's Jews made up almost half of the Jewish population of the entire country in the 1920s and 1930s. The identification of "Jew" with "New Yorker" was thus not unnatural. When Jesse Jackson referred to New York City as "Hymietown" in the presidential campaign of 1984, he was using a characterization that was not common, but the underlying reality was familiar to most Americans. When they said "New Yorker," their image a good deal of the time was that of a New York Jew.

The Jews of the rest of the country were not very different from the Jews of New York City. Most non–New York Jews had entered the country as immigrants through New York, had lived there for a while or had relatives who lived there, or in search of opportunity would possibly live there again at some time in the future. Expatriate New York City Jews—and there were many in the retirement communities of Florida, in the movie and clothing and real-estate industries of booming California, scattered through the university towns of the country as these exploded in the 1950s and 1960s—stuck out like a sore thumb, with their New York accents ("Brooklynese" it was often called), their liberal politics, their passion for corned beef and bagels and lox, their nostalgia for New York. The reduction of New York City's prominence in the American Jewish population thus did very little to reduce the popular association of "Jew" with "New Yorker." That more Jews now lived in Miami or Los Angeles, Ann Arbor, Columbus, Bloomington, or Urbana-Champaign, only strengthened the association of New York City with Jews: they had brought the city with them. The major concentrations of Jews outside of New York City were in large measure colonies of New York City Jews.

The calculation of the Jewish population of the United States in the 1985 *American Jewish Year Book* by state[12] showed New York State far in the lead, with 10.6 percent of its population Jewish, New Jersey next with 5.8 percent, Florida next with 5.2 percent. New Jersey's Jews are in large measure an extension of the New York City metropolitan Jewish complex. The concentrations of Jews in Florida (559,000) and California (793,000), the two states next to New York (1,880,000) in Jewish population size, are in large measure colonies of New York City, still organizing circles of graduates of Brooklyn's Erasmus High School and other organizations symbolizing their link to New York.

Demography is not destiny, or not the only element in destiny, but it is important. In 1981, it was estimated there were 1,159,000 Jews in New York City and that they comprised almost one-sixth of New York City's population; another 672,000 Jews lived in Westchester, Nassau, and Suffolk counties. But Jews were far more prominent than that if one takes into account measures of potential influence. In key Manhattan they made up more than a fifth of the population. Jews were considerably older than the area population. In the eight-county area (the city, plus Nassau, Suffolk, and Westchester), 29 percent of Jews were over 55, against 23 percent of the entire population; only 16 percent were under 14 years of age, against 21 percent of the whole population. They were better educated: 24 percent of male household heads had graduate degrees, 35 percent bachelors, 15 percent some college; only 26 percent were high school graduates or less, and one may assume that most of these were to be found among the 17 percent of adults who were foreign born. In Manhattan, a startling 36 percent of the male household heads had a graduate degree, 39 percent had a four-year college degree, another 13 percent some college. Only 12 percent had a high school education or less. In contrast, in the United States generally, only one in six adults over 25 had four years of college or more. Among Jewish male heads of households, 4 percent in the New York metropolitan area had M.D. degrees, another 3 percent Ph.D. or Ed.D. degrees.[13]

This educational advantage translated into an income advantage. The Jewish median income of $34,000 far exceeded the national median of $20,000. A more properly limited comparison suggests an 8 percent advantage in earnings of urban Jews over urban non-Jews in the states of New York, New Jersey, and Connecticut.[14]

Jews are thus older, better educated, better off. They thus vote in large numbers, provide financial support for—and influence—political candidates, are concentrated in business, the professions, and the law, and exhibit a high concentration among elites generally. How high this concentration is may be startling. In the late 1960s, Jews made up 10 percent of faculties in American colleges and universities, but more like one-third of faculties in high quality institutions and an even higher percentage in law schools and medical schools.[15] A recent research undertaking showed, not surprisingly, that only 1 percent of the military elite (high level officers) were Jewish. But Jews comprised 8 percent of the business elite, 21 percent of the federal civil service elite, 26 percent of the media elite, 40 percent of corporate lawyers, 48 percent of a "public interest" elite, 58 percent of the makers of prime-time television, and 59 percent of the makers of high-drawing movies.[16] All this means a high potential for influence in the political arena, the national economy, and the cultural realm.

Politics

The story in politics is perhaps the clearest. Until the 1930s, as I have pointed out, Jewish numbers did not do much to give Jews major weight in the affairs of New York City, let alone the nation. But New York City Jews had a number of bases of power and prominence on which to expand their role in the city, to the point where the reflection of that role in the nation became significant.

Jews created and led the major needles-trades unions—the International Ladies Garment Workers Union, the Amalgamated Clothing Workers Union, and lesser but not insignificant unions in New York, such as the Hatters and Furriers. These were ideological unions, the first three Socialist or social-democratic, the fourth Communist. The Jewish labor movement played an important role in New York City and New York State. With the election of Franklin D. Roosevelt in 1932, and the simultaneous election of Herbert Lehman as governor of New York State, Jewish organized labor leaders, who had been embroiled so long in factional struggle between Socialists and Communists, achieved positions of influence. Their members were still so attuned to regarding the Democratic party organization in New York City with distaste that the American Labor party had to be organized to give them a line on which they could vote for Roosevelt and Lehman (and also La Guardia—Jewish workers would not very likely vote on the Republican line). When the American Labor party was taken over by Communists and fellow travelers, or at least those who tolerated them, the Liberal party was formed. These were purely local manifestations. But Jewish labor leaders played a national role when the CIO was formed and big labor became a substantial force in national politics in the Roosevelt years, and beyond.

The decline in the numbers of Jewish workers and trade unionists in New York City after World War II was precipitous. Even as retired workers, however, their political weight was formidable. The shift from proletarian to middle class did nothing to change the pattern of Jewish allegiances and voting. The Jewish teacher or accountant or dentist or lawyer or doctor voted pretty much as his clothing-trades father voted. Why Jewish voting behavior and political outlook did not change as Jews rose socio-economically remains one of the perplexing questions of American political sociology. But the fact remains, as Milton Himmelfarb once summed it up, Jews have the income of Episcopalians and vote like Puerto Ricans.[17]

Is the explanation Jewish religious ethics? Hardly. The Orthodox tend to be the least liberal Jews. Is it the heritage of discrimination? This may play a more substantial role. But neither the distant past of the Prophets nor the current circumstances of American Jews is sufficient to explain the persistence of leftism and liberalism among American Jews. More significant is the near background of Jewish history. Generally speaking, European conservative parties were anti-Semitic, while liberals and socialists exhibited greater friendliness to Jewish interests. A powerful Jewish socialist subculture was carried to the United States and expanded here by Eastern European immigrants. In the most extended study of this phenomenon, Arthur Liebman summed up the matter as follows: "The key to understanding the relationship between the Jews and the Left in America lies in the class-linked socialist subculture that a portion of the Jewish community erected on these shores after the turn of the century. This subculture as an entity in and of itself . . . was the crucial factor in the making of generations of Jewish Leftists."[18] I agree. This doesn't answer every question, such as, why Jews continued to be marked by this subculture as they moved very far from the working class, but I believe this was the heart of the matter. One would have to add that the Democratic party, as the party of big-city immigrants, was there to capture Jewish allegiance as the Socialist party declined.

Whatever the explanation, the facts are clear. The liberalism of American Jews remains one of the prominent features of the American political scene. It has long been expected to disintegrate as Jews have become prosperous in business and independent professionals, but Jews diverge in their liberalism from these ordinarily conservative occupational groups. There was some modest Jewish defection from Harry Truman in 1948, but this was a defection only to the even more liberal Henry Wallace, supported by the Communists. There was some defection to Eisenhower in 1952 and 1956, but the majority of Jews supported Adlai Stevenson, and Jews voted even more strongly for John F. Kennedy in 1960 than Irish Catholics did. Jews had no problem supporting Lyndon Johnson and Hubert Humphrey massively in 1964 and 1968, but by the time McGovern ran for the Democrats in 1972, some issues had risen to prominence which diluted Jewish support for liberal and left positions across the board: the problem of Israel, and tensions with blacks over affirmative action, and black nationalists' sympathy for anti-Israel national liberation movements.

The most substantial break in Jewish support for a Democratic national presidential candidate came in Carter's second run in 1980, when U.S. votes in the U.N. against Israel and a meeting between U.N. Ambassador Andrew Young and a representative of the PLO sharply weakened support for Carter among Jews.

New York State was crucial for Carter and thus New York City's Jews became crucial. To secure their support, Carter tried to win over Edward I. Koch, the Jewish mayor, who he hoped would reassure New York Jews he was friendly to Israel. Koch played Carter unmercifully, squeezing from him both commitments on Israel and benefits for a New York City struggling to recover from the financial and economic crisis of the mid-1970s. As Carter told Koch on one of his many visits to New York City during the campaign, ". . . I need your help because whenever you say something up here it affects me all over the country, like in Florida. I need help with the Jewish community."[19] New York City, parochial as its interests were, at least as its mayor expressed them, was important not only because the Jewish vote could swing the second largest state, but also because of the importance of the Jewish vote—so closely linked to New York—in Florida. Indeed, the first thing a Democratic candidate wants from the Jewish mayor of New York is an electioneering trip to Florida. Thus, despite earlier strains between them, Mayor Koch went to Florida for Democratic candidate Dukakis: "One moment speaking Yiddish and the next posing in a boat that is used to chase drug traffickers, Mayor Koch of New York campaigned here today for Michael S. Dukakis, the Democratic Presidential candidate. . . . [F]or audiences filled with former New Yorkers, his visit was a welcome breath of New York in this land of palm trees."[20]

Whatever the fate of Governor Dukakis nationally, he did not have much to fear when it came to Jews. Despite concern about Jesse Jackson's role in the Democratic campaign among a significant minority of Jews, Dukakis won considerably greater support among Jewish voters

(64 percent) than among Catholics (47 percent) and white Protestants (33 percent).[21]

As we may see from the political career and role of Mayor Koch, the political influence of New York Jews seems to have changed in character, and perhaps to have declined. When Jewish influence was exercised by labor leaders in the New Deal, it formed part of a major national consensus, in the Depression and in war. Jewish liberal internationalism after World War II continued to reflect an important national consensus. Two things have happened to make Jewish influence in American politics, and particularly its exercise through the Jewish population base in New York City and New York State, somewhat more restricted in scope. One is the increasing dominance of the problem of the security of Israel, which played a rather modest role in the entire array of Jewish political interests through the 1960s. Note that there was relatively little Jewish influence on Eisenhower to moderate his insistence on Israel's withdrawal from Sinai in 1957, and no discernible weakening of Jewish support for Kennedy in 1960 despite his support of the Algerian rebellion. It was the Six-Day War in 1967 that made Israel the preeminent issue in Jewish political attitudes, for despite Israel's overwhelming victory, the period of threat that preceded the war raised the chilling possibility of another holocaust. That episode—and the more dangerous and more hard-fought war of 1973—maintains Jewish watchfulness over politicians' attitudes towards Israel at a high level of sensitivity. This changes the general character of Jewish influence, which was less parochial in appearance when it was connected with other major interests through the labor movement and liberal internationalism.

In New York City in particular the powerful impact of Israel on Jewish political attitudes is combined with antagonism toward black demands, as expressed in Mayor Koch and his conflict with Jesse Jackson. This Jewish conflict with blacks is at its peak in New York City, because it is there that there is still a very large Jewish lower-middle class, of civil servants and shopkeepers, who either come into direct conflict with affirmative action demands and requirements, or who bear the brunt of black juvenile delinquency and crime.[22]

Manhattan East Side and West Side Jews, living in the most prosperous and best protected parts of the city, worry less about blacks, and were made uncomfortable by Mayor Koch's unrestrained advocacy of Jewish interests and opposition to affirmative action, and by the style of his advocacy of Israel. They would have preferred the kind of argument that might go down at a meeting of the Council on Foreign Relations. But the poorer, more Orthodox Jews of Brooklyn were for him unreservedly.

Whatever the differences in tone and style, the issue of Israel, for both poorer and more prosperous Jews, is paramount, and both major parties have their feet held firmly to the fire, not only by the Jewish vote, which is important in New York, New Jersey, Florida, and California, but by Jewish contributions, which play a major role, particularly in the Democratic party. There have been startling estimates of the proportion of Democratic funds raised among Jews (equally startling estimates of the amount of funds raised by Michael Dukakis among Greeks, a much smaller group). Whether these estimates reflect ethnic pride, hyping the power of the group, or alternatively complaints by those politicians who have been hurt by Jewish opposition because they did not toe the line on Israel, it would be hard to say: this is not the kind of figure that can easily be ascertained.

There is Jewish influence on American politics, as there is influence from every ethnic and religious group. Jewish influence, however, is exercised with more intensity, because the problem of Israel's security is ever-present in Jewish minds, because the issue is on the permanent agenda of international politics, because Jews as a prosperous group can raise a good deal of money for candidates, because Jews as a result of the number of lawyers and businessmen among them form a larger percentage of those active in politics as financial backers and as candidates for elective and appointive office.

Jewish influence has in general been exercised on the liberal side of political issues, and on the side of Israel. These two interests once went together. They have since diverged. The tension between support for Israel and liberalism increased when a nonliberal and nationalist coalition took office in Israel in 1977, and increased further as American policy accepted the PLO as a legitimate negotiating partner, and as extreme Orthodox groups, whom the overwhelming majority of American Jews oppose, have increased their power in Israel. Non-Jewish liberal and left forces are increasingly critical of Israel. These tensions force American Jews to choose between their liberalism and their support for Israel. As they make different choices, the weight of Jews in American politics will be increasingly divided. The return to power in Israel of a more moderate national government in 1992 brought Jewish liberalism and commitment to Israel back into some degree of harmony.

But in the long term, it seems inevitable that Jews will in greater numbers move into the Republican party (some Jewish intellectuals already have). This may dilute their influence—or, some would argue, will spread it, because the two parties will have to compete more for Jewish support. In the Democratic party, Jewish weight has already declined, as a result of rules changes and the rise of new minorities within the party. These changes suggest that Jews will not be as influential in the future in politics as they have been through most of the postwar period.

Economics

One sees no such weakening—yet—in the Jewish role in the city's economy, and in the significance of Jewish New York in the national economy. In the 1950s and 1960s the children of prosperous Jewish small businessmen, who entered the newly opened elite colleges, disdained taking over their fathers' businesses and poured into the professoriat or into corporate law offices that were now open to Jews. A shift from business, even small business, into academia and medicine and law did not portend either maintenance or increase of Jewish weight in the economy. But as matters turned out, business school and law were crucial launching grounds for the massive reshaping of the American economy that has occurred over the past decade. Since the early 1980s, Jews for the first time in the nation's history have played a remarkably important role at the peak of the American economy.

According to the *Fortune* findings of the mid-1930s, Jews were to be found principally in clothing, merchandising, entertainment. These might have been considered fairly marginal in the 1930s. In the postwar period of increasing affluence and consumerism, Jewish absence from heavy industry hardly limited the rise of Jewish influence in the economy. Jews had early established dominance in the movies. The early history of the movies was in New York City, but by the twenties production had moved to Hollywood. Most of the Jews who went into and created the Hollywood studio system, interestingly enough, came from clothing and merchandising. The link between them would seem to be obscure, but apparently it was crucial: The movies were not only a matter of artistry but also of styling, merchandising, building theaters, distributing movies, creating chains, advertising the product, getting it before the masses. Merchandising provided Jewish entrepreneurs with the required skills, and the movies became a Jewish industry almost from its origin.

Despite the move of production to Hollywood, distribution, advertising, merchandising, and financing remained in good part in New York. With the rise of radio in the 1920s, a new industry in which Jews were prominent was created. The links with Hollywood were of course strong. In the postwar era, the rise of television added another major branch of the entertainment industry. Whether it was movies, or radio, or TV, or recording, or cable, or Broadway musicals, or whatever, through all the shifts and transformations Jews continued to play a major role in entertainment as an industry. Artistic talent, of course, could surface anywhere, and did. Production, distribution, advertising, financing, were in large measure Jewish. The New York–Los Angeles axis dominated entertainment, and Jews were to be found in central positions at both ends.

Was there something about Jewish experience that made Jews particularly adept in shaping the entertainment of a mass society, and keeping up with all its twists and turns and transformations?

Neil Gabler thinks there was.[23] These movie entrepreneurs, born in small East European towns, coming to this country as immigrants, working in clothing manufacturing and sales, furs, or scrap metal, were deeply appreciative of the opportunity given to them in this country. They became in some respects more American than the Americans, but their accents and immigrant origins did not recommend them to the older Americans. Louis B. Mayer took as his birthday (he claimed to have forgotten what it was in Europe) the Fourth of July, and ran a huge party each July 4, for himself, for his family, for the studio, and for America. In the movies they created an ideal America. Gabler argues they were not only skillful salesmen, merchandisers, money-raisers, institution-builders, entrepreneurs: they had a vision, and that vision determined what they put on the screen in the days of Hollywood's glory, in the 1930s and 1940s before Hollywood was challenged by television and the studio system collapsed.

The entertainment industry, whatever its opportunities for the imaginative entrepreneur, was however dangerous for the image of the group that was so prominent in it. The American Protestant ethic does not look kindly on the hedonism and unconventionality that are inevitable in entertainment, and the Jewish moguls and the movies were often under attack for undermining sexual morals, despite the overall pollyannish tone and piety that men like Zukor, Laemmle, Mayer, and Goldwyn favored. The media are often under attack for undermining morals and those who run them become the target of these attacks. If they are Jews, as they so commonly are, there may be an anti-Semitic twist, as in the criticism of the movie *The Last Temptation of Christ*.

When we consider a more central role that New York Jews have come to play in the economy, the conflict between what we may conceive of as old American values and modern entrepreneurship is rather sharper. In the thirties, we have pointed out, the Jewish role in banking was limited. There were the important investment banks of Kuhn, Loeb and Lehman Brothers with their German-Jewish origins and still with

German-Jewish connections, but banking as a whole was *judenrein*. This was to change after the war. The change was not simply a matter of the circulation of elites: It involved new approaches in banking and finance which transformed a conservative and stable business into a maelstrom of change and uncertainty. Or perhaps the world itself changed and banking simply had to adapt.

Jews were prominent in this adaptation. There were many phases in the series of transformations that during the postwar period have shaken the investment banking, securities, and bond industries, and the currency, stock, and commodities markets. The latest phase, scarcely more than ten years old, was one of huge leveraged buy-outs which preceded the collapse of the junk-bond market and real-estate industry in 1990 and 1991. There was and remains great uncertainty as to whether we have reached a phase that portends some enormous collapse, whether these enterprises are simply exercises in greed, or whether they are indeed part of an essential or necessary restructuring of American industry that will make it more efficient and competitive.

Whatever the judgment of history on $20-billion buy-outs, they presented themselves to the popular mind as enterprises in which New York Jewish financiers and lawyers, interested only in money, restructured or perhaps demolished well-known firms that were run for the most part by non-Jews in America's heartland. We may trace this impact on finance by Jewish bankers thirty years back to the career of S.M. Warburg. Warburg was a member of an old Hamburg Jewish banking family, with connections in New York. He became a refugee from Hitler and created a major merchant bank in London. He worked simultaneously in New York as a partner in Kuhn, Loeb. He is credited by Jacques Attali as being the inventor of the unfriendly takeover.

He "attempted and succeeded in bringing off a great 'first' in the history of world capitalism: arranging for a company to be bought on the Stock Exchange by foreign interests, against the will of its directors." This was the purchase of British Aluminium for Reynolds in the United States, and it did not help Warburg's image that the directors were led by Lord Viscount Portal of Hungerford, former chief of staff of the RAF. Warburg "was the first to have made use of the press against the institutions, to organize companies on a world scale, to jostle elites who were settled in their certainties, and with an ordinary telephone call, move private capital from one country to another and sweep away company chiefs." This coup took place in 1958–1959. From then on, writes Attali, "it was no longer shameful [in the City] to get up early and to work late . . . no management or heir was safe from a coup d'état." This is not only Attali's judgment. In an obituary on Warburg in 1982, the *Financial Times* of London wrote: Warburg "was bitterly resented by his opponents as a gun-toting, parvenu financier. This . . . reflects the extraordinary stuffiness of the City establishment in the late 1960s and its isolation from the central stream of international finance."[24]

The émigré Warburg made London, in an England stripped of its empire and declining (relatively) economically, a center of world banking, particularly by exploiting the opportunities given by the presence in Europe of large sums in expatriated overseas dollars, Eurodollars, which made it possible to raise great amounts of capital for public authorities and businesses, relatively independently of national restraints.

This did not happen without pain. No establishment is overturned without pain: Warburg "would remember hearing . . . many openly anti-Semitic remarks directed against him, the foreigner trying to sell one of the nation's jewels to foreigners."[25]

The thirty-year-old story sounds eerily familiar, except that the management of the takeover was undertaken by an elegant and aristocratic German Jew rather than by East European Jews.

Attali argues that Warburg and his fellow German-Jewish bankers "were more concerned with what they were doing than the money they were making, trying their utmost to ensure that fair exchange prevailed over violence, circulation over immobility, life over death."[26]

One wonders whether the same case will ever be made for the takeover artists who are the subject of Connie Bruck's *The Predator's Ball:* Michael Milken, of Drexel, Burnham (despite the name, a Jewish-owned firm), and the raiders and corporate restructurers with whom he has worked—Saul Steinberg, Ivan Boesky, the Belzberg brothers, Ronald Perelman, and others, almost all Jewish. Having demonstrated that one could take over enormous companies with high-risk bonds, secured by the companies' assets, in leveraged buy-outs, Drexel, Burnham was followed in these enterprises by the most respectable American banks, which once would have spurned such activity. "Milken's machine," writes Bruck, "would stir hatreds and prejudices as bitter as any social revolution. . . . The denizens of corporate America would be challenged, and some of them dispossessed. In their place would come Milken's own—a band of mainly small-time entrepreneurs, raiders, greenmailers, the have-nots of the corporate world."

Describing an early take-over in Milken's career, Bruck writes: "On April 2, 1985, the conference room on the eighth floor of the no-frills National Can headquarters in southwest Chicago was packed with the usual armies of deal advisers—M & A Lawyers from Skadden, Arps, Slate, Meagher and Flom as well as from Paul, Weiss, Rifkind, Wharton and Garrison, and investment bankers from Salomon Brothers. There were some new investment-banking faces too, troops who were still a little green but who had launched a juggernaut that was commanding the attention, and fear, of corporation chieftains across the country. . . .

"Two weeks earlier, Triangle Industries headed by Nelson Peltz and Peter May, had made a Drexel-backed offer for all outstanding shares of National Can . . . Frank Considine, the silver-haired patrician CEO of National Can, . . ." and so on.

Sometime after the deal had been consummated, May is quoted by Bruck as saying: "I'm sure he thought of us as two Jewish guys from New York he'd never heard of, and we were the last thing he wanted."[27]

Deals and takeovers were often perceived as assaults by New York deal-makers, lawyers, and financiers against heartland industrialists. "Here's this poor guy from Hammermill [Talbot Duval, its CEO]," Bruck quotes an informant, "a real Ivy League guy . . . he's sitting there thinking that the world works the way it always has, with his golf club and his graduating class, and he never raises his voice—and all of a sudden, he's got Carl [Icahn], who is such a fighter. . . ." Icahn told Duvan he "wanted to piece off the company. He said. 'I'm only in this for the money. I don't care anything about the paper business.' "

One close associate of Icahn's recalled that Laurence Tisch, Chairman of Loew's and now of CBS, Inc., said. . . ., "Tell Carl to cut this out. It's not good for the Jews."[28]

One could, of course, find Jewish firms, lawyers, and financiers on both sides of these battles, perhaps older and more established German Jews against newer and harder-driving East European Jews. But the dramatis personae were very often as these stories in Bruck's book have it—WASP descendants of founding entrepreneurs or their managers, and Jewish corporate raiders—and in the biggest buy-out launched to date they remained the same. It was Ross Johnson of RJR-Nabisco and a Board of Directors that contained perhaps one Jew that dealt with Peter A. Cohen of Shearson Lehman (the successor firm to Kuhn Loeb), and Salomon Brothers, and with Henry R. Kravis and George Roberts of Kohlberg, Kravis and Roberts (KKR). KKR's huge war chest contained contributions from major pension funds and university endowments. Everyone joined the game New York Jewish firms and entrepreneurs set afoot.

With what consequences, we will have to wait for history to tell us. It takes no prescience however to note that today's high finance, whatever it does for or to the country, nails down in the American mind how different New York is—and how different it is because it is in part a Jewish city. As talk developed of a possible buy-out of Sears, one money manager was quoted in the *Wall Street Journal:* "God, I hope that (the takeover) doesn't happen. . . . We're talking about middle America here. . . . People wouldn't stand for this." The *Wall Street Journal* reporter commented: "Some pros see the problem as a reprise of the age-old tensions between Wall Street and Main Street."[29] Wall Street in the old battles was attacked by anti-Semites as Jewish when it wasn't. Now it is.

Culture

Trade-book publishing—the publishing of current books, fiction and nonfiction, for bookstores, as against the publishing of textbooks, Bibles, and other items that will generally not be reviewed in magazines and newspapers—stands at the intersection between business and culture. It has been centered in New York City for many decades, and was until the 1950s a business which had a decidedly minority Jewish presence. There were a number of Jewish-owned trade-book firms in early postwar New York: Alfred A. Knopf, Random House, Simon and Schuster, and Viking, all established in the 1920s. John Tebbel, in his history of American publishing, notes that B.W. Huebsch, who began his publishing career in the early 1900s and merged with Harold K. Guinzberg's Viking firm in 1925, was apparently the first Jew to enter general publishing, and comments that this was "a fact remarkable only because his entry cracked the solidly Gentile facade of the business, at the same time subtly rebuking the unacknowledged anti-Semitism prevalent in the trade during the early part of the century. It was not until the twenties that this unhealthy climate began to change." This may be too early to date the change. Tebbel later notes that Alfred A. Knopf organized in 1927 "a new kind of bookmen's lunch club . . . the Book Table, distinct from the Publisher's Lunch Club, which was not notable for the number of its Jewish members."[30] Along with Knopf and Viking, with their especially strong lines of European writers, other new entries into publishing in the 1920s which established a Jewish presence in that business were Henry Simon and Max Schuster, who founded Simon and Schuster, and Bennett Cerf and Donald Klopfer, who began with the Modern Library and founded Random House.

If one can define a Jewish thrust in publishing in New York, it would consist of two elements: first, an orientation toward the new and avant-garde; but second, and quite different, the development of new "products" and new approaches to marketing, as in the crossword puzzle books that were Simon and Schuster's first success, and the establishment in the 1920s of the Book-of-the-Month Club. The two were often combined, as in the Modern Library, which brought classics and daring European and American writers to a large public at low prices. But even as late as the early 1950s, New York tradebook publishing was largely a non-Jewish affair, a quiet business much like New York banking before the revolution, in which tweed-clad editors had long lunches with writers in from the country, and retired to wood-paneled offices to read manuscripts at leisure.

All this was to change. Publishing had always been a business, of course, but one in which the business side was rather subordinated. Tebbel asserts that "it was [Leon] Shimkin [who came to work at Simon and Schuster in 1924] who introduced a new concept to publishing—the businessman as publisher."[31] Shimkin's successes at S&S included Dale Carnegie's *How to Win Friends and Influence People* and J.K. Lasser's series on how to make out your income tax. Shimkin and S&S were involved in the first successful and sustained mass paperback publishing operation, Robert De Graff's Pocket Books, launched on the eve of World War II.

After the war, in the 1950s and 1960s, publishing was transformed into a business in which the last thing an editor could do in his office was to read a manuscript. This was much regretted—as was the transformation in banking brought about in the 1970s and 1980s—by those who remembered the halcyon days but it happened, and bright Jewish publishers in New York, exploring new kinds of books and new kinds of markets, were in large measure responsible. Jason Epstein, just out of Columbia, where he had been a classmate of Norman Podhoretz, John Hollander, and others who were to achieve prominence in various fields, and where he had received the excellent undergraduate education in the humanities that the Columbia University of Jacques Barzun and Lionel Trilling was then providing, joined Doubleday in the early 1950s, its first Jewish editor. He was seized with the passion to do for the United States what Penguin Books had done for England: publish good books, old and new, in paperback formats at low prices. (The Modern Library was then still in hard covers, and did not publish new books.) He was able to convince the chief powers at Doubleday to back him in launching Anchor Books, the first of the quality paperback lines. He hired me away from *Commentary*, where I was an editor, to assist him. I was the second Jewish editor at Doubleday, and the one-block move from *Commentary* at the American Jewish Committee to Doubleday—from 56th and Third Avenue to 57th at Madison—was a revelation to me. It was a move from an entirely Jewish to an almost entirely non-Jewish world.

Publishing was changing so rapidly that Jason Epstein had very little time to enjoy his position as a pioneer with a unique product. Immediately other bright young men saw the opportunity in quality paperbacks and jumped into the business, the first being young Arthur Cohen, a recent graduate of the University of Chicago, who launched Noonday. The number of new paperback lines exploded rapidly. The success of Anchor and its competitors was attributable in large measure to the simultaneous explosion in college enrollments. Courses such as Jason Epstein had taken at Columbia, in which students covered the humanities from Homer and Aristophanes to Gide and Faulkner, guided him in what he published.

Simultaneously, the social sciences were also exploding. One of the first great Anchor successes was *The Lonely Crowd,* by David Riesman, Nathan Glazer, and Reuel Denney, which I, as one of the co-authors, reduced and reworked from the original 1950 Yale University Press edition for the paperback edition in 1953. Soaring enrollments and expanding courses in the humanities and social sciences brought success to Anchor and many of its innumerable competitors, and transformed the face of American publishing.

New York Jews were cropping up everywhere in publishing in the 1950s. Arthur Rosenthal, with a deep interest in psychoanalysis, launched Basic Books and the Basic Book Club. His first great success was Ernest Jones' biography of Freud. He acquired Irving Kristol—formerly an editor of *Commentary,* founder of *Encounter,* and editor of *The Reporter*—as his chief editor, and Basic Books became the leading publisher of the kind of social science that tries to bridge the gap between the academy and the lay reading public. (Rosenthal was to become in time publisher of Harvard University Press.) Jeremiah Kaplan, a drop-out from City College, traveling as a fund collector for a Jewish organization, was visiting friends at the University of Chicago—expatriate New Yorkers Daniel Bell and Martin Diamond—who were teaching in its admirable required program of social science courses for undergraduates. They told him that the social science classics they needed—such as works of Emile Durkheim and Max Weber—were simply not in print in the United States, and there would be a market for these then obscure (to Americans) European social theorists. The University of Chicago courses would provide a modest base. Kaplan then launched the Free Press, bringing out reprints of Durkheim, and immediately grabbing on to the boom in sociology. He republished Talcott Parsons' enormous and obscure *The Structure of Social Action,* went on to publish other works of Parsons, for which it turned out there was a substantial market in the burgeoning social sciences. He became the publisher of Robert Merton, the brilliant teacher and theorist at Columbia University, of Edward Shils, and many leading figures in the social sciences, and went on to become president of Macmillan and publisher of the International Encyclopedia of the Social Sciences.

These and other publishers were exploiting the divide between the "New York intellectuals," who have recently been discussed at great length, and the American college and university, bringing the knowledge and energy of the first to the second. In time, figures in the New York intelligentsia such as Edmund Wilson and Lionel Trilling—brought to large audiences by Anchor—were to become the guides of young Americans interested in exploring literature and ideas. The editors and writers for *Partisan Review*—Phillip Rahv, William Phillips, and others—discovered, somewhat to their astonishment, that they could become professors at good colleges and editors of books in which major publishers might be interested.

The quality paperback revolution was only one event in the transformation of American publishing. It was also being transformed in other ways: for example, the creation of celebrity books, books written by ghosts, marketed in new ways to reach huge audiences, and Jewish agents and publishers were as active in that sphere as in the more rarefied sphere in which the best that had been written and thought was brought to large audiences in and outside of colleges and universities.

The Jewish role in what Serge Guilbaut has called New York's "stealing of the idea of modern art" was also marked. Thus, Guilbaut attributes a key role to Samuel Koontz, collector and art dealer, who in 1942 "challenged the New York art community to react to the death of Paris by creating something new, strong, and original."[32] One of the first galleries to show abstract art was Peggy Guggenheim's "Art of This Century." And among the artists who played a key role in promoting this art were Mark Rothko and Adolph Gottlieb.[33] Jewish dealers, publicists, gallery owners, and artists were part of the conquest of modern art.

Perhaps most important were Jewish critics. Meyer Schapiro, Clement Greenberg, and Harold Rosenberg defined first for the New York intelligentsia, and rather more important, for dealers and collectors, what was new and exciting and breakthrough in art. In 1945, Clement Greenberg was an editor at *Partisan Review,* wrote columns on art for *The Nation,* but made his living at the *Contemporary Jewish Record* and its successor, *Commentary;* Harold Rosenberg worked for an advertising agency, and was known as a universal intellectual in the Village; Schapiro had an academic appointment at Columbia, and taught Romanesque Art, but few in the New York intellectual circle knew much about that. He was an expert on Marxism, and much else, lectured on modern art to crowded classes at the New School, and passed judgment on new artists coming on the scene. A transformation equivalent to what occurs in Proust's *Remembrance of Things Past* to Madame Verdurin's little circle was to propel them all to wider and more powerful stages in the 1950s and 1960s. Clement Greenberg became a consultant to leading art dealers; Rosenberg began to review art for *The New Yorker;* and Meyer Schapiro hovered over the scene, defining with his monumental knowledge and authority what was worthy in the enterprise of advanced, experimental art.

These are some sketches, scarcely more than that, of the role that New York Jews played in a few areas of culture in the 1940s, 1950s, and 1960s. These were of course also areas of business. Books must be produced, advertised, distributed, sold, as well as contracted for and written; art needs dealers, publicists, purchasers, curators, serving to define what is good and what is better, and providing a living not only to artists but to a host of others. The primacy in publishing and culture had passed from Boston to New York, the largest city, long before Jews played any role in either. Did it matter that in the postwar world a largely Jewish group of intellectuals and cultural entrepreneurs began to play a major role in these fields? Did it change the course of culture? Did it affect its character?

New York's primacy, one must conclude, was determined by factors other than the ethnic and religious background of the individuals who became so prominent in these fields in the two decades after the war. But there was, I believe, a distinctive contribution to be attributed to the Jewish component. One must recall that in the twenties and thirties genteel culture still dominated colleges and universities and publishing houses and galleries. They were not attuned to the new and experimental. The New York intellectuals looked more to Europe than the United States. But they also knew they had to find in the United States, in American culture, roots for the new they advocated. Their radical political interests prevented them from becoming simply Europhile snobs. For the genteel tradition they had nothing but disdain. It offered them nothing and was anti-Semitic to boot. Their careers, if there were to be careers, as intellectuals, as teachers, as publishers, as critics, had to be founded on the advocacy of the new, but their generally socialist background kept them from being advocates of the most extreme and most "irresponsible" aspects of the new in art and culture (for example, Dada and Surrealism). They tried to give a social meaning and significance to the new, as against celebrating pure sensation and rebellion.

By the 1960s, they were becoming an establishment themselves. In the 1970s and 1980s, whatever the New York intellectuals had had to offer was already somewhat old hat. The social criticism of Edmund Wilson and Lionel Trilling was history, rapidly being replaced by semiotics and deconstructionism. Abstract Expressionism was now classic, while wave upon wave of short-lived styles passed over the modern art scene. Modernism, which the New York intellectuals had embraced wholly, trying their best to deal with the anti-Semitism of some of its leading prophets and exponents, was being replaced with postmodernist fashions for which they had little enthusiasm.

But whatever the modesty of their role in the late 1980s, they had extended the boundaries of American culture in creating a market for the new in field after field, and in establishing it in college curriculums.

Conclusion

I have dealt with a rather elusive topic. My aim of course has been to go beyond the simple recording of who among New Yorkers active and influential in politics, business and finance, and culture were Jews. One reason this would not by itself be very revealing is that just *how* they were Jewish matters in trying to discern a Jewish influence. Did it matter that Robert Moses and Walter Lippman, both of whom had no connection with the Jewish community, and denied or evaded any connection with Jewishness, were of Jewish origin? What could it mean to say they were "Jewish" and to include them in some account of the Jewish factor in New York's influence on the nation? In contrast, most of those I have referred to were Jewish in a common and distinctive manner. They were East European Jewish immigrants, or the children or grandchildren of such immigrants, emerging from a common culture, facing similar circumstances in getting an education, choosing or finding an occupation or profession or career, establishing success or prominence. Whatever their latter-day relationships to Jewishness, Jewish religion, or a Jewish community, they knew themselves as, and others knew them as, Jews, and this was no simple matter of naming: the name referred to a culture and a community.

Thus when we say they were Jews we are not simply recording a demographic feature of no great significance or consequence. My argument has been that the fact that they were Jewish mattered in some way. New York City was different because of that Jewishness, and its influence on the nation was different from what it might have been had there not been this large Jewish component in its population and its elites. There is no way of testing this, obviously. We cannot perform the experiment of contrasting the real New York with an imagined New York without Jews or with fewer Jews. We can contrast New York's influence on its hinterland with those of other world cities, with many fewer Jews, or no Jews at all. The experiment—not attempted in this chapter—would show that all dynamic world cities have somewhat similar influences on the countries of which they are a part. They are "advanced" in business techniques and culture, they are centers from which innovations in various spheres spread, because the creative concentrate there, and techniques of diffusion are developed there.

Did it matter that New York was so markedly a *Jewish* city? It mattered quite clearly for New York City's politics. The great metropolis may be generally a center for the new in business and culture, but it is not necessarily such a center for politics, nor are its politics necessarily to the left of the nation's. Here the Jewish influence was most marked. In business and culture, New York played the role a great city must, and the Jewish influence was more subtle—one finds a greater thrust to the most daring efforts in finance and merchandising, a greater push to the liberal and the avant-garde in culture, connected at the same time with a certain bourgeois moderation, as I have indicated.

Cities are not only the product of their size and their economic function. Who populates them matters. Who makes up their elites matter. Those who have tried to divine a city's ethos have been persuaded of this: Puritan Boston was different from Quaker Philadelphia, Digby Baltzell argued, because they were first settled by Puritans and Quakers, and that meant something for their future development.[34] Boston lost its cultural primacy to New York, Martin Green argued, not only because New York became a larger city, but because Boston's elite suffered from a crucial defect in relating to modern culture.[35] Others have commented on the role of Jews in the remarkable cultures of Vienna, Berlin, Budapest. There were, and are, even more Jews in New York, and they have given a distinctive spin to New York's influence on the nation.

Notes

1. Glazer, Nathan, "City College," in Riesman, David, and Verne A. Stadtman, eds., *Academic Transformations* (New York: McGraw-Hill, 1973), pp. 71–98.
2. Wechsler, Harold S., *The Qualified Student: A History of Selective College Admission in America* (New York: Wiley-Interscience, 1977), chapter 7; Jones, Theodore Francis, *New York University, 1832–1932* (New York: New York University Press, 1933), pp. 225–235, 381–387.

3. See, for example, Bayor, Ronald H., *Neighbors in Conflict: The Irish, Germans, Jews, and Italians of New York City, 1929–1941* (Baltimore, MD: Johns Hopkins University Press, 1978).
4. Glazer, Nathan and Daniel P. Moynihan, *Beyond the Melting Pot* (Cambridge, MA: MIT Press, 1963, pp. 147–148, and footnotes therein.
5. Lowi, Theodore, *At the Pleasure of the Mayor: Patronage and Power in New York City, 1898–1958* (Glencoe, IL: The Free Press of Glencoe, 1964), p. 198, and throughout.
6. Wechsler, *The Qualified Student*, pp. 194–204.
7. Feingold, Henry, *The Politics of Rescue: The Roosevelt Administration and the Holocaust, 1938–1945* (New Brunswick, NJ: Rutgers University Press, 1970); Wyman, David S., *The Abandonment of the Jews: America and the Holocaust, 1941–1945* (New York: Pantheon, 1984).
8. Trilling, Diana, "Lionel Trilling, A Jew at Columbia," *Commentary*, March 1979, pp. 40–46; Hook, Sidney, *Out of Bounds* (New York: Harper & Row, 1987), chapter 16, pp. 529–535.
9. Glazer and Moynihan, *Beyond the Melting Pot*, p. 151.
10. Rosenwaike, Ira, *Population History of New York City* (Syracuse, NY: Syracuse University Press, 1972), pp. 86–87, 123–125; Rischin, Moses, *The Promised City: New York's Jews, 1870–1914* (Cambridge, MA: Harvard University Press, 1962), pp. 194, 297–298.
11. Ritterband, Paul, and Steven M. Cohen, "The Social Characteristics of the New York Area Jewish Community, 1981," in *The American Jewish Year Book, 1984* (New York and Philadelphia: American Jewish Committee and the Jewish Publication Society of America, 1983), p. 129.
12. *American Jewish Year Book, 1985*, p. 180.
13. Ritterband and Cohen, "The Social Characteristics of the New York Area Jewish Community," pp. 147, 150, 156, 136.
14. Ritterband and Cohen, *Ibid.*, p. 137; Barry R. Chiswick, "The Labor Market Status of American Jews: Patterns and Determinants," *American Jewish Year Book, 1985*, p. 139.
15. Ladd, E. C. Jr., and S.M. Lipset, *The Divided Academy* (New York: McGraw-Hill, 1975), p. 151; Ladd, E. C., Jr., and S.M. Lipset, "Jewish Academics in the United States: Their Achievement, Culture and Politics," *American Jewish Year Book*, vol. 72 (1971).
16. Lerner, Robert, Althea K. Nagai, and Stanley Rothman, "Marginality and Liberalism Among Jewish Elites," Center for the Study of Social and Political Change, Smith College, unpublished paper, 1988.
17. Kristol, Irving, "Liberalism and American Jews," *Commentary*, October 1988, 86:4, pp. 19–23; Lichter, Nagai, and Rothman, "Marginality and Liberalism."
18. Liebman, Arthur, *Jews and the Left* (New York: John Wiley, 1979), p. 3. See,

too, Glazer, Nathan, *The Social Basis of American Communism* (New York: Harcourt, Brace and World, 1962), chapter 4.

19. Koch, Edward I., *Mayor* (New York: Simon & Schuster, 1984), p. 272.
20. "Koch, in Miami, Tempers Tough Talk," Schmalz, Jeffrey, *New York Times*, October 18, 1988: Section B, p. 3.
21. New York Times/CBS News exit poll, *New York Times*, November 10, 1988, Section B, p. 6.
22. See Rieder, Jonathan, *Canarsie: The Jews and Italians of Brooklyn Against Liberalism* (Cambridge, MA: Harvard University Press, 1985).
23. Gabler, Neal, *An Empire of Their Own: How the Jews Invented Hollywood* (New York, Crown, 1988).
24. Attali, Jacques, *A Man of Influence: The Extraordinary Career of S. G. Warburg* (Bethesda, MD: Adler and Adler, 1987), pp. 233, 234, 235.
25. *Ibid.*, p. 233.
26. *Ibid.*, p. *xvi*.
27. Bruck, Connie, *The Predator's Ball: The Junk Bond Raiders and the Men Who Staked Them* (New York: The American Lawyer/Simon & Schuster, 1988), pp. 19–20, 105, 136.
28. *Ibid.*, pp. 156, 157, 160.
29. Salwen, Kevin G., "Investors Fret Over Possible LBO Curbs," *The Wall Street Journal*, November 10, 1988.
30. Tebbel, John, *Between Covers: The Rise and Transformation of Book Publishing in America* (New York: Oxford University Press, 1987), pp. 157, 231.
31. *Ibid.*, p. 236.
32. Guilbaut, Serge, *How New York Stole the Idea of Modern Art* (Chicago: University of Chicago Press, 1983), p. 65.
33. *Ibid.*, p. 67.
34. Baltzell, E. Digby, *Puritan Boston and Quaker Philadelphia* (New York: The Free Press, 1979; Boston, Beacon Press, 1982).
35. Green, Martin, *The Problem of Boston* (New York: W.W. Norton, 1966).

9

On Metropolitan Dominance: New York in the Urban Network

Paul DiMaggio

The chapters in this volume collectively depict a New York that remains at the peak of the U.S. urban system, and whose claim to the status of "global city" is secure. Yet they also make it clear that, at least in some domains, New York, if not quite in decline, is not as dominant as it was at mid-century.

For example, New York's dominant position in finance appears relatively secure, and is perhaps reinforced by the rise of new communications technologies and by the internationalization of capital markets. In manufacturing, however, New York has lost ground and fallen behind much of the United States and the industrialized world. In politics, New Yorkers still occupy key positions in the economic-policy establishment; yet the voices of New Yorkers are both weaker and less harmonious in the areas of foreign and domestic policy than they were half a century ago. New York remains the center of the nation's art market, trade book

My ideas on these topics were formulated in the stimulating atmosphere of the meetings of the Metropolitan Dominance section of the Social Science Research Council's Committee on New York City, and consequently owe much to the other authors in this volume, who were seated around the table. For probing comments on an earlier draft, I am indebted to Martin Shefter and to participants in the Yale Sociology/ISPS Workshop on the City: Neil Bennett, Steven Brint, Deborah Davis, Paul Johnston, Caroline Persell, and Doug Rae.

publishing, and highbrow journalism; but city institutions no longer dominate the mass media as they once did.

The diagnosis, then, is mixed. Moreover, the prognosis is uncertain. To clarify matters, we need ways to think about how changes in New York's position in one realm influence its position in any other: how, for example, shifts in the city's economic standing shape its political fortunes. We must ask how the internal contours of New York, as subject and object of metropolitan competition, have changed, and with what implications for the city's capacity for inter-urban struggle. And, insofar as New York's position has declined, we must ask whether the city has been superceded by some even more central place, or whether, instead, the system as a whole has become less hierarchical and more horizontally differentiated.

It follows that this chapter has a double purpose: first, to synthesize the conclusions of the chapters that have preceded it; and, second, to develop an analytic scaffolding that can support such a synthesis. The latter consists largely of a distinction among three kinds of metropolitan dominance—structural, strategic, and cognitive—which vary in the extent to which they are, first, self-renewing or self-attenuating, and, second, convertible into one another or inert.

New York will remain economically dominant because its economy revolves around goods and services that are demanded by an unusually broad range of national and international enterprises. New York's position as a cultural center has eroded somewhat and may continue to do so, but will rest secure so long as economic wealth is converted into cultural distinction. By contrast, New York's political clout has declined, largely because New Yorkers failed to renew it and to convert it to economic advantage for the city as a whole.

The relative social fragmentation of New York, compared to other major cities, serves it well in the economic realm, but places it at a political disadvantage. Whether New York remains America's first city depends on whether its elites can forge political alliances with one another and with other organized New York interests. The issue is one of identity, not capacity: it will depend on whether the city's elites choose to act politically *as New Yorkers,* rather than as representatives of finance or other industries, a national business class, ethnic or racial groups, or sub-metropolitan political entities.

Varieties of Metropolitan Dominance

This volume is the product of a set of conversations organized by the Social Science Research Council under the rubric "Metropolitan Dominance." That phrase, which may have a sinister ring to readers unfamiliar with central-place theory, has not been featured in the foregoing chapters. But the problem of metropolitan dominance—how to explain the changing position of a metropolitan area (New York City) in the national and global economy, culture, and polity—has animated the papers herein.

Discussions of urban systems are replete with spatial imagery. We say, for example, that New York is dominant within a city system, or sits astride the urban hierarchy, or is central to our national politics or culture. Such phrases are evocative, but they can mean, and in this volume do mean, several things.

At its simplest, "dominance" refers simply to numerical superiority, as when one metropolitan area exceeds others in population or volume of trade. This definition of dominance fails in two ways to capture the phenomenon we are pursuing. First, at least in culture and politics, sheer quantitative superiority cannot be equated with national leadership. Second, dominance is a relational concept (a dominant metropolis is dominant over other places); quantitative indices refer, at best, to the outcomes of relational processes by which superiority is achieved, but tell us little about the processes themselves.

The imagery of "network" lies just beneath the surface of dominance.[1] New York is influential in culture and politics because it is central to elite circles in which significant opinion is formed; it is economically prosperous because it is a "node" through which international traffic must flow. But merely declaring that New York's position is a function of its pattern of interactions with other places, although it gets us closer, is not enough. For although urban networks (patterns of relationship among places and actors that inhabit them) figure into any kind of metropolitan hierarchy, different forms of dominance require us to think about networks in different ways. (See Table 1 for a schematic representation of the typology that follows.)

Structural Dominance

In geography and sociology, dominance is the product of central positions in relational networks. Particular "nodes" of the networks and the defining relations among them are regarded as stable: in the city system, the units that are connected are cities or SMSAs, and the key "ties" are flows of trade and information. A place is dominant, or "central," insofar as other places depend on it for information, goods, and services to a greater extent than it depends on them.[2]

Structural dominance or centrality (I shall use the two as synonyms) yields benefits. As Ronald Burt has demonstrated in other contexts, insofar as actors in other places must go through middlepersons in a dominant metropolis in order to transact with one another (and thus exercise less choice among interaction partners than those at the center), the latter can in effect extract a "tax" from more marginal players. Dominance is in this sense a matter of position, a location in social or physical space, that enables an actor (or set of actors) to command a particularly large proportion of the flow of goods, money, and services. Note that such processes have a marketlike quality: structural dominance emerges from ongoing relations among many pairs of actors, rather than from an overarching design.

Strategic Dominance

By contrast, one can conceive of networks as protean with respect both to the "nodes" or actors and to the types of relationships that constitute them. Such networks require more energetic management, either through imperative coordination (not available to cities in an urban system, except insofar as they can co-opt the central state) or through the fashioning of coalitions. Dominance in this sense, which I shall call strategic dominance, differs from structural dominance (which may facilitate it) in several ways.

First, coalitions are special kinds of networks in that relations between any two actors may be actively manipulated by a third: coalitions are "cobbled together" and coalition members participate in a set as a coalition itself, rather than as transactors in a series of dyadic exchanges. Second, the media of exchange are diverse, and it is up to participants

Table 1 Varieties of Dominance

	Nodes	Relations
Structural	Fixed population of specialized actors	Fixed set of specialized ties
Strategic	Changing population of specialized actors	Strategic manipulation of types of resources
Cognitive	General population of unspecialized actors; communications media	By-product of specialized and general social relations, and relations to media ("two-step flow")

to discover media through which they can reach accommodations. (If an economic network rests on flows of goods and services, a strategic network can combine exchanges of capital [low-interest loans to induce business participation], jobs [patronage or other boodle to entice local politicos], and votes [log-rolling for pet projects]). Third, the population of "nodes" that establish the network is less fixed, precisely because entrepreneurs use new media of exchange to bring in new players. Consequently, the distribution of power is less rigidly determined, more susceptible to gaming.

Strategic dominance, then, is a product of agency, not just position. Structural dominance matters, because actors from central places can bring more resources to the table than those in structurally peripheral locations. But the exercise of strategic dominance may operate adventitiously to set parameters for the routine exchanges out of which structural superiority emerges, laying down the tracks (sometimes quite literally, as in the case of centrally planned transportation routes) that bear the traffic of short-term transactions.

Cognitive Dominance

Metropolitan dominance also entails cognitive influence: a center's reign over the national imagination, such that it is the place where innovation occurs, tastes are defined, and models originate to be replicated elsewhere. This form of dominance also works through networks; but they are less readily perceived, for two reasons. First, their membership is not delimited: compared to networks of exchange or of command or coalition, cognitive influence is exerted alongside, and as a by-product of, myriad social, professional, avocational, and incidental interactions of everyday life. Consequently, there is relatively less division of labor or elite closure in cognitive influence processes: whereas most participants in exchange or strategic networks occupy specialized roles (purchasing agent or banker, legislator or lobbyist), anyone can participate in the flow of opinion and ideas. Second, cognitive networks are literally "mediated": the press and broadcasters diffuse ideas and models in a structured but impersonal way, the familiar two-step flow, to local opinion leaders and from them to people who listen to them.[3]

Cognitive dominance cannot be reduced entirely to such networks, however, for it rests on the willingness of outsiders to view New York–generated ideas or styles as credible. This willingness is itself a product of the institutionalization of legitimate cultural authority, either of the urban area itself (such that residency in a center itself places a halo over practitioners of some craft, as in the case of "New York Abstract

Expressionists" or "Parisian designers") or of particular urban institutions (e.g., New York's philanthropic foundations or financial institutions).[4] Cultural authority works both to disseminate messages and models from a center (for example, by attracting the media to New York as a source of quotable experts or talk-show guests) and to enhance the credibility of those messages in the view of those who receive them.

Control of Positions

The overrepresentation of New Yorkers in the Washington domestic, foreign, and economic policy establishments is an *indicator* of strategic dominance (see Kurth, chapter 4; Shefter, chapter 5). But observers often treat it as a *form* of metropolitan dominance. This is potentially misleading, for the presence of New Yorkers in national institutions, although perhaps an indicator of dominance, does not constitute a mechanism of dominance. For one thing, New Yorkers tapped for positions of national leadership rarely use their jobs to further the interests of the city. (For example, it was under the chairmanship of New Yorker Nancy Hanks that the National Endowment for the Arts clarified its policy of emphasizing regional artistic development.) Second, control of national positions is inherently unstable. Where New Yorkers have remained nationally prominent, as in banking regulation, their presence reflects a cross-effect of stable patterns of structural dominance.[5]

Forms of Metropolitan Dominance in Economy, Politics, and Culture

The terms "structural," "strategic," and "cognitive" may seem forced, because of the palpable affinity between each form of dominance and one of the functional domains (economics, politics, and culture) around which this volume is organized. Is not structural dominance merely a synonym for economic centrality, strategic dominance a synonym for political control, and cognitive dominance another way of referring to cultural hegemony?

It is essential to avoid confusing these analytic categories, which refer to distinct processes of influence, with the actual content of the political, economic, and cultural realms. Although each form of dominance is the pivotal mode of domination within a particular functional domain, each is also present to some degree within each of them. (See Table 2.)

Economy

The economy is the principal site in which structural dominance is exercised. Networks of economic exchange entail relations among producers and consumers of goods, services, and finance that range in intensity from single exchanges to the relational contracts characteristic of high finance. (By relational contracts I mean, long-term associations based on substantial mutual knowledge and trust.) New York's centrality in such networks is largely self-reinforcing, due primarily to the existence of agglomeration economies that induce new firms in thriving industries to locate in New York and lower the costs of doing business there. As Kahler (chapter 2) and Vogel (chapter 3) demonstrate, such economic dominance is strongest in the financial and business-service sectors.

Nonetheless, if structural processes are central to New York's economic influence, they are reinforced by strategic networks based on authoritative command. Decisions that shape the economic fates of individuals throughout the world are made in New York City boardrooms of major banks and industrial firms. Similarly, finance is characterized by less formal but highly instrumental strategic relationships, which may involve either short-term agreements or long-term associations between New York financial institutions and ones headquartered elsewhere (as when banks collaborate to finance major corporate acquisitions).[6] Indeed, the modest decline in the number of Fortune 500 corporations headquartered in New York may be an illusory indicator of the city's fortunes. The mergers and acquisitions of the 1980s probably increased the number of regional enterprises controlled by many of the remaining New York–based corporations; and mergers effected elsewhere were often managed and organized by New York–based financial institutions.[7] New York's economic centrality is also reinforced by networks of cognitive influence: consider, for example, the success of New York brokerage firms in creating new financial products that were imitated nationwide in the 1980s.

To be sure, outside of finance, U.S. business culture is largely decentralized: few companies noted for innovation in workplace management, for example, are located in New York; and the leading business schools in which business ideology is created and transmitted are scattered across the country. Nonetheless, the city remains a meeting place for business peak associations (for example, the Conference Board and the Business Roundtable, in each of which New York companies play prominent roles) that socialize corporate leadership and define the political positions of big business as a whole. And New York's stranglehold

Table 2 Forms of Dominance and Functional Domains

Domain:	Economy	Polity	Culture
Form of Dominance:			
Structural	**Centrality in* economic transaction networks**	Centrality in elite policy networks/ ability to organize policy initiatives	Agglomeration and market centrality in media, advertising, art, and publishing
Strategic	Headquarters control; role NYC banks in mobilization of large-scale capital	**Role in national politics, augmented by financial resources and votes**	Foundations, cultural projects
Cognitive	Innovation in financial instruments; business peak associations; management consulting	Cultural authority of policy centers and foundations; media, press, and intellectuals	**Fashion, design Foundations Nonprofits The arts**

*The major form of dominance for each sector is in bold.

over the business-services field ensures that management nostrums reach New York quickly and are diffused nationwide by New York–based consulting companies.

Politics

The political realm is the primary arena within which strategic dominance operates. Because New York is not a capital, its political influence rests not on command but on the capacity of its agents to build coalitions in national decision-making forums that defend and extend the city's interests. As Shefter (chapter 5) notes, New York politicians have played key roles in both Democratic and Republician coalitions: in the former, from Van Buren through Tammany Hall to FDR's New Deal; in the latter, during the heyday of Republican internationalism, from Theodore Roosevelt and Stimson to Dewey and Rockefeller.

If strategic dominance is pivotal to the political realm, however, other mechanisms also play a role. New York's structural dominance of the economy created wealth that enabled New Yorkers to offer indispensable donations to national political parties and, for a time at least, to identify the interests of the city's industries and financial institutions with those of the nation. Structural dominance of national policy networks has also been important: Consider, for example, the influence that political centrality conferred on New Yorkers in the National Civic Federation during the Progressive Era, or on the major New York foundations during the 1950s and 1960s, when they organized and tested social programs that the federal government later adopted.

Nor is cognitive dominance absent from politics. First, as Baughman (chapter 6) notes, the city's dominance of the news media enables New York to define the nation's social agenda to a disproportionate extent. Local problems are especially salient to New York reporters and news executives, and the concentration of news-gathering organizations in New York enables them to cover local events intensely. Moreover, due to the three-hour gap between the coasts, even with the rise of Atlanta-based CNN and the defection of some network operations to Washington, D.C., New York stories (and New York experts commenting upon them) are more likely to appear on the evening news or in early morning papers than are events that take place on the West Coast. (That is one reason that network coverage of California so often highlights relatively timeless lifestyle stories.)[8]

Second, quite apart from the structural centrality of members of the New York policy elite, the cultural authority of such New York institutions as philanthropic foundations and policy centers invests their spokespersons' diagnoses and prescriptions with gravity, credibility, and a magnetic appeal to media opinion-makers (whose attention, in turn, has reinforced that authority). This process is itself enhanced by the fact that New York remains a center of intellectual journalism (including policy journalism, although Washington challenges New York's lead) and one of the few places where one can earn a living as a member of the "intelligentsia" without university affiliation.[9] As a result, new ideas diffuse quickly within the city and are disseminated elsewhere by many means.

Culture

The primary locus of cognitive dominance is the cultural realm. Here, New York remains the center of innovation, the place where styles are generated or imported from Europe first. New York's influence stems from dense agglomerations of commercial and "serious" artists and critics in many media, the cultural authority of its arts schools and non-profit institutions, and that of its publishing houses and journals of opinion. (To be sure, California challenges in New Age thought and youth culture. But note that, in the latter, after California's reign during the late 1960s, New York reestablished hegemony with disco and, through its linkages to Europe, punk; and, with help from the new immigration, has stayed in the musical vanguard in house music, industrial music, and hip-hop.)

Nonetheless, as Herman Melville wrote, "intellectual superiority . . . can never assume the practical available supremacy over other men, without the aid of some sort of external arts and entrenchments, always, in themselves, more or less paltry and base . . ."[10] Indeed, as Baughman suggests (chapter 6), sheer structural dominance—economic centrality to the media, the art market, advertising and design, and in publishing—underlies much of New York's pivotal role in U.S. culture. New York has also exercised strategic dominance in this field: As Zolberg points out (chapter 7), only the Ford Foundation could have coordinated the rise of the American nonprofit stage. Similarly, New York philanthropic, arts, and humanities figures were instrumental in creating and molding the National Endowments for the Arts and Humanities, and New York congressional representatives have been among those agencies' strongest backers.

Forms of Dominance and New York's Trajectory

Because the city's position rests on different forms of dominance, which have different tendencies and interact with one another in different ways, it is difficult to generalize about New York's trajectory. Different forms of dominance renew themselves to different degrees, a fact which lies behind what Martin Shefter (chapter 1) aptly calls the "dialectic of domination and diffusion." Concretely, structural dominance tends to be self-renewing, generating multiplier effects over time. Cognitive dominance is self-attenuating or entropic. (It is more difficult to generalize about strategic dominance, for reasons that I shall go into below.) Similarly, structural dominance is readily convertible into cultural and, to a lesser extent, strategic dominance, but these relationships are largely intransitive. The relative balance between self-renewing and convertible forms of dominance, on the one hand, and self-attenuating and inert forms, on the other, has important consequences for the long-term role of New York City in national and international affairs.

Structural Dominance

Economic geographers have demonstrated extraordinary stability of the U.S. urban hierarchy as a network of economic exchange. Structural dominance in the economy renews itself by establishing agglomeration economies in goods, information, and human capital that attract additional trade and information and induce new firms to locate in an urban area (thus converting structural to strategic dominance through command). Moreover, as Alan Pred has argued, structural dominance enables urban places to capture not only multiplier effects of local business activity but multiplier effects of activities conducted elsewhere, as well.[11] Thus, even as California banks and Chicago commodity markets challenge New York financial institutions, growth in those areas yields more business for the city's financial and business services industries. As in finance, New York's structural dominance of markets in art, advertising, and publishing also tends to be self-renewing.

Indeed, in the economic realm, New York's wealth of financial institutions places the city in particularly good stead because of the peculiar nature of the commodity in which they traffic. As Beth Mintz and Michael Schwartz have argued, capital's fungibility makes it a uniquely important basis of centrality.[12] Thus, even if New York were to become as dependent upon financial services as Detroit was on automobiles or Pittsburgh on steel, its product—capital and financial services—would provide a stronger foundation for continued superiority in the urban hierarchy. Similarly, legal services, information, and business consulting, three other sectors in which New York is prominent, have markets that span many industries, also enhancing the centrality and stability of the city's economy.[13]

Structural centrality to elite policy networks is also potentially self-renewing, as sponsorship and mentoring bring new generations into positions of informal influence. Three features of the American polity, however, make it difficult for New Yorkers and their institutions to maintain centrality in this way. First, the decentralization of U.S. higher education means that experts move frequently, requiring New York–based institutions to seek expertise beyond the city's borders, inhibiting the development of close-knit policy communities, and delocalizing expertise. Second, the nationalization of policy formation in a weak-party, strong-executive system without a powerful permanent bureaucracy, has led to an almost quadrennial reshuffling of policy networks, as waves of experts crash onto the Potomac's shores at four-year intervals.[14] Third, the interaction between these first two factors has led to a proliferation of competing university centers and Beltway think tanks that also destabilize traditional elite and networks (Kurth, chapter 4).

To be sure, the reproducibility of structural dominance is only a tendency, albeit a very strong one, even in the economy and culture. As systems grow, the proportion (but not the amount) of activity dominated by the center stands to decline, due to the proliferation of midsized places growing more rapidly than the center and to the capacity of those places, once they reach a threshold size, to support a broader range of commercial and cultural activities. For example, between 1950 and 1980, a period of massive expansion in domestic passenger air service, New York area airports remained the most central in the United States, but their degree of centrality declined by just over 20 percent.[15]

Moreover, exogenous change (for example, the rise of Pacific Rim economies and the resultant boost to Los Angeles in international trade) may also challenge a center's structural dominance (see Vogel, chapter 3). Whether tendencies towards self-renewal of structural advantage counterbalance structural consequences of system growth depends, first, on the nature of exogenous change and, second, on the ability of central places to use strategic dominance to reinforce their structural advantage.

Structural dominance is not only more self-renewing than other forms. It is also more easily convertible into other types of dominance. In the economic realm, for example, geographers have demonstrated the incentives for headquarters to occupy central places in the urban system, thus adding direct command to the indirect influence accruing from centrality itself. As we have seen, structural dominance in cultural markets is at the root of New York's influence over ideas and style; and the wealth accrued from trade and finance has supported the city's leading nonprofit cultural institutions throughout the century. Similarly, economic centrality provided the capital that fueled New York's rise to political prominence, and the structural centrality of New Yorkers to elite political networks, from Elihu Root to Franklin Roosevelt to John J. Rockefeller, Jr., enabled such leaders to coordinate national policy coalitions for decades, thus providing New York institutions with substantial strategic dominance as well. Structural dominance is also convertible into political representation, for executives seeking appointees in both private and public sectors know and rely on organizations and persons at the center of specialized networks.

Cognitive Dominance

By contrast, cognitive dominance is more entropic and less convertible. To be sure, the capacity of New York intellectuals (in the arts, politics, or management) to set agendas and focus attention of elites elsewhere is considerable; and when New Yorkers define the terms of national discourse and taste along lines in which the city excels, such processes have a self-renewing quality. Moreover, the cultural authority of New York figures and institutions places them at the center of ongoing exchange networks, generating structural centrality (as when representatives of New York nonprofit organizations are plucked for corporate board positions; or the cultural authority of New York consultants or artists generates trade for New York service firms or art galleries). But, overall, the reproducibility and convertibility of cognitive dominance are modest compared to the multiplier- and cross-effects of structural dominance.

This is the case because cognitive dominance, unless backed up by structural or political dominance, leads to diffusion of the very innovations that make a city central. Paradoxically, the greater the extent to which elites in other cities embrace values, styles, practices, and forms of organization pioneered in New York, the greater the extent to which the city's cognitive dominance diminishes.

By way of illustration, consider the nonprofit arts boom of the 1960s and 1970s (Zolberg, chapter 7). New Yorkers were instrumental in increasing institutional support for the arts in both the private and public sectors. The New York State Council on the Arts, created by Nelson Rockefeller in 1959, served as a model for the National Endowment for the Arts. That agency's formative leadership came out of New York's art world: first, Roger Stevens, a New York theatrical figure, and then Nancy Hanks, a long-time Rockefeller aide. The NEA used federal funds to encourage all fifty states to establish arts agencies on the New York model, creating independent sources of support for local and regional art worlds. Under the direction of W. McNeil Lowry, New York's Ford Foundation virtually created a national nonprofit theatre with a massive program of developmental grants in the 1960s (ironically building the "regional stage" with New York money). Soon thereafter, corporate art supporters created a New York–based Business Committee for the Arts to encourage company sponsorship of arts events and the growth of corporate art collections, which, especially in the Midwest and Southwest, bolstered the rise of regional aesthetics.

The results demonstrate the "dialectic of domination and diffusion" nicely. During the century's first half, structural dominance of American economic life made New York a magnet to artists, a principal center of art collecting, and, with Broadway generating productions that toured America's cities on the theatrical road, the hub of the American stage. After World War II, the city achieved structural dominance of the art market with the rise of Abstract Expressionism and the international style, a development that caused the decline of regional realism and gave the city a virtual monopoly over contemporary visual art. During the 1960s and 1970s, structural dominance was converted to cognitive and (in government and foundation programs) strategic dominance.

New York–based models and expertise flowed to the hinterlands. By the 1980s, vital regional art worlds again challenged New York's hegemony in the visual arts; and, whereas Broadway was once the source of plays that toured the country, resident theatres from New Haven to Seattle had become a principal source of productions for Broadway's commercial stage.[16]

Cognitive influence in the political and cultural spheres is also entropic because the very success of central models is liable to breed conflict and countermobilization. The influence of postwar liberalism as the taken-for-granted worldview of much of the New York–based media inspired strong counter-reaction once those media exposed southeastern and western audiences to ideas that many northeasterners accepted without question. Similarly, the art censorship conflicts of the early 1990s had less to do with changes in the level of social tolerance than with the fact that an expanded and increasingly pervasive system of nonprofit arts institutions exported cosmopolitan artists and art works to places where, a few years earlier, people would never have encountered them. Thus the very success of New York in exerting cognitive dominance triggers the emergence of new identities defined in opposition to metropolitan models.

The entropic tendencies of cognitive dominance can be counteracted to the extent that cognitive centrality is embedded in other forms of control. Strategic dominance is one such possibility: The influence of the New York–based mass-communications media, for example, was bolstered for years by the success of its lobbyists in impeding the development of cable as a viable programming alternative. Similarly, structural dominance in the art market ensures that New York artists remain prominent, despite the development of competing art worlds elsewhere.

To maintain cognitive dominance a city must generate steady streams of innovations, so that as old styles, models, and tastes are assimilated by the hinterlands, new ones emerge in their place. In this respect, compared to European capitals, New York suffers from the decentralization of American higher education and from the uniquely broad role of universities as incubators of innovation in everything from technology to art and business practices. Except in such fields as the visual arts, advertising, and finance, in which structural dominance and specialized training institutions ensure indigenous innovation, New York must import or co-opt experts trained or stationed elsewhere to supplement the contributions of men and women at distinguished local institutions. To an extent, the great private foundations (Rockefeller, Russell Sage, Ford, and a few others) and the institutions they created (the Council on

Foreign Relations, the Population Council, and the Social Science Research Council) have served as functional equivalents to universities in the political domain. But ultimately, even in such areas as business consulting, where practitioners package and retail methods developed at leading business schools throughout the country, New Yorkers often rely on experts located elsewhere.

Strategic Dominance

It is less easy to generalize about the effects of strategic dominance on a city's fortunes, because those effects vary so much. Strategic dominance *can be* self-renewing: success in forming coalitions gives institutions and their representatives skills and contacts that can be reused. On the other hand, because strategic dominance requires resources to bring to the table, it is vulnerable to exogenous change. Consider, for example, the influence of the westward migration of voters on the relative ability of New York- and California-based politicians to broker coalitions in presidential politics.

Similarly, strategic dominance *may be* convertible into other forms of dominance. Participation in coalitions enhances organizers' structural centrality, increasing the likelihood that they will serve as brokers in subsequent negotiations. And brokers can use strategic positions to enhance their cities' structural centrality, as when legislators acquire industrial-development or other pork-barrel funds for their districts as a condition of participating in larger coalitions. Private interests may also convert strategic to structural dominance, as some foundations did in the 1920s when they arranged for respected New Yorkers to be placed on governing boards of agencies they supported; or as New York banks did in the 1970s, when they coalesced to frustrate the Hunt brothers' attempt to corner the silver market, protecting the interests of New York investors.[17]

Although strategic dominance can be converted into structural dominance (and from there to cognitive influence), such conversion does not necessarily occur, for three reasons. First, as Shefter points out (chapter 1), when used to advance policies with national rather than local objectives, strategic dominance is a nonrenewable resource. During the postwar era, New York elites built coalitions for liberal domestic and foreign policies by providing inducements to politicians from other regions—public works, military contracts, transportation enhancements—that undermined New York's structural interests.

Second, the "New York City interest" is often not clear. Should New York's Washington advocates in the 1970s have fought for federal industrial programs to save lower-Manhattan manufacturing firms or for housing subsidies to accelerate gentrification? In this, as is often the case, New Yorkers had many interests, some of them in direct opposition to one another.

Third, urban dominance is an aggregate concept, the result of the positions and actions of thousands of individuals, firms, and institutions. Many of these actors are largely indifferent to the "New York City interest" even when it can be clearly discerned. Whereas the *structural* centrality of a powerful New York firm is likely to yield jobs and tax revenues for the region, it may use its *strategic* position to advance policies that profit the company's shareholders at the expense of the region and its inhabitants. These issues—the extent to which New York City can be said to have coherent interests, and the extent to which New York–based actors attempt to advance such interests—are sufficiently important to bear closer inspection.

Cohesion, Fragmentation, and the Decline of Place

One can view a metropolis in two ways: as a community of actors competing collectively against other cities; or as a set of populations competing against one another. For the most part, the preceding essays take the first view. Focusing upon the city itself as a unit of analysis, the authors clarify much about New York's changing fortunes, but at the risk of obscuring the multiplicity of actors and interests that "New York" comprises.

Two issues are at stake here. First, in what sense is a city or metropolitan area an "actor"? To what extent do cities have (or do their inhabitants act collectively as if they have) objective functions? And insofar as they do, to what extent do urban actors maximize from the standpoint of the city as opposed to some other unit of analysis? This is the problem of cohesion versus fragmentation in urban systems.

The second issue is broader: how have changes in the focal points of identity and agency since the early twentieth century, when geographers began writing about central places, affected the relationship between metropolitan dominance and urban fortunes? How has system-level change altered the reproducibility and convertibility of different forms of dominance, with what implications for New York's role in the twenty-first century? Is the imagery of a city system in which the vertical axis dominates the horizontal—i.e., of an "urban hierarchy"—the best way to understand the world in which we live? Or do we need new models that emphasize horizontal differentiation among plural "centers," only some of which are "metropolitan places" in the ordinary sense of that term?

Cohesion and Fragmentation

As early as 1870, New York's elite was notably fragmented in comparison to the upper classes of other major American cities.[18] Whereas Boston's Brahmins and Chicago's vigorous business class exercised stewardship over their cities' institutions, New York's multiple elites operated independently and often at cross-purposes. Today, this tradition is reflected in the querulous nature of New York politics, the difficulty of coordinating city-wide solutions to urban problems (even the fiscal crisis of the 1970s required the political equivalent of martial law in the form of the Municipal Assistance Corporation), and the always lively and sometimes poisonous quality of inter-group relations.

How has the fragmentation of New York's social mosaic, at both the elite and popular levels, affected New York's capacity to compete with other American cities? When New York's dominance is enhanced by the successes of individual firms, or where projects require only a critical mass as opposed to unanimous support, elite fragmentation may be a boon.[19] The reason for this is that fragmentation hones the competitive skills of elites at the same time it provides maximum autonomy for entrepreneurship. Because this is the case for structural dominance, the form of dominance that is most self-renewing and convertible, on balance fragmentation may have been in New York's interest. Fragmentation is also consistent with the exercise of cognitive dominance in most spheres.

Moreover, although New York's elites found it difficult to act decisively at the local level, early in this century fragmentation probably contributed to the city's structural centrality to national enterprises and campaigns. For one thing, fragmentation led New Yorkers to go outside their city's boundaries to build coalitions more than did members of more solidary elites. When Bostonians invested outside their city in the second half of the nineteenth century they sent family members to the copper mines or railroads to supervise their investments. By contrast, New Yorkers built coalitions, providing capital for elites in other cities and sending their children to schools where they would mingle with, influence, and even marry into, the upper classes of Boston, Cleveland, Chicago, and Philadelphia. With such commercial and school ties, and philanthropic foundations, as a base, they were well positioned to seize leadership in the first part of this century. An exemplary if atypical figure was Elihu Root, who played significant roles in building national coalitions in politics (as secretary of state), economic reform (as a founder and principal of the National Civic Federation), and culture (as founder and central figure in the American Federation of Arts). Indeed, the tendency, even then, for New Yorkers to resolve their disagreements in courts of law rather than private clubs may have also reinforced the capacity of members of New York's elite (an unusual proportion of whom were lawyers) to broker national coalitions.[20] As Shefter (chapter 5) notes, a later generation of New York lawyers played prominent roles in organizing the New Deal coalition.

Even today, fragmentation poses little direct danger to structural dominance in the economic or cultural realms. As Shefter suggests, the very fluidity of New York's elite social structure and the concurrent lack of effective social control facilitate innovation. If many entrepreneurs fall in combat, the survivors are well poised to compete in the national and international arenas. This phenomenon is as visible in finance, where in the 1980s outsiders like Saul Steinberg or Salomon's Lewis Ranieri created financial instruments that bolstered New York's dominance, as in the arts, where New York remains the center of the avant-garde.[21]

When the New York interest demands not just competitive wit and critical mass, but also elite cohesion and social control, so that the city presents a united front in corporate action, New York's fragmentation is a liability. For example, one faction of wealthy New Yorkers created a successful art museum, the Metropolitan Museum of Art, as early as Boston and before Chicago. But when rapid mobilization was necessary in the competition for the 1891 World's Fair, Chicago left New York in the dust.[22] The difficulty New York's institutions have in enunciating consensus positions places the city's strategic dominance constantly at risk.

New York interests retain substantial clout in government, although not as much as they had during the heyday of the New Deal. (Even then, as Kahler points out in chapter 2, economic policies championed by New York elites may have assisted other cities more than New York itself.) City interests also retain strategic dominance in much of the private sector. Corporate takeovers organized by New York banks have shaped communities large and small, and New York corporate headquarters command enterprises throughout nation and world. But whether their activities redound to the benefit of the city as a whole is another issue. Although "New York capital" has always been powerful, the political roles of a New York firm closely held by men and women with metropolitan roots and a multinational headquartered in the city may be very different.

Urban Identity and the Decline of Place

Theorists of "postmodernism" have written much about the "eclipse of place."[23] By this, they mean at least three different things. The first, which need not detain us here, refers to architectural and cultural homogenization attendant to the rise of postmodern shopping malls and other redevelopment schemes. The second refers to a decline in the effect of location on the behavior of economic or political actors. Third, the phrase connotes an increase in the extent to which business is conducted and fateful decisions are made in distinctly national or global, as opposed to local, institutions.

It is a commonplace that the advance and integration of computing and telecommunications technologies has made time and space less forbidding barriers to interaction and administration, a fact to which the rise of multinational enterprise testifies. Capital's greater mobility cuts New York both ways. On the one hand, the city retains its centrality in the flow of capital between the United States and Europe, and its financial and business-service operations hold a privileged position in international communication and transportation networks, thus permitting some city interests to gain from these developments. On the other hand, the multinational's loyalty is to shareholders and management, not to the city in which it makes its home. Indeed, when one speaks of multinationals, the meaning of place is notoriously slippery. Is a Delaware-chartered company with headquarters in New York, most of its personnel working in branches around the globe, and much of its stock owned by pension funds located in cities throughout the United States (but managed by New York financial institutions) a "New York company" in the same sense that the Morgan and Chase banks were in the 1920s? Which is the New York institution: a New York daily newspaper owned by a London or Los Angeles communications conglomerate, or a national newspaper owned by a New York–based company? The internationalization of capital is reflected not only in the relocation of corporate headquarters, but in the failure of New York's business community to control urban growth as effectively as it did during the prime of the New York Regional Plan. As David Harvey has put it, "The communities of money and capital are communities without propinquity."[24]

One can calculate the contribution of such firms to structural dominance in the economy by conventional means. But their impact on the city's strategic and cognitive dominance is less easily judged. Moreover, the same capital mobility that has enhanced the ability of New York's financial institutions to tap global markets has made the city's hold on its corporate enterprises tenuous. If New York's major businesses hold back from collective efforts to address the city's domestic problems—something their capacity to relocate gives them every incentive to do—the cost to the city may become so great as to erode the structural advantages that New York maintains.

The declining significance of place to New York's elite has a social, as well as an economic and organizational, side. The executives of New York–headquartered enterprises live for the most part in suburbs outside the city and, in many cases, the state. This peculiarly American division of home and workplace, and splintering of authority between central cities and suburban political jurisdictions, likewise militates against elite political mobilization around urban identities.

Spatially rooted identities are, of course, far from dead among the majority of New Yorkers. Indeed, among poor and working-class New Yorkers, a resurgence of the primordial politics of ethnicity, race, and place—a *sub-urbanization* of political identity that parallels the *suburbanization* of elite residence—threatens the viability of "New York" as a political subject as severely as the delocalization of corporate decision-making.[25]

If one facet of the eclipse of place is a decline in the "New Yorkness" of local institutions, another, especially relevant to structural dominance and the ability of city interests to use the political system, is the movement of agency and identity from local to national levels. The most obvious shift has been the movement of formal system governance functions from central metropolitan areas to Washington. This happened first in finance. From the Civil War onward, the fiscal power of New York's bankers, closely tied to European capital, enabled them in effect to set fiscal policy for the nation as a whole. Once J.P. Morgan, Jr., the central figure in the financial coalition of the 1920s, failed to stem the Great Depression, the formalization of financial policy shifted control to the Federal Reserve. Similarly, the centrality of New York institutions—at first, such firms as United Fruit, with their private foreign policies, and later the Council on Foreign Relations—to foreign-policy formation also succumbed to Washington and the defense and intelligence establishment of the cold war (Kurth, chapter 4). By the Great Society era, Washington agencies and think tanks likewise supplanted New York institutions in the field of social policy making. In each case, the shift initially enhanced New York influence, as New Yorkers took on key positions in national institutions and New York–based policy models gained public endorsement. But in each case this transitional stage was followed by a decentering of strategic control.

By and large, then, the action has shifted: But to where? Certainly not to Washington as an urban center, though federal government expansion has had a positive impact on that city's bedeviled economy. Rather, it has been absorbed by supralocal institutions to which place is decreasingly relevant.

Although change is most visible in the public sector, it is evident in the private as well. As academic anti-Semitism abated, the Jewish intellectual community of which Glazer writes (chapter 8) gravitated to universities around the nation. If, in the early progressive era, men like Root or John D. Rockefeller, Jr., could forge national networks around their personal and institutional affiliations, by the 1950s universities and professional associations replaced elite networks as the scaffolding around which professional communities arose. Again, New York fell behind less because competing centers emerged than because agency and identity became supralocal.

Conclusion

New York retains its structural dominance of the economy on a solid foundation of finance and business services, two industries notably resistant to long-term fluctuation of demand. Indeed, the city's structural dominance, according to conventional measures of central-place geographers, may be enhanced by the increasing integration of the world economy. Thus New York's long-term prosperity, at least as compared to heartland U.S. cities, seems secure. Moreover, the convertibility of structural into strategic and cognitive dominance likewise bodes well for New York's survival as a global financial capital.

New York retains substantial cognitive dominance as well, due in large part to its structural superiority in key cultural industries. On the other hand, the self-limiting quality of cultural dominance, per se, and the decentralization of cultural authority within a far-flung system of public and private universities, ensures that American culture, in the broadest sense, will be increasingly multicentric.

New York's weakness is in converting structural to strategic dominance. In part, this is a function of the perennial fragmentation of the city's most prominent interests, which impedes collective mobilization for the city's benefit at the federal level. In part, it reflects the weakening urban identities of significant components of the city's dominant coalition, especially the corporate sector. As the globalization of enterprise enhances New York's economy, it threatens the city's polity. Unless political coalitions within the metropolitan area satisfy the needs for services of New York's poor, working-class, and lower-middle-class communities, the city's structural advantages in economic competition may be undermined by social disorganization and political chaos. In other words, if the economic benefits of New York's metropolitan dominance fail to trickle down to the city's working population, elites may discover that the misery of the underclass and working poor have trickled up.[26]

As the authors of this volume's essays suggest, New York's fate parallels that of the nation as a whole. As the American century closes, the United States shifts from an economic and political hegemon to the role of *prima inter pares*. Likewise, New York, the capital of the American century, becomes only the dominant, no longer the hegemonic, American urban place.

To be sure, this analogy is not inevitable. Lesser powers than the United States have maintained unchallenged urban centers: Paris and Tokyo come readily to mind. But in such societies, structural dominance in economics, politics, and culture has been reinforced by strategic control (such cities are centers of government as well as private initiative) and by centralized cultural authority. Absent such institutional means of counteracting the self-attenuating character of cognitive dominance, and without the effective exertion of strategic dominance to assert a collective urban interest, New York will never occupy the place in American culture and politics that it did at the height of the American Century. But neither will any other city.

Notes

1. See Knoke, David, *Political Networks: The Structural Perspective* (New York: Cambridge University Press, 1990) for a fine overview of network approaches to power and politics.
2. For purposes of exposition, I ignore variation within the geographic and sociological literatures and elide the differences between them. In general, sociologists have paid more attention to the technical development of network analysis as an abstract tool than geographers; the best exposition of relevant analytic principles is Ronald L. Burt's *Structural Holes* (Cambridge, MA: Harvard University Press, 1992). Substantive differences are largely a matter of emphasis and convergence is visible. For example, early work in geography emphasized the role of spatial distance in defining urban location, whereas network analysts focused on relational distance between units in a sociomatrix, defined on the basis of pairwise similarity between actors' transaction patterns taken as a whole, often expressed as Euclidian distance. With the development of central place theory, however, geographers, too, began to highlight the importance of transactional intensity, as distinct from spatial distance, in defining the shape of urban networks; see

King, Leslie J., *Central Place Theory* (Newbury Park, CA: Sage Publications, 1988); and Morrill, Richard, Gary L. Gaile, and Grant Ian Thrall, *Spatial Diffusion* (Newbury Park, California: Sage Publications, 1988).

A notion related to centrality is that of hierarchy: a multilevel replication of relationships in the form of an inverted tree, with actors at the highest level accruing superiority as a result of being at the culminating point in a series of exchanges. See Simon, Herbert, "The Architecture of Complexity," in *The Sciences of the Artificial*, 2nd ed. (Cambridge, MA: MIT Press, 1981), pp. 193–229. Centrality and hierarchical superordination are in a sense the same thing: one can see this graphically if one rearranges the downward lines of an inverted tree (appropriate for the special case of organization charts, in which levels are connected by relationships embodying formal authority rather than simple exchange) by making the limbs go out in all angles from the center. They are not one and the same, however, because hierarchy, as ecologists and early central-place theorists conceived of it, entails the more exacting requirement of homologic replication between levels. For example, early central-place theory posited nested sets of places, each with homologous ties to those immediately below them in the urban hierarchy (as well as to smaller places in their immediate hinterlands). Nonetheless, the gravitation of sociological network analysts to measures of centrality that weight the importance of ties by the prominence of each actor with whom another is tied captures something of this vertical imagery, if not the structure (rarely observed in informal networks, as distinct from natural systems or formal organizations) of homologic replication. See Bonacich, Philip, "Power and Centrality: A Family of Measures," *American Journal of Sociology* 92 (1987):1170–1182.

3. On the two-step flow, see Lazarsfeld, Paul F., Bernard Berelson, and Hazel Gaudet, *The People's Choice* (New York: Columbia University Press, 1948). Once again, the resonance between a sociological network approach and geography's central-place theory is marked. For one thing, rates of interaction between opinion leaders in different places are higher than rates of interaction between non-elites; and one can easily imagine that the position of a locality's opinion leaders in a national elite network is closely aligned to the position of their SMSA in the interurban network. There are no doubt as many levels of opinion leadership as there are levels in the urban hierarchy; and one may consider an opinion leader's following as a kind of human "hinterland."
4. On cultural authority, see Starr, Paul, *The Social Transformation of American Medicine: The Rise of a Sovereign Profession and the Making of a Vast Industry* (New York: Basic Books, 1982), p. 11. On the notion of "centers," see Shils, Edward, "Center and Periphery," ch. 4 in *The Constitution of Society* (Chicago: University of Chicago Press, 1972).
5. Even if New Yorkers tried to reproduce New York control of particular offices (and there is no evidence that they do) and succeeded 80 percent of the time (and there is no evidence that they could), within two decades

two thirds of the New Yorkers would be replaced by persons originating elsewhere. (If the probability of retention of a New York office holder or the succession of a New Yorker by another New Yorker from one presidential term to another is .8, the probability of retention of New Yorkers over 20 years [five presidential terms] is $.8^5$ or .328.)

6. Mintz, Beth and Michael Schwartz, *The Power Structure of American Business* (Chicago: University of Chicago Press, 1985).
7. On the centralizing effects of the merger movement, see Logan, John R., and Harvey L. Molotch, *Urban Fortunes: The Political Economy of Place* (Berkeley: University of California Press, 1987), pp. 201–202.
8. Tuchman, Gaye, *Making News* (New York: Free Press, 1978).
9. See Kadushin, Charles, *The American Intellectual Elite* (Boston: Little, Brown, 1974).
10. Melville, Herman, *Moby Dick*, Charles Fedelson, Jr., ed. (Indianapolis, IN: Bobbs-Merrill Co., Inc., 1964), p. 198.
11. Pred, Allan, *Urban Growth and City-Systems in the United States, 1840–1860* (Cambridge, MA: Harvard University Press, 1980), p. 121.
12. Mintz and Schwartz, *The Power Structure of American Business*, p. 37.
13. Logan and Molotch, in *Urban Fortunes*, p. 262, note that "producer services . . . cluster in the largest places and seem to have had the least tendency to dispersal."
14. See Nathan, Richard F., Fred C. Doolittle, and Associates. *Reagan and the States* (Princeton: Princeton University Press, 1987).
15. Irwin, Michael D., and John D. Kasarda, "Air Passenger Links and Employment Growth in U.S. Metropolitan Areas." *American Sociological Review* 56 (1991):524–537, Table 2, p. 529. (Due to a typographical error, the column for 1980 is labeled 1960).
16. On the visual arts, see Crane, Diana, *The Transformation of the Avant-Garde: The New York Art World, 1940–1985* (Chicago: University of Chicago Press, 1987); and Martorella, Rosanne, *Corporate Art* (New Brunswick, NJ: Rutgers University Press, 1990).
17. On the foundations, see DiMaggio, Paul, "Creating an Organizational Field: American Art Museums, 1920–1940," in *The New Institutionalism in Organizational Analysis*, Powell, Walter W., and Paul DiMaggio, eds. (Chicago: University of Chicago Press, 1991); on the mobilization of bankers to discipline the Hunts, see Mintz and Schwartz, *The Power Structure of American Business*, pp. 93–94.
18. On fragmentation of New York's upper class, see Beisel, Nicola, "Class, Culture, and Campaigns Against Vice in Three American Cities, 1872–1892," *American Sociological Review* 55 (1990):44–62; Hammack, David C., *Power and Society: Greater New York at the Turn of the Century* (New York: Russell Sage Foundation, 1982); and Jaher, Frederic Cople, *The Urban Estab-*

lishment: Upper Strata in Boston, New York, Charleston, Chicago, and Los Angeles (Urbana, IL: University of Illinois Press, 1982).

19. See Oliver, Pamela, Gerald Marwell, and Roy Teixerira, "A Theory of Critical Mass. I. Interdependence, Group Heterogeneity, and the Production of Collective Action," *American Journal of Sociology* 94 (1985): 502–531.
20. Hammack, *Power and Society*, pp. 53–54.
21. See Lewis, Michael, *Liar's Poker* (New York: Penguin, 1989).
22. Bender, Thomas, *In New York Intellect: A History of Intellectual Life in New York City, from 1750 to the Beginnings of Our Own Time* (Baltimore: Johns Hopkins University Press, 1987), Thomas Bender has argued that the inability of New Yorkers to coalesce around single efforts was particularly fateful in higher education, where New York failed to develop a college as attractive to national elites as Yale, Harvard, or Princeton.
23. Harvey, David, *The Condition of Postmodernity: An Enquiry into the Origins of Cultural Change* (Cambridge, MA: Basil Blackwell, 1990); see Lash, Scott, *Sociology of Postmodernism* (New York: Routledge & Kegan Paul, 1990); and Zukin, Sharon, *Landscapes of American Market/Place* (Berkeley: University of California Press, 1991).
24. Harvey, David, *Consciousness and the Urban Experience: Studies in the History and Theory of Capitalist Urbanization* (Baltimore: Johns Hopkins University Press, 1985), p. 254.
25. See Mollenkopf, John Hull, "The Place of Politics and the Politics of Place," in *Power, Culture, and Place: Essays on New York City*, Mollenkopf, J.H., ed. (New York: Russell Sage Foundation, 1988), pp. 273–284.
26. I am grateful to Doug Rae for suggesting this formulation. For a sustained treatment of these issues, see the papers in *Dual City: Restructuring New York*, Mollenkopf, John H., and Manuel Castells, eds. (New York: Russell Sage Foundation, 1991).

Name Index

A

ABC, 125, 129, 130
Acheson, Dean, 71, 82, 87
AFL-CIO, 101, 175
Amalgamated Clothing Workers Union, 100, 174
American Association of Social Workers, 99
American Enterprise Institute (AEI), 88, 93
American Federation of Arts, 210
American Honda, 142*n*
American-Israel Public Affairs Committee (AIPAC), 90
American Jewish Committee, 168, 169, 185
American Museum of Natural History, 9
American Society of Composers, Authors and Publishers (ASCAP), 121, 127
American Symphony Orchestra League, 153
American Telephone and Telegraph, 124
Anchor Books, 185, 186
Anti-Defamation League, 169
Arnez, Desi, 124
Artists Club, 16
Art of This Century Gallery, 17
Associated Press, 119
Association for Improving the Condition of the Poor, 99
Attali, Jacques, 181–182

B

Bagehot, Walter, 51
Baker, James, 111–112
Balanchine, George, 1
Ball, Lucille, 124
Baltzell, Digby, 190
Bank of America, 65
Bank of England, 12, 13, 43, 52
Bank of the United States, 10
Barbirolli, John, 164*n*
Barnes Collection, 149
Barr, Alfred, 163*n*
Bartles & Jaymes, 132
Barzun, Jacques, 185
Basic Book Club, 186
Beame, Abraham, 35
Bell, Daniel, 186
Belzberg Brothers, 182
Benjamin, Walter, 1
Bennett, James Gordon, 96
Bensel, Richard, 11
Berle, Milton, 124, 125, 126
Berlin, Irving, 170
Bernstein, Leonard, 102
Board of Trade: London, 6
Boesky, Ivan, 182

Book-of-the-Month Club, 185
Bowman, Isiah, 74
Brandeis, Justice Louis D., 171
Braudele, Fernand, 28, 45*n*
Breton, André, 16
British Aluminum, 181
Broadcast Music Inc., 127
Brookings Institution, 87–88, 93
Bruck, Connie, 182–183
Bryce, James, 3, 4, 118, 133
Brzezinski, Zbigniew, 85, 86
Bundy, McGeorge, 85, 86
Bureau of Labor Statistics, 132
Burt, Ronald, 196
Bush, George, 20, 21, 92, 104, 108, 132, 165*n*
Business Committee for the Arts, 205
Business Roundtable, 199

C

Cable News Network (CNN), 130, 141*n*, 201
Caesar, Sid, 125
Cannell, Stephen J., 133
Capital Cities Communications, 130
Carnegie, Dale, 185
Carnegie Endowment for International Peace, 88, 93
Carnegie Foundation, 104, 164*n*
Carson, Johnny, 126, 129
Carter, Jimmy, 21, 89, 106, 176
CBS Records, 132
Center Theater, 124
Central Bank, 106, 110
Central Intelligence Agency, 82, 85
Cerf, Bennett, 118, 184
Cezanne, 150
Chase Manhattan Bank, 41, 105, 211
Chicago, University of, 186
Chicago Board of Trade, 67
Chicago Mercantile Exchange, 67
Churchill, Winston, 80
Citibank, 66, 68
City College, 168, 186
Clayton, Will, 82
Cohen, Arthur, 186
Cohen, Peter A., 183
Columbia Concerts Corporation, 153
Columbia Records, 154
Columbia University, 83, 85, 103, 169, 170, 185, 187
Commission for Cultural Affairs of the City of New York, 166*n*
Committee on Economic Security, 101
Community Concerns, 153
Conference Board, 199
Considine, Frank, 183
Coolidge, Archibald Cary, 74
Coughlin, Father Charles, 170
Crane, Diana, 158
Cunningham, Merce, 1

D

Davis, Elmer, 119
Davis, John W., 74
Davis, Norman, 74
De Graff, Robert, 185
De Mille, Cecile B., 122
Denney, Reuel, 186
Desilu, 125
Destler, I. M., 111
Dewey, Thomas, 101, 200
Diamond, Martin, 186
Dillon, Read Ltd., 58
Dinkins, David, 42, 112
Disney, Walt, 125
Doubleday Books, 185
Downtown–Lower Manhattan Association, 38
Dreier, Kathryn, 149
Drennan, Matthew, 36
Drexel Burnham, 109, 182
Drury, Alan, 127
Duchamp, Marcel, 16, 149–151, 162*n*
Dukakis, Michael S., 176–178
Dulles, John Foster, 83–84
Durkheim, Emile, 186
Duval, Talbot, 183

E

Eastman, Max, 10
Eberstadt, Ferdinand, 82
Eisenhower, Dwight D., 72, 83, 84, 85, 176, 177
Ellington, Duke, 121
Emergency Financial Control Board, 38
Epstein, Jason, 4, 185, 186
Erasmus Hall High School (Brooklyn), 173
Ernst, Max, 16

F

Fainstein, Norman I., 42
Fainstein, Susan S., 42
Fauves, 150
FCC. *See* Federal Communications Commission
Federal Communications Commission, 124, 129, 130
Federal Emergency Relief Administration, 100
Federal Home Loan Bank Board, 100
Federal Radio Commission, 120
Field Foundation, 102, 104
First Boston Corporation, 109
First National City Bank, 105
Fitzgerald, F. Scott, 122
Flynn, Ed, 101
Ford Motor Company, 90
Foreign Policy Association, 91
Forrestal, James, 82, 100
Fox (television network), 130
Frankfurter, Felix, 171
Free Press, 186
Freud, Sigmund, 186
Frohnmeyer, John E., 165*n*

G

Gabler, Neal, 122, 180
Gauguin, 150
General Electric, 105
General Motors, 84, 90, 105
Georgetown University Center for Strategic and International Studies (CSIS), 88, 89, 93
Gershwin, George, 170
Gilman, Richard, 160
Ginsberg, Benjamin, 115*n*
Glazer, Nathan, 186
Gleason, Jackie, 125
Goldman, Sachs, 62, 109
Goldwater, Barry, 84
Goodman, Paul, 102
Gorbachev, Mikhail, 89
Gottlieb, Adolph, 17, 187
Gourevitch, Peter, 113*n*
Graham, Martha, 165*n*
Greeley, Horace, 10, 96
Green, Martin, 190
Greenberg, Clement, 17, 187, 188
Greenspan, Alan, 2, 109, 110
Groton, 73
Guggenheim Museum, 17, 150
Guggenheim, Peggy, 17, 187
Guggenheim, Solomon, 150
Guilbaut, Serge, 151, 187
Guinzberg, Harold K., 184
Gunther, John, 123

H

Hamilton, Alexander, 97
Hammack, David, 8, 24*n*
Hammer, Armand, 163*n*
Hammerstein, Oscar, 10, 170
Hanks, Nancy, 156, 198, 205
Harding, Warren, 12, 86
Harold Pratt House, 81
Harriman, Averell, 13–14, 71, 82, 100
Harrington, Michael, 102
Hart, Lorenz, 170
Harvard University, 74, 85, 169
Harvard University Press, 186
Harvey, David, 211
Hatters and Furriers Union, 174
Hearst, William Randolph, 9, 96
Heilbrun, James, 158
Heclo, Hugh, 44*n*

Hennings, C. Randall, 111
Henry, O., 10
Heritage Foundation, 89
Hewitt, Abram, 98
Hillman, Sidney, 101, 104
Himmelfarb, Milton, 174
Hitler, Adolph, 13, 181
Hock, Sidney, 170
Hollander, John, 185
Hoover, Herbert, 12, 119
Hoover Institution, 88, 89
Hopkins, Harry, 13, 100, 101
Huebsch, B. W., 184
Hughes, Charles Evans, 12, 75
Hull, Cordell, 78, 79, 83
Humphrey, Hubert, 176
Hunt Brothers, 207

I

IBM, 105
Icahn, Carl, 183
ILGWU, 31
IMF. *See* International Monetary Fund
International Bank for Reconstruction and Development (World Bank), 81, 82
International Encyclopedia of the Social Sciences, 187
International Ladies Garment Workers Union, 174
International Monetary Fund (IMF), 81, 82; location of, 14
International Trade Organization (ITO), 81

J

J. M. Kaplan Fund, 102
J. P. Morgan & Co., 8, 12
Jackson, Andrew, 10, 98
Jackson, Jesse, 172, 176, 177
Jacobs, Jane, 29
Javits, Jacob, 156
Jay, John, 97
Jefferson, Thomas, 7
Jewish Museum, 163*n*
Joffrey Dance Company, 165*n*
Johns Hopkins University, 74
Johnson, Lyndon Baines, 15, 20, 87, 176
Johnson, Ross, 183
Jones, Ernest, 186
Judson, Arthur, 153, 154, 156, 157, 160, 164*n*

K

Kandinsky, Virgil, 150
Kaplan, Jeremiah, 186
Katzenstein, Peter, 43
Katznelson, Ira, 114*n*
Kennan, George, 71, 82, 83
Kennedy, John F., 18, 20, 85, 102, 103, 176, 177
Kernell, Samuel, 114*n*
Kern, Jerome, 170
Kerner Commission, 104
Kikko, 62
Kindleberger, Charles, 52, 76–77
King, Martin Luther, 102
Kissinger, Henry, 85, 86, 94*n*
Klopfer, Ronald, 184
Knight-Ridder, 128
Knoedler & Co., 163*n*
Knopf, Alfred, 118, 184
Knox, Frank, 79
Koch, Edward I., 38, 42, 112, 176–177
Kohlberg, Kravits and Roberts, 183
Koontz, Samuel, 187
Kravits, Kenry R., 183
Kristol, Irving, 186
Kuhn, Loeb & Co., 8, 171, 180, 181, 183

L

Labor, Department of, 100
La Guardia, Fiorello, 79, 101, 104, 170, 174

Lamont, Daniel, 98
Lampard, Eric, 6
Lardner, Ring, 119
Lasser, K., 185
League of Nations, 74, 80
Lear, Norman, 130
Leffingwell, Russell, 74
Léger, Fernand, 16
Lehman, Herbert, 79, 171, 174
Lehman Brothers, 171, 180
Leveson, Irving, 39
Levin, Gerald M., 141*n*
Liebman, Arthur, 175
Lincoln, Abraham, 96
Lindsay, John V., 35, 104, 156
Lippman, Walter, 171, 189
Loew's, Inc., 122, 183
Lovett, Robert, 13, 71, 82, 100
Lowry, W. McNeil, 155, 205
Luce, Henry R., 17, 96, 118–119

M

Macmillan, 187
Martorella, Roseanne, 159
Marx Brothers, 135*n*
Massachusetts Institute of Technology, 85
Masuda, Shigeru, 59
May, Peter, 183
Mayer, Louis B., 180
McArthur, Douglas, 83
McCarthy, Joseph, 15, 83
McCloy, John J., 13, 71, 82, 87, 92, 100
McGovern, George, 176
MCA, 125
Meany, George, 101
Melville, Herman, 202
Merrill Lynch, 68, 109
Merton, Robert, 187
Metro-Goldwyn-Mayer, 122, 124
Metropolitan Museum of Art, 9
Metropolitan Opera, 9, 156
Milken, Michael, 109, 182
Mintz, Beth, 203
Miro, Joan, 16
Mobilization for Youth program, 103, 104
Modern Library, 184–185
Mollenkopf, John, 31, 36
Mondrian, Piet, 16
Montgomery, David, 96
Morgan, J. P., 148, 161*n*–162*n*, 212
Morgan, J. P., Jr., 73
Morgan Guaranty, 105, 211
Morgan Stanley, 109
Morgenthau, Henry, Jr., 82
Morris, William, 163*n*
Moses, Robert, 171, 189
Moynihan, Daniel P., 103
Mumford, Lewis, 118
Municipal Assistance Corporation, 38, 209
Musée des Arts Décoratifs, 162*n*
Museum of Non-Objective Art, 17, 150

N

National Can Company, 183
National Civic Federation, 200, 210
National Commission on Civil Disorders, 104
National Concert and Artists Corporation (NCAC), 154
National Consumers' League, 99
National Institutes of Mental Health, 103
National Resources Planning Board, 100, 102
National Security Advisors, 85, 86
National Security Council, 82
National Urban Coalition, 104
New Museum of Contemporary Art, 160
New School for Social Research, 188
New York City Opera, 165*n*

New York Federal Reserve Bank, 106, 115*n*
New York Philharmonic Symphony Orchestra, 9, 153, 154, 160
New York Regional Plan, 211
New York State Council for the Arts, 156, 205
New York Telephone, 65–66
New York University, 169
Nichols, Nicholas J., Jr., 141*n*
Nikkei, 67
Nippon Life Insurance Company, 62
Nissan, 142*n*
Nitze, Paul, 82
Nixon, Richard, 106
Nomura Securities Company, 62, 66
Noonday, 186
Norman, Montagu, 13
North Atlantic Treaty Organization (NATO), 82

O

Ochs, Adolph, 9
O'Keeffe, Georgia, 149
OPEC, 90
Ormandy, Eugene, 164*n*

P

Paley, William, 96, 153, 154
Parker, Dorothy, 10
Parsons, Talcott, 186
Paul, Weiss, Rifkind, Wharton and Garrison, 182
PBS. *See* Public Broadcasting System
Peltz, Nelson, 183
Penguin Books, 185
Perelman, Ronald, 182
Perkins, Frances, 13, 100
Peterson, Paul, 23*n*
Phelps, William Lyon, 121
Philadelphia Orchestra, 153, 164*n*
Phillips Collection, 149
Phillips, Kenneth, 66
Phillips, William, 187
Picabia, 151
Picasso, Pablo, 150
Pocket Books, 185
Podhoretz, Norman, 185
Pollock, Jackson, 17
Population Council, 207
Portal, Lord Viscount, 181
Port Authority, 34, 35
Pred, Allan, 4, 203
Presidents Committee on Juvenile Delinquency (PCJD), 103
Proust, Marcel, 188
Public Broadcasting System, 129
Publisher's Lunch Club, 184
Pulitzer, Joseph, 9, 96

Q

Quinn, John, 148–150, 153

R

Rahv, Phillip, 187
Random House, 184
Ranieri, Lewis, 210
RCA-NBC, 130
RCA Victor, 154, 166*n*
Reagan, Ronald Wilson, 20, 21, 86, 89, 92, 104, 105, 106–111, 132
Reconstruction Finance Corporation, 100
Reynolds Co., 181
Rice, Grantland, 119
Riesman, David, 186
Riney, Hal, 132
RJR-Nabisco, 183
Roberts, George, 183
Rockefeller, David, 38, 86, 91
Rockefeller, John J., Jr., 204, 213
Rockefeller, Nelson Aldrich, 17, 84, 86, 94*n*, 150, 155, 156, 200, 205
Rockefeller Brothers Fund, 155
Rockefeller Foundation, 104, 155, 206
Rodgers, Richard, 10, 170

Roosevelt, Franklin Delano, 13, 18, 73, 76, 78, 79, 80, 93*n*, 97, 99–101, 112, 171, 174, 200, 204
Roosevelt, Theodore, 11–12, 74, 200
Root, Elihu, 11–12, 74, 204, 213
Rosenberg, Harold, 17, 187
Rosenthal, Arthur, 186
Rostow, Walt, 85
Rothko, Mark, 187
Royal Institute of International Affairs, 74, 77
Rubin, Lawrence, 152
Runyon, Damon, 119
Russell Sage Foundation, 100, 206

S

Salomon Brothers, 55, 109, 182, 183, 210
Sarnoff, David, 154, 156, 160
Schapiro, Meyer, 187, 188
Schuster, Max, 184
Schwartz, Michael, 203
Sears, 183
Senate Foreign Relations Committee, 83
Shales, Tom, 130
Shearson Lehman, 62, 109, 183
Shefter, Martin, 24*n*, 25*n*, 115*n*
Shils, Edward, 187
Shimkin, Leon, 185
Silverman, Fred, 130
Simon, Henry, 184
Simon and Schuster, 184, 185
Skadden, Arps, Slate, Meagher and Flom, 182
Skocpol, Theda, 114*n*
Slawson, John, 169
Smith, Red, 119
Social Science Research Council, 194, 207
Sony Corporation, 130, 132
Sotheby's (London), 159
Southern, Hugh, 156
Spelling, Aaron, 130
Stahr, Monroe, 122
Stanton, Frank, 125
Starr, Roger, 32, 34
Steiglitz, Alfred, 148
Steinberg, Paul, 182
Steinberg, Saul, 210
Stern Foundation, 104
Stevens, Roger, 156, 205
Stevenson, Adlai, 176
Stimson, Henry L., 11–12, 13, 75, 79, 100, 101, 200
Stokowski, Leopold, 164*n*
Strong, Benjamin, 13
Studio Gallery, 149, 150
Sumitomo Bank, 62

T

Taconic Foundation, 102
Tebbel, John, 184, 185
Terasawa, Yoshi, 66
Thomas, Theodore, 9
Thomas A. Edison Studios, 124
Tilden, Samuel, 98
Tilly, Charles, 4
Time, Inc., 131, 141*n*
Time-Warner, 131
Tinker, Grant, 130
Tisch, Laurence, 183
Tobier, Emanuel, 33
Toscanini, Arturo, 154, 164*n*
Triangle Industries, 183
Trilling, Lionel, 170, 185, 187, 189
Truman, Harry S., 13, 82, 85, 175
Tweed, William M., 146–147
Twentieth Century Fund, 100

U

Union League Club, 146
United Fruit, 212
United Press, 119
U.S. Census Bureau, 158
U.S. Department of Commerce, 100
U.S. Department of Defense, 32, 82, 85

U.S. Department of Justice, 100
U.S. Department of State, 2, 12, 80, 85, 100, 101, 151
U.S. Department of the Treasury, 80, 95, 97, 105, 107, 109–111
U.S. Department of War, 80

V

Van Buren, Martin, 10, 11, 97–98, 99, 112, 200
Vandenberg, Arthur, 83
Van Gogh, Vincent, 150
Vernon, Raymond, 7, 15–16
Viking, 184
Villard, Oswald Garrison, 119
Vogel, David, 114*n*
Volcker, Paul, 2, 21, 106, 109, 111–112
Volkswagen, 132

W

Wagner, Robert F., 14, 101, 102, 104
Wakeman, Frederic, 123
Waldinger, Roger, 33, 37
Wallace, Henry, 176
Warburg, Paul, 74
Warburg, S. M., 181–182
Warner Brothers, 122, 124, 125
Warner Communications, 131
Washington State Arts Commission, 165*n*
Weber, Max, 186
Wechsler, Harold, 169
Welk, Lawrence, 126
White, E. B., 123
White Citizens Council, 22
Whitney, Gertrude Vanderbilt, 149, 150
Whitney Museum of American Art, 17, 149, 150, 152
Wilson, Charles, 84
Wilson, Edmund, 187, 189
Wilson, James Q., 23*n*, 25*n*, 114*n*
Wilson, Woodrow, 80
Witte, Edwin, 100
WNET television, 129
Woodrow Wilson Foundation, 74
Woollcott, Alexander, 121
Works Progress Administration, 13, 100
World Bank, 14, 81, 82
WWJ radio, 120
Wynn, Ed, 121, 124

Y

Yale University Press, 186
Yamaichi, 62
Young, Andrew, 176

Z

Zeron Capital Management Inc., 59
Zolberg, Vera, 9

Subject Index

Boldface numbers refer to figures and tables.

A

Abstract Expressionism, 1, 16, 151, 152, 189, 198, 205
academics as foreign policy elite, 85–86
acquisitions: banking, 50
actors, 122, 123
adaptation: international relations of New York, 29–30, 38, 41–43
advertising: employment, 149; industry, 42, 132, 142*n;* New York as center for, 118; political campaigns, 98; radio, 120; television networks, 132
Ad Week, 140*n*
aerospace industry, 32
Africa: primitive art of, 148
agencies: advertising agencies, 98, 118, 162*n*
agrarian population. *See* agriculture
agriculture: banking system, 12; elites, 73; exports, 56; political campaigns and, 98; subsistence for, 1800s, 97; trading, 53
airlines: cargo, internationalization, 18; domestic passenger service, 204
air pollution: controls, 133
airports: business interests, 35; construction of, 17
Albany Regency, 11, 98
Alberta: television production, 133
Algerian rebellion, 177
Algonquin Roundtable, 10
Alliance for Progress, 86
All in the Family, 126
American capital: disappearance of, 78
American Century, 1, 71, 73, 214
The American Commonwealth, 3
American Labor Party, 31, 169, 174
American Revolution, 6, 73
Amsterdam: international economy, 28
Ann Arbor: Jewish population, 173
anti-Semitism, 168–169, 171, 175, 180, 184, 188–189
Antwerp: economy, 28, 45*n*
apparel industry, 18, 33–34, 36–38, 40, 41, 100
Arab-Israeli conflict, 89–90
Armory Show of 1913, 148
art and artists: abstract art, 149; agglomerations, 201; American scene painters, 151; Boston, 149; business, art as, 158–159; censorship, 206; center of, 194; collectors, 149, 158; criticism, 148–149, 201; dealers, 158; financial houses and art markets, 22–23; France, 16; galleries, 152; grants to, 21; international market, 22; international trends, 159; investments in art,

art and artists (*continued*)
146; life style, 22, 157–158; Los Angeles, 165*n;* nonprofit organizations, 205; patronage, 146–149, 155–157; Philadelphia, 149; post-World War II period, 16–17, 205; regional artistic development, 198; restrictions on, 2; San Diego, 158; San Francisco, 158; "satellite trades," 149; social life, 10; Soviet Union, 151; "tradition of the new," 151; World Wars, 151
art museums: modern art, 160; New York City, 145, 146–153; regional, 158
Asia: economic growth, 40; futures, 67; immigrants, 2; migration, 37, 38; trade with, 49, 68; urban development, 28; U.S. foreign policy, 83
Atlantic Alliance, 86
automobile industry: absence of Jews in, 169; Detroit, 203; free trade, 90; Japan, 132
avant-garde art, 151
avant-garde music, 154
"awesome foursome," 85

B

backlash: residential neighborhoods, 42–43
"back office" operations, 38, 41
Bahamas: banks and banking, 57
balance-of-payments deficit, 19, 105
balance of power: business community, 108
balance-of-trade: positive, 50; surplus, 49
Baltimore, Maryland: newspapers, 8
banks and banking: acquisitions, 50; Arab-Israeli conflict and, 90; Bahamas, 57; California, 65, 203; Cayman Islands, 57; Chicago, 64; Civil War, 96, 212; crises of 1929–1933, 78; Dallas, 65; deregulation, 68; domestic regulation, 43; dominance, rise to, 4; establishment of New York-based, 31; expansion abroad, 105; financial panics in U.S., 12; foreign, 64, 68; Great Britain, 52, 53; Hamburg, 181; headquarters, 64–65; industry, conflict with, 74; influence of, 2; interstate, 43–44, 50, 105; investment, 56–57, 109; Japan, 59–60; Jews in, 169, 180–182; loans to Europe, 76, 77, 78; London, 8, 55; Los Angeles, 64, 68; mergers, 50; money-center, 44, 108; motion picture industry, 122; nineteenth century, 7; Northeastern states, 65; opportunities for, 89; overseas operations, 106; Pacific Basin, 50–51; panic, 1907, 52; Sunbelt, 65; "super-regional," 44; underwriting, 109; United Kingdom, 53; U.S. central bank, proposal of, 12
Barney Miller, 126
Battery Park City, 38
Bauhaus movement, 163*n*
Beyond the Melting Pot, 169
Biennial art exhibits, 152
"big bang" day (October 27, 1986), 55
"bipartisanship" era: in American foreign policy, 83
Birmingham, Alabama: civil rights demonstrations, 15
Black Ball line, 7
Blacks: Jews and, 177; musicians, 120; population, 172; poverty, 42
blue-collar workers, 36
Bohemianism, 10
bonds: bull market, 106; Eurobond market, 53, 58, 62; government bond trading, 62; high-risk, 182; Japan, Treasury bond purchase, 107–108; "junk bonds," 67, 181; market, decline in, 111; U.S. Treasury, 58; *Wall Street Journal*, 128; yen-dominated, 60; zero coupon bonds, 68

border cities, 29
Boston Globe, 128
Boston, Massachusetts: art and artists, 149; Brahmins, 209; challenge to New York national influence, 10; cultural dominance, 118; cultural life, 10; elite cultural institutions, 9; military spending, 32; municipality-elite relations, 147; museums, 210; newspapers, 8, 119; in the nineteenth century, 3; Puritans, 190; railroads, 7–8; symphony orchestras, 160; upper classes, 7, 209
Brahmins, 209
Bretton Woods system of currency exchange, 1–2, 18, 30, 52, 82, 86, 105
Broadway: California and, 122; mass culture and, 131; modern composers, 154; musicals, 10, 170; productions, 160; television's reliance on, 124; touring plays, as source of, 205–206
Brooklyn, New York: back-office employment moved to, 41; high schools, 173; manufacturing, 36; Orthodox Jews, 177
budget, deficit, 38, 89, 107, 109, 111
bull market (stocks), 39, 106
Burbank: *Tonight Show* relocation, 126
Bush administration: foreign policy, 92; National Endowment for the Arts (NEA), 165*n*
business clubs: discrimination, 168
business community: balance of power, 108
business services: internationalization, 41; sectors, 39

C

cable television, 130, 131
California: advertising industry, 142*n*; banks and banking, 65, 203; costs of doing business, 133; defense manufacturers, 14; economic expansion, 32; financial institutions, 40; growth, 2; motion picture industry, 121–122, 124; music, 127; New Age culture, 202; news, 201; prestige, 129; retirement communities, 172; social trends and fads, 132; technology revolution, 65; television industry, 124, 126
Canada: television production, 133
capitalism, 28
capitalization: New York Stock Exchange, 57
capital markets: internationalization of, 57; size of U.S., 58
Car 54, Where are You?, 126
Caribbean: migration, 37; military intervention, 75
Carnegie Hall, 102
CBS. *See* Columbia Broadcasting System
censorship: art, 206; music, 127
Central America: military intervention, 75
Central Park, Manhattan, 147
central place theory, 214*n*
charitable foundations: civil rights policies, 20; restrictions on, 2
Charlotte (N.C.) News, 123
Chicago, Illinois: advertising agencies, 162*n*; banks and banking, 64; business class, 209; commodity markets, 203; commodity trading, 51; corporations, number of, 8; cultural dominance, 118; elite cultural institutions, 9; financial institutions, 40; museums, 210; challenge to New York national influence, 10; upper classes, 209; World's Fair, 210
Chicago Daily News, 119
Chicago Tribune, 128
China: economy, 75; military intervention, 75; U.S. foreign policy, 12, 83
Chinese-Americans: entrepreneurs, 38

"city-pairs": Los Angeles–San Francisco's challenge to New York's national influence, 10; New York–Washington axis, 11–17
city-states, 28
civil liberties jurisprudence, 21
Civil Rights Act, 15
civil rights movement: campaign financing, 102; demonstrations, 102; desegregation, 15; emergence of, 15; legislation, 104; policy, 21; role of New York institutions, 20, 104
Civil War: antiwar feeling, 72; banks and banking, 96, 212; coverage, 10–11; Great Britain, Southern states trading with, 73; industrial economic growth, 56; manufacturing after, 32
cognitive dominance, 197–198, 201–202, 204–207; of nonprofit organizations, 205
Cold War: AFL-CIO and, 101; art and artists, 16, 151; consensus, 20; domestic support for, 13; foreign policy elite, support, 84, 89; impact on New York, 81–82; liberalism, 30; military spending, 31; mobilization of support for, 100; new Cold War, 89; organized labor, 14
colleges and universities: cognitive dominance, 206; decentralization, 203; discrimination in admissions, 168–171; single efforts, inability to coalesce, 217*n*
Columbia Broadcasting System (CBS), 153; CBS Records, 132; censorship, 127; classical record industry, 166*n*, 183; communication technology and, 120; conflict of interest, 129; network news programs, 130; popular film series, 125
Commentary, 185, 186, 187
"commercial Keynesianism," 101
Committee on Economic Security, 101
commodities: flow to Europe, 6; futures markets, 67; trading, 51
Common Market, 132
communications: international, 4; revolution, 211; technology, 112, 193
Communism: anti-Communism, 30–31
Communist Party, 174
competition: advantages of New York, 36; American industry, 58; foreign, 18; immigration and, 37; London, 55; Soviet Union, 31
composers, 152–153, 170
computer: technologies, 112
Congress: art, lobbies for subsidies, 148; currency enactments, 1860s, 96; Democrats, 107; federal job programs, termination of, 102
"consensus" era in foreign policy, 83
conservative evangelical movement, 2
consulting companies, **200**
consumers, 100, 105
Contemporary Jewish Record, 187
Convention Center, 38
corporate raiders, 67
cotton: export, 7, 56; southern cotton growers, 14
Council on Foreign Relations: challenges to, 85; creation of, 206–207; expansion of, 76; foreign policy centers, 87; foreign policy elite, influence on, 71; foreign policy formation, 212; founding of, 74–75; Jews and, 177; New Deal, 101; "1980's Project," 89; Trilateral Commission, 90–91; U.S. policymakers, influence on, 81; War and Peace Studies Project, 80, 81, 89; Washington foundations, comparison to, 88; Washington office, 93; world economy between Britain and U.S., 77; World War II, 80
creditors: Japan as, 50; United States as, 50, 73–74
criticism: arts and artists, 148–149, 201; literature, 1

Cuban missile crisis, 15
Cubism, 150
cultural influence of New York City, 10, 145–166; business, art as, 158–159; contemporary cultural standing, 157–161; Jewish population, 184–189; life style of artists, 22, 157–158; location, significance for cultural institutions, 159–161; mass culture, 117–143
culture: access to institutions, 102; commercial primacy and, 8; federal policies, 21–22; forms of dominance, 201–202, 203; nineteenth century, 11; post-World War II period, 16. *See also* art and artists; dance; literature
currency: convertibility, 18; dollar as key international currency, 14, 16, 30; foreign currency trade, 57; gold, 30; sterling, 30, 52, 55; yen, 60, 63

D

Dadaists, 150, 188
Daily Variety, 127
Dakar: economy, 28
dance: companies, modern dance, 1, 22; regional companies, 160
Dawes Plan (1924), 76, 77
debt: Third World countries, 44
decentralization: higher education, 203; manufacturing and, 32–33
decline of place, 208–209, 211–213
defense policy: expansion of, 87; expenditures, 32, 44, 89; leadership, 82. *See also* military
deficit. *See* balance-of-payments; budget; trade
Democratic Party: base for, 73; Congress and House, 107; 1800s, 10, 98; free trade coalition, 78; hegemony, 108; Jews, 169, 174, 178; 1940s, 102; 1972 presidential campaign, 176; political campaigns, 96; strategic dominance, 200; urban-liberal wing, 101; World War II, 80
"demonstration project," 104
depression and recession. *See* Great Depression; recession
deregulation: banks and banking, 68; financial markets, 19, 55, 57; Reagan administration, 92; telecommunications, 65–66
desegregation: Supreme Court decision, 15
détente, 84–85, 88, 89
Detroit: absence of intellectual influence, 4; automobile industry, 203; music, 127; New Deal, 105; radio stations, 120
"dialectic of domination and diffusion," 205
direct-mail: political campaigns, 96
"disintermediation," 108
division of labor: labor pool, 7
dollar: crises, 106; decline in value of, 19, 49–50; export by banks, 106; key international currency, 14, 16, 30; pressures on, 105; replacement of sterling, 52; restriction on capital outflows, 35; shortage, 84; surplus, 84; value, climbing of, 110–111; world trade, dollar-based, 59; yen and, 63, 107, 109, 111. *See also* currency
dominance, rise of New York, 6–11. *See also* metropolitan dominance
Dominicans in the United States: entrepreneurs, 38
dual city, 42
duty-free assembly plants, 29

E

East Asia: post-World War II period, 16
East European Jewish population, 168, 172, 183, 189
East Side, Manhattan, 177
East Village, Manhattan, 152

eclipse of place. *See* decline of place
economic institutions: elite, 14
Economic Opportunity Act, 103
economic order, U.S., 11–14, 30
"economic royalists," 100
economy: agglomeration economics, 199; decline of, 27, 35; development programs, 41; dominance of United States, 40; forms of dominance, 103, 199–201; international strategy and New York economy, 35–44; international system, role in decline of, 27; New York Jewish population and, 179–184; 1970s, 2; output, 105; restructuring of, 18; Senegal, 28; Seville, 28
education: higher education, expansion, 22
1812 war, 7
electronic markets, 68
Electronic Media, 133
electronics industry, 32
elite: arts, financing of, 146, 148–149; business, 33, 34; cultural institutions, 9; decline of place, 212; economic elite, 30; economic institutions, role in, 14; foreign policy, 20, 31; fragmentation, 209–210; Jewish population, 79, 92, 170, 174; manufacturers and, 33, 34; multinational corporations, 15; municipality-elite relations, 147; national government, support of, 12; national politics, influence, 112–113; as New Yorkers, 194; post-World War II period, 44; structural centrality to networks, 203; voters, 108; Washington, D.C., 15; WASPs, 79; World War II, during, 11. *See also* foreign policy elite
employment: advertising, 149; art and artists, 149, 165*n;* banking and finance, 64; classical musicians, 154; discrimination in, 171; immigrants, 37; level of, 105; publishing industry, 36, 41
Encounter, 186
England: cultural capital, 118; museums, 162*n;* theater, imports from, 160
entertainment industry: conglomerization movement, 2; Jews, 180
entrepreneurs: Chinese-American, 38; immigration, 38, 44; Jewish, 121
environmental policy, 104
Erie Canal, 10, 34
ethnic groups: foreign policy and, 97; local politics, 31; Puerto Ricans, 172
Eurobonds, 53, 58, 62
Eurocurrency, 53, 55, 106, 112
Eurodollars, 55, 182
Euromarkets, 35
Europe: art and artists, 149, 160; commodity flow, 6; foreign policy toward, 76; isolationism, 83; post-World War II period, 16; rebuilding of economy, 106; rival to New York, 43; urban development, 28; U.S. bank loans to, 76, 77, 78; U.S. economic involvement, 30; U.S. foreign economic policy, 12
European Community: gross national products, 53
European immigrants in New York City: music, 147
expansion: political backlash, 43
exports: agricultural products, 56; cotton, 7, 56; Germany, 54; Japan, 54, 63; London, 51; market for, 77; West Germany, 63

F

facsimile transmission (fax), 133
fads, 132
fashion industry, 22, 41, 42
federal farm credit system, 105
federal job programs, termination of, 102
federal mortgage insurance programs, 101
Federal Reserve: access to, 2; creation

of, 12–13; inflation, 108; influence of, 105, 109; New York representation in national affairs, 95, 97; power of, increase, 21; shifting of control to, 212; shrinkage of foreign markets, 78; strengthening of, 77; Treasury nexus, 110, 111; Wall Street influence, 112
Figurative Realism, 163*n*
financial center, New York City as, 56–59
financial crisis of 1969–1975, 44
financial district, 38
financial institutions, 199; structural dominance, 203
financial markets: deregulation of, 57; internationalization, 20, 22, 36, 41, 59; Japan, 62; liberalization, 62; London, 62
financial panics, 11, 12, 52
financial representation, New York, 1980s and 1990s, 104–113
Financial Times, 182
The Fire Chief, 121
fiscal crisis of 1975, 27
"flexible response," 86
Ford Foundation: antipoverty program, model for, 15; "gray areas" program, 103, 104; innovativeness, 206; nonprofit theatre, 205; opera, 165*n;* performing arts, support for, 104, 155, 164*n*
foreign capital: U.S. financial markets, 111
foreign currency trade, 58
foreign debt, 50
foreign exchange: futures, 51; Japan, 60; support for, 77
foreign investments: U.S. dependence on, 58; U.S. pension funds, 57
foreign markets: shrinkage, 78
foreign policy: allies, support of, 61; Arab-Israeli conflict, 89–90; crisis in, 86; expansion of, 87; Iranian hostage crisis, 86; 1920s, 12; post-World War II period, 14; Vietnam War, 20, 86–88
foreign policy centers, 87–88
foreign policy elite, 71–94; academics as, 85–86; arms control, 88–89; Cambridge, 85–86; Cold War, 81–82, 84, 89; consensus foreign policy, 76; Council on Foreign Relations, 71, 74–75; economic policies, 210; finance versus industry, 75; fragmentation, 2; free trade and, 73, 90–91; Great Britain, 80; Middle East, 89–90; national government, access to, 100; New Deal and, 101; origins of, 72–73; post-World War II period, 31, 79–85; privatized, 75–76; protectionism, 73, 90–91; regional divisions of New York, 82–84; Wall Street, allegiance to, 92; Washington, D.C., rise of, 84–85; world economy between Britain and U.S., 76–77; World War II, 13
Fortune, 120, 125, 169, 179
Fortune 500 companies, 18, 36, 199
"Forward to Richmond" campaign, 96
foundations support for the arts, 155–157
fragmentation: metropolitan dominance of New York, 209–210
France: artists, 16; international art auction market, 151; museums, 162*n;* reparation payments, 78; repayment of war debts, 76. *See also* Paris
Frankfurt, Germany: banking, 8; prosperity, 18
free trade, 16; coalition, 78; protectionism versus, 73; world market and, 90–91
futures: foreign exchange, 51; markets, 67

G

garment industry. *See* apparel industry

General Agreement on Tariffs and Trade (GATT), 81, 82, 105
German population, New York: isolationism, 31; Jewish population, 168–171, 180–182; music, 147
Germany: artwork borrowed from, 150; defeat of, 14; exports, 54; France, defeat of, 16; Louvre accord and, 111; prosperity, 18; U.S. bank loans to, 76, 77, 78; World War II, 11
gilt (government securities) markets: Great Britain, 55
Glass-Steagall Act, 105
"global city," 193
global financial center, 49–70
"global office," 38
global order, 17–23
GNP. *See* gross national product (GNP)
gold: currency, 30; Great Britain, 52; trading, 53
government securities: sale of, 13
government support for the arts, 147, 155–157
"gray areas" program: Ford Foundation, 103, 104
Great Britain: banks and banking, 52, 53; commercial links to New York, 6–7; cultural influence, 10, 118; decline of industry, 58; foreign policy elite, 80; gilt (government securities) markets, 55; gold standard, 52; gross national product (GNP), 53, 54, 56; investments, 54; lend-lease aid to, 101; links with New York, 1820s–1920s, 97; manufactures, 52; news from, 8; overseas trade and investments, 52; public policy, 54; public schools, 73; reparation payments, 77–78; Southern states, trade with, 73; transfer of international leadership from, 11, 14, 50; world economy between Britain and U.S., 76–77. *See also* London
Great Depression: corporate community, 67; failure to stem, 212; impact on New York, 77–78; influence of New York political forces, 13; Jewish population, 177; motion picture industry, 122; protectionism and, 79; radio programs during, 120; transfer of international leadership, 11; and transition of world financial center, 52
Great Society, 103, 212
Great White Way, 120
Greenwich Village, Manhattan, 10
gross national product (GNP): Great Britain, 53, 54, 56; Japan, 61, 62; Pacific Basin, 49; United States, 56, 62
Growing Up Absurd, 102
Guggenheim Museum: collection, 152; founding of, 149

H

Hamilton-Dorgan bill, 110
Harlem, 120
hegemony: Democrats, 108; functions, 82; investment banking, 109; mass culture, 131; reestablishment, 202; short-term phenomenon, 133; stable world economy, 77; Tokyo as a challenge to New York, 59; United States as hegemonic power, 50
Herald Tribune, 119, 128
higher education. *See* colleges and universities
highways, 4, 17, 101
Hispanic population: poverty, 42
Hollywood, California: actors, 158; Jewish population, 168, 179; migration from New York, 131; motion picture industry, 22, 121–122; music, 127; political contributions, 20; tv-movies, 133
Hong Kong: urban development, 28
households: heads of, 173

House of Representatives (U.S.): Democrat majority in, 107
housing: discrimination in, 171; subsidies, 34
Houston, Texas: auctions, 159; intellectual influence, 4; Republican Party, 105
How New York Stole the Idea of Modern Art (Guilbaut), 151
How to Win Friends and Influence People (Carnegie), 185
The Hucksters, 123
Hyde Park, 73

I

I Love Lucy, 124, 125
"I love New York" campaign, 39
immigration: Asian, 2; economy and, 37; entrepreneurs, 38, 44; influence on economy, 41; labor, low-wage, 33, 40; laws, 38; Miami, 37; policy, 21
imports: Japan, 63; surge in, 34
Impressionists, 150
Indochina: military containment, 84
industrialists: foreign policy elite, 75
industrialization: trade among industrialized countries, 32
Industrial Relations Counsellors, 101
industry: banks in conflict with, 74; Civil War, 73; consensus foreign policy, 76; defense, 89; Jews in management, 169; New England, 73; Wall Street influence, 2
inflation: decline in, 111; double-digit, 106; Federal Reserve, 108; pressures, 105; Supply-Siders, 107
influence: international relations of New York, 29–30
infrastructure: construction of, 17; London, 51
intellectual influence: change in, 4; Ithaca, New York, 4; Jewish population, New York, 213; New Haven, 4; Palo Alto, 4; publishing industry, 187–189
interest rates: ceilings on, 105; rising of, 111; savings deposits, 55
international bank lending: Japan, 61; London, 57; Wall Street, 58
international influence of New York, 1–25
internationalism, 73–79; foreign policy disputes, 75; policy of, 1; political campaigns, 96
internationalization: financial markets, 20, 22, 36, 41, 59; and New York influence, 18–19; requirements of, 44–45
international monetary system: Bank of England, 13
international order: financial community and, 105
international relations of New York, 29–35
international strategy and New York economy, 35–44
international trade, 18
interstate banking, 43–44, 50
investment banks, 56–57, 109
investments: art, 146; Great Britain, 54; Japan, 61
Irish population, New York: isolationism, 31
isolationism, 73–79; Europe, 83; foreign policy disputes, 75; political campaigns, 96; Treaty of Versailles, blocking of, 12
Israel: Arab-Israeli conflict, 89–90; creation of, 31; impact on Jews in U.S., 177–178; 1967 war, 177; United Nations, 176
Italy: artwork borrowed from, 150

J

Japan: American banks and brokerage firms, 109; automobile manufacturers, 132; banks and banking, 59–60; creditor, 50; eco-

Japan (*continued*)
nomic growth, 40, 41; exports, 54, 63; financial markets, 62; foreign-exchange controls, 60; gross national product (GNP), 61, 62; imports, 63; international bank lending, 61; massive trading surplus, 61; musical instruments, manufacture of, 160; overseas investments, 40; prosperity, 18; rebuilding of economy, 106; rival to New York, 43; Treasury bond purchase, 107–108; Treasury Department pact with, 107; U.S. foreign policy, 83; world capitalist system, future role in, 63–64
Jay Treaty, 97
Jersey City, New Jersey: back-office employment moved to, 41
Jewish population, New York: Arab-Israeli conflict and, 89; Bloomington, Indiana, 173; colleges and universities, admissions to, 168–171; Columbus, Ohio, 173; Connecticut, 173; cultural influence, 184–189; demography, 171–174, 189; East Europeans, 168, 172, 183, 189; economics and, 179–184; educational advantages, 173–174; elites, 79, 92, 170; employment discrimination, 171; entrepreneurs, 121; German Jews, 168–171, 180–182; housing discrimination, 171; intellectual community, 213; internationalism, 31; Israel, impact of, 177–178; labor movement, 174; Left in America and, 175; liberalism, 168, 177, 178; Miami, 173; medical schools, 174; Nassau County, 173; national influence, 167–192; Orthodox, 175, 177, 178; politics, 167, 169, 174–179; post-World War II period, 168–171; presidential candidates, support for, 176; publishing, 184–187; Socialism, 174; trade unions, 170, 174–175; Urbana-Champaign, 173; voters, 175–178; WASP-Jewish coalition, 17
journalism: center of, 194; "the new journalism," 128; newspapers, 119–120; New York as center, 119
junk bonds, 67, 181
juvenile delinquency, 103

K

"key currency" plan, 14, 16, 30
Kojak, 126
Korea: musical instruments, manufacture of, 160
Korean War, 86

L

labor force: immigrants, 33, 40; skilled labor, 44
labor markets, 4
labor unions: apparel industry, negotiations, 100; moves by manufacturing to avoid unionization, 33–34; post-World War II period, 14; power of, 34; Reagan administration, 108
Ladies Home Journal, 118
The Last Temptation of Christ, 180
Late Night with David Letterman, 132
Latin America: economy, 75; foreign policy toward, 76; migration, 37, 38; reparation payments, 78; U.S. foreign economic policy, 12, 30
law schools: Jews and, 174
LBOs. *See* leveraged buyouts
leveraged buyouts (LBOs), 67, 168, 181, 182
liberalism: Cold War, 30; internationalism, 31; Jewish population, New York, 168, 177, 178
liberalization: financial markets, 62
Liberal party, 169–170
Life, 128
light manufacturing, 18

Lincoln Center, 155–157
literature: criticism, 1; Society portrayed in, 3
loans: bank loans to Europe, 76, 77, 78
location, significance for cultural institutions, 159–161
London: adaptation, 45; American banks and multinationals, 35; auctions, 159; banks and banking, 8, 55; "big bang" day (October 27, 1986), 55; Board of Trade, 6; competition, 55; equity market, 53; exports, 51; financial center, as, 51–56, 58, 63; financial elite, 73; financial markets, 19, 62; foreign asset deposits, 53; industrial growth, 56; infrastructure, 51; international art auction market, 151; international bank lending, 57; international capital market, 44; international economy, 28; internationalization of financial markets, 36; long-term capital market, 52; national regulatory authorities, 43. *See also* Great Britain
"London plan": of newspaper circulation management, 8–9
The Lonely Crowd (Riesman), 186
Look, 128
Los Angeles, California: advertising industry, 132; art dealers, 158; artists, 158, 165*n*; auctions, 159; banks and banking, 64, 68; centers for performing art, 155; challenge to New York international strategy, 40, 41; challenge to New York national influence, 10; costs of doing business, 133; economy, 204; entertainment industry, 180; finance of trade and investment, 65; growth, 2; immigration, 37; Jewish population, 173; motion picture industry, 121, 123; music, 127; Pacific Basin market for mass culture, 132; preeminence of, 27; prestige, 129; regional financial centers, 50; rival to New York, 69; television industry, 124
Los Angeles Times, 128, 140*n*
Louvre accord, 111
Lux Radio Theater, 122

M

McCarran-Walter Act of 1952, 34
Madison Avenue, 118, 132
Madison Square Garden, 102
magazines. *See* periodicals
Man Against Crime, 124
manufacturing: decline in, 32–38, 41; Great Britain, 52; international trade, 18; liberalized trading system, 34; small manufacturing, 4, 34, 41. *See also* specific industries
maquiladora industry, 29
marine terminals: business interests, 35
"market for corporate control," 107
Marshall Plan, 18, 76, 79, 82, 86
Marxism, 2, 188
mass culture, New York City and, 117–143
mass transit, 34
mercantile elite: political leaders linked to, 97
merchandise: trade deficit, 50
mergers: banking, 50; mass culture and, 130–131
metropolitan dominance of New York: cognitive dominance, 197–198, **200**, 204–207; cohesion, 209–210; control of positions, 198; culture, 201–202, 203; decline of place, 208–209, 211–213; "dialectic of domination and diffusion," 205; economy, finance, 193; foreign trade, 7; forms of, 198–208, **200;** forms of dominance, 199–201, 203; fragmentation, 209–210; functional domains, forms of dominance and, **200;** politics, forms of dominance, 200–201; stage, 205; strategic domi-

metropolitan dominance of New York (*continued*)
nance, 196–197, **200**, 207–208; structural dominance, 195–196, 199, **200**, 202–204; trajectory, 202–208; urban networks, 193–217; varieties of, 195–198, **196**
metropolitan elites: policies of, 101; political campaigns, 96
Metropolitan Museum of Art: contemporary artists, 148, 149; creation of, 210; elite cultural institution, 9; elites connected with, 148; establishment of, 146; Jewish trustees, 170; other museums and, 150
microcosm, city as, 3
middle class: GOP coalition, 107; home owners, 105; reformers, 31; Roosevelt administration policies, 101; voters, 108
Midwest: artists, 158; industrialists, 101; industry, 73; regional elite, 83
military: arms control, 88–89; assertive U.S. posture, 20; bases, benefits of, 29; containment, 84; conventional forces, 83–84; defense manufacturers, 14; expenditures, 18, 31, 32, 105, 107, 108; institutions, 12; intervention, 75; Jews in, 174; massive retaliation, 84; nuclear deterrence, 83; overseas expenditures, 18; spending, 32; supplies, 1700s, 6; technology, 108
"military-industrial complex," 72
Milwaukee, Wisconsin: television advertising, 132
Milwaukee Journal, 140*n*
Minimalism, 163*n*
minorities: foreign policy and, 97; musicians, 127; national attention to problems of, 102
modern art: museums, 148–153, 160; rise of, 145; Russia, artwork borrowed from, 150
MoMA. *See* Museum of Modern Art (MoMA)
monetary policies, 12, 29
money-center banks, 44, 108
motion pictures: industry, 121–124; Long Island, New York, 135*n*; production, 118; television and, 125
Mr. Peepers, 124
multinational corporations: Arab-Israeli conflict, 89–90; headquarters, 18, 210; imports, 34; London, 35; post-World War II period, 15; rise of enterprise, 211
municipal government: office districts and, 4
Museum of Modern Art (MoMA), 17; collection, 162*n*; education by, 152; founding of, 149; loan program, 150
music: Broadway, 10; classical music, 153–155, 159, 166*n*; disco, 202; elite cultural institutions, 9; European and German immigrants, 147; Hollywood, migration of musicians to, 131; industry, 122; Jews, role in, 170; minority artists, 127; Nashville, 127; patronage, 146–147, 152–153, 155–157; popular music, 127; regional orchestras, 160; songwriters, 120; tape recordings, 166*n*. *See also* symphony orchestras
Musical America, 153

N

Nasdaq market, 68
national and urban development, 28–30
National Broadcasting Company (NBC): censorship, 127; conflict of interest, 129; network news programs, 130; radio, 120; symphony orchestra, 154; television series, 124
National Endowment for the Arts (NEA): "artist," defined, 163*n*; creation of, 202; matching contributions, 156, 165*n*; models for, 104,

205; 1960s, 21; policies of, 156–157; regional artistic development, 198
national influence of New York, 1–25
national mediation, 28–29
national politics and New York City, 95–115
nation-states, 28–29
NBC. *See* National Broadcasting Company (NBC)
NEA. *See* National Endowment for the Arts (NEA)
neighborhoods: backlash, 42–43
Neo-Expressionism, 163*n*
Neo-Impressionists, 150
network analysis: cognitive dominance, 197–198, 204–207; imagery of, 195; nodes of, 195; sociological network analysis, 215*n;* strategic dominance, 196–197, 207–208; structural dominance, 195–196, 202–204
network news, 96, 130, 201
networks, 130, 132; radio, 121, 122, 123, 127; television, 123–127
New Deal: art and artists, 151; center of power, 15; creation of, 13; domestic reforms, 14; financial interests during, 112; impact on New York, 78–79; local bastions of, 105; music, funding, 154; political influence of New York, 99–102; pro-growth coalition under, 31; promises of, 79; strategic dominance, 200; transportation regulation, 17–18; Wall Street, 16, 105; weakening of political forces, 21
New Jersey: manufacturing, moves from New York to, 34
"the new journalism," 9, 128
newspapers: cultural leadership, 127–128; journalism, 119–120; local news, 131; nineteenth century, 8–9; "the new journalism," 9, 128; popularity, 131; tabloids, 98
New York City. *See* specific topics throughout this index
New Yorker, 118, 129, 188
New York Times: competition, 142*n;* cultural leadership, 127–128; emergence as national newspaper, 2; letters to, 102; prestige, 131; ranking of, 140*n*
New York–Washington axis, 11–17
Nikkei stock index, 59
"1980's Project": Council on Foreign Relations, 89
Northeast Asia: rebuilding of, 18
Northeastern states: banks and banking, 65; decline of industralization, 64; economic shift, 50
nuclear deterrence, 82, 83–84

O

ocean cargo: internationalization, 18
Oceania: primitive art of, 148
off-Broadway, 154, 160
off-off-Broadway, 160
oil: Arab-Israeli conflict, 89–90; denomination in dollars, 63; price, decline in, 65, 90
On Our Own, 126
opera companies, 154, 165*n*
The Other America, 102

P

Pacific Basin: banking, 50–51; economic growth, 40, 49; finance of trade and investment, 65; gross national product (GNP), 49; growth, 64, 69; mass culture of U.S., market for, 132
Pacific Rim: economy, 204; U.S. trade with, 68
Palestinian Liberation Organization, 176, 178
panics: financial, 11, 12, 52
Paris, France: art, usurpation of dominance by New York, 151; artwork borrowed from, 150; wealth, 22
Partisan Review, 187

patronage of art and music, 146–153; foundation and government support, 155–157
Pattern art, 163*n*
Pennsylvania: art museums, 149; industry, 73; manufacturing, moves from New York to, 33
pension funds: foreign investment in, 57
performing artists: California, centers for performing art, 155; life style, 158; support for, 104, 164*n*
periodicals: art criticism, 148–149; city magazines, 129; mass circulation magazines, 118, 128; political campaign advertising, 98; publishing industry, 128–129
Philadelphia, Pennsylvania: advertising agencies, 162*n;* art and artists, 149; Bank of the United States, 10; challenge to New York national influence, 10; cultural dominance, 118; cultural life, 10; elite cultural institutions, 9; intellectual influence, 4; newspapers, 8; nineteenth century, 3; Quakers, 190; symphony orchestras, 160; television industry, 124; upper classes, 7, 209
philanthropic foundations, 198
Plaza agreement, 111
policy elite: structural centrality, 201. *See also* foreign policy elite
policy networks, 203
political campaigns: centralized organizations, development of, 98; conflict, 42; direct-mail, 96; financing by New York, 96; moderates, 96; 1980s, 105
political influence of New York: conditions of, 95–97; financial representation, 1980s and 1990s, 104–113; New Deal, 99–102; 1960s, 102–104; party representation, 1820s–1920s, 97–98; presidential representation, 1930s–1970s, 99–104
political order, 14–16
political parties: New York representation, 1820s–1920s, 97–98. *See also* specific party
politics: forms of dominance, 200–201
popular culture: demand for, 132; development of, 9; loss of hegemony, 131; mass culture, New York City and, 117–143
Populist era, 72
Portuguese monarchy, 28
post-industrial transformation, 36
postmodernism, 211
post-World War II period: art and artists, 16–17, 204; elites, 44; foreign policy elite, 79–85; foreign policymaking, 14; French repayment of war debts, 76; Great Britain, growth, 53; international growth, 18; international relations of New York, 30–35; international security, 16; Jewish population, influence of, 168–171; manufacturing, decline in, 33; mass culture, 123; planning, 15; political coalition, 34; reparation payments, 77–78; Wall Street, 105; "Wise Men," 97, 100
poverty: antipoverty program, 15; arts, depiction in, 102; Black population, 42; Hispanic population, 42; legislation, 104; regions, 17; working poor, 214
The Predator's Ball (Bruck), 182
Progressive Era, 98, 201
protectionism: Council on Foreign Relations, 74; foreign policy elite, 90–91; free trade versus, 73; Great Depression, 79; international relations of New York, 43; Republican Party, 75; trade law, 78
Protestant ethic, 180
Public Affairs Program: Ford Foundation, 103
public relations firms: political campaign advertising, 98
public sector unions, 42
publishing industry: book publishers,

131; center of, 194; conglomerization movement, 2; crossword puzzle books, 184; cultural authority, 201; dominance of New York, 118–119; employment, 36, 41; humanities, 186–187; Jewish influence, 184–187; music publishers, 122; newcomers to, 42; paperbacks, quality, 187; periodicals, 128–129; social sciences, 186–187; theater publishers, 131; trade book publishing, 184–195, 194

R

racial liberalism, 104
radio, 120–121; Jews in, 170; migration from New York, 122; performers, 163*n*; popular music, 127; symphony music, 156; television and, 123
Radio City, 120
railroads: corporations, 8; nineteenth century, 7–8; trucks supplanting, 34
Reagan administration: decline of New York, 20; financial sector, 107–111; fiscal policy, 21; foreign policy, 92; new Cold War, 89
recession: 1981–1982, 39
"recession proof" services, 39
Reciprocal Trade Agreements, 78
regional divisions of New York, 82–84
regional elites: Midwest, 83
regional financial centers, 50
Regional Plan of 1929, 33
"Remember the Maine" campaign, 96
Remembrance of Things Past (Proust), 188
reorganization of corporations, 19, 109
The Reporter, 186
Republican Party: base for, 73; Jews, 169, 178; 1940s, 102; nineteenth century, 10, 97; political campaigns, 96; protectionism, 75; Senate recapture, 106; strategic dominance, 200; Supply-Siders, 107; Wall Street, 14; World War II, 80
residential property: backlash in neighborhoods, 42–43; space, use for, 41
Rhoda, 126
Ring Around Manhattan, 65
Rockefeller Center, 120, 124
Roosevelt administration: financial system, reorganization, 18; Great Britain, alliance with, 80; labor relations practices, 100; New Deal coalition, 96; social policy complex, 99, 101
Russia: artwork borrowed from, 150

S

SALT I, 88
San Francisco, California: advertising industry, 132; art dealers, 158; challenge to New York national influence, 10; growth, 2; neighborhoods, 43; prestige, 129
Saturday Evening Post, 124, 128
Saturday Night Live, 132
savings deposits: interest rates, 55
SEATO treaty, 84
Seattle: dance companies, 165*n*
"securitization," 108
Selma, Alabama: civil rights demonstrations, 15
Sephardic Jews, 172
Seven Years' War, 6
small manufacturing, 4, 34, 41
Smithsonian Agreement, 86
Smoot-Hawley tariff, 78
SMSAs, 96, 215*n*
social disorganization, 214
social fragmentation, 194
Socialist Party, 169, 174, 175
social policy complex, 99
social policy elites, 101
Social Security Act, 13

social trends and fads, 132
"Société Anonyme," 149
sociological network analysis, 215*n*
SoHo, Manhattan, 152, 159
songwriters, 170
Southern states: artists, 158; civil rights movement, 102; Democratic Party, 98; foreign policy and, 97; Great Britain, trade with, 73; regional financial centers, 50
South Street Seaport, 38
Southwestern states: economy, 65
Soviet Union: arms control and, 88–89; art, control of, 151; competition with, 31; containment of, 14; Cuban missile crisis, 15; Jewish population, 31. *See also* Cold War
Spanish monarchy, 28
spatial distance and urban location, 214*n*
speculators, corporate, 67
St. Lawrence Seaway, 34
St. Louis Star, 119
Stanley, 126
state arts agencies, 156
steel industry, 203
sterling: currency, 30; decline of, 55; lending, 52; replacement of by dollar, 52
Stock Exchange, 181
stock index trading, 51
stock market crash: 1929, 13, 77–78; 1987, 111
strategic dominance, 196–197, 200, 207–208
structural dominance, 195–196, 199, 202–204
The Structure of Social Action (Parsons), 186
Sun, 8
Sunbelt: banks and banking, 65; economic expanson, 32; growth of, 27; political campaigns, 96; regional financial centers, 50; Supply-Siders, 107
Sunday Today, 130
"super-regional" banks, 44
"super service center," Manhattan as a, 36
Supply-Siders, 107
surplus: balance-of-trade, 49; massive trading, 61
Surrealism, 150, 188
symphony orchestras: government subsidies, 147; Jewish trustees, 170; New York City, 145, 146–148, 153–155; regional, 160
syndicated reruns, 126

T

takeovers, corporate, 109, 181, 183
Tammany Hall, 11, 97, 200
tape recordings: music, 166*n*
tariff: border cities, 29; protection, 30; reductions, 18; Smoot-Hawley tariff, 78
taxation: cuts in, 107, 108
technology: communications, 112, 193; computer, 112; defense and, 32; military, 108; radio, 121; revolution in, 65
telecommunications: deregulation, 65–66
teletypes, 123
television: advertising, 132; Bronx, New York, 124; cable television, 130, 131; civil rights demonstrations, 102; detective shows, 138*n*; motion pictures and, 125; New York–based series, 126; New York vs. California as center of industry, 129–130; production, 123–127, 133; syndicated reruns, 126; West Virginia, 124
Tet offensive, 1968, 96
textile industry: free trade, 90
Thailand: military containment, 84
theaters: 1800s, 11; regional, 160. *See also* Broadway
Third World countries: debt crisis, 44; overthrow of regimes, 2

thrift institutions, 105, 109
Time Magazine, 118–119
time zone: trading and, 54
Tin Pan Alley, 120, 122, 165*n*, 170
Tokyo: auctions, 159; challenge to New York, 51; equity market, 53; as financial center, 36, 40, 59–64; financial markets, 19, 50, 55; national regulatory authorities, 43; prosperity, 18; rival to New York, 69; stock market, 57, 60, 61
Tonight Show, 124, 126
tourism: attracting tourists, 30; damage to, 42; economic development programs, 41; encouragement of, 39; international economy, dependence on, 44
trade: agriculture, 53; deficit, 49, 50, 107, 108; government bonds, 62; international equity trading, 54; massive trading surplus, Japan, 61; metals, 53; protectionism, 78; time zone, 54. *See also* free trade
trade unions: Jewish, 170, 174–175
Traditionalists, 107
transportation: 1800s, 7; mass transit, 34; New Deal regulation, 17–18
Trilateral Commission: Council on Foreign Relations, 90–91
trucks: railroads, supplanting of, 34

U

United Charities Building, 99
United Kingdom: banking center, 53
United Nations: creation of, 82; international security, organization of, 81; Israel, 176
United States: allies, support of, 61; Asia, trade with, 68; bank loans to Europe, 76, 77, 78; creditor, as, 50, 73–74; economic dominance, 40; foreign debt, 50; foreign investors, dependence on, 58; foreign trade, 49; global financial center, 49–70; gross national product (GNP), 56, 62; importer, as, 50; Jewish population, 173; national politics and New York City, 95–115; succession of Britain, 14; world economies and, 18; world economy between Britain and U.S., 76–77
universities. *See* colleges and universities: funding for, 22; technology-defense nexus, 32
upper classes: Cleveland, Ohio, 209; coherency of, 7; Jewish entrepreneurs, 121
Upper East Side, Manhattan, 159
Upper West Side, Manhattan, 42
urban development, 28–30
urban identity: decline of place and, 211–213
urban networks, 4
urban policies, 38
urban studies, 3
USA Today, 128
U.S. Treasury bonds, 58

V

vaudeville performers: radio, 120–121; television, 124
Venice: adaptation, 44–45; economy, 28
Vietnam War, 20, 71, 86–88
voters: Jewish population, 173–178; national politics, voice in, 96
Voting Rights Act, 15

W

wages: immigrant labor, 33, 40
Wall Street: allegiance to foreign policy elite, 92; decline of, 61; Federal Reserve influenced by, 112; future of, 67; growth of, 56–57; influence of, 2, 10, 20, 112; international bank lending, 58; internationalism, 1; Jewish influence, 170; "market for corporate control,"

Wall Street (*continued*) 107; national corporations and, 8; national government, access to, 100; New Deal, 105; October 1987 crash, 111; post-World War II period, 105; priorities of, 105; reorganization of corporations, 19; Republican Party, 14; restrictions upon, 16, 105; takeover boom, 109; Traditionalists, 107; "Wise Men," 97, 100
Wall Street Journal, 2, 128, 131, 184
War and Peace Studies Project: Council on Foreign Relations, 80, 81, 89
Washington, D.C.: art museums, 149; centers for performing arts, 155; cultural influence, 10; elites, 15, 84–85; news, 201; newspapers, 119; New York–Washington axis, 11–17; nineteenth century, 3; nonprofit organizations, 20; political opinion center, 19; relationship with other cities, 31
Washington Post, 130, 140*n*, 142*n*
WASPs, 17, 79, 147
wealth: within cities, 3; concentration in New York, 22; cultural institutions, 9; national power and, 96; patronage of the arts, 147
Weimar Republic: U.S. bank loans to, 76
welfare establishment: New Deal, 13; political mobilization around, 42
Western Europe: rebuilding of, 18; trade with U.S., 49
West Side, Manhattan, 42, 177
Whig Party, 10, 98
white-collar workers, 37, 38
"Wise Men": post-World War II period, 97, 100
working poor, 214
World, 119
"world city" strategy, 39, 42
world market: free trade and, 90–91
World's Fair: 1891, 210; 1939–1940, 79
World War I: art and artists, 151; economic assets of U.S., 77; foreign reserves, 52; free trade and protectionist coalitions, 73–74; international monetary system, 13; U.S. intervention, 12
World War II: art and artists, 16, 151; Council on Foreign Relations, 80; debates on military procedure, 80–81; defense spending, 32; Democratic Party, 80; Federal Emergency Relief Administration, 100; Great Britain, transfer of international leadership, 11; precipitation of, 13; publishing industry, 185. *See also* post-World War II period
WPA artists, 16
writers: life style, 22; periodicals and newspapers, 119; social life, 10; strikes, 141*n*

Y

yen: dollar agreement, 107, 109, 111; dollar and, 63; international use of, 60; rising in value, 159
Young Plan (1929), 76

Z

zero coupon bonds, 68
zoning code, 1916, 33